Tony Ortega is executive editor of *The Raw Story* and former editor-in-chief of *The Village Voice*. He's been writing about Scientology throughout his career, and also operates his own website with breaking news about the church at www.tonyortega.org. He lives in New York City. *The Unbreakable Miss Lovely* is his first book.

THE UNBREAKABLE MISS LOVELY

HOW THE CHURCH OF SCIENTOLOGY
TRIED TO DESTROY PAULETTE COOPER

TONY ORTEGA

SILVERTAIL BOOKS • *London*

First published in Great Britain and the United States by Silvertail Books in 2015
www.silvertailbooks.com
Typeset in Ehrhardt Monotype
ISBN 978-1511639-37-8

For Arielle, Benjamin, and Rebecca

CONTENTS

FOREWORD

I f you write about Scientology, one of the first names you hear is Paulette Cooper's. As soon as people find out that you're looking into the famously secretive and litigious organization, you're asked, "Do you know what happens to people who investigate Scientology? Haven't you heard about Paulette Cooper?" Her story is still spoken of with fear today, more than 40 years after her book, *The Scandal of Scientology*, was published.

When I began writing about Scientology in 1995, I was aware in rough terms of what Paulette had been through. I knew that thanks to her book she had become the target of the most notorious campaign of harassment and retaliation ever carried out by a group well known for the lengths it will go to in order to bully the people it considers enemies. But I didn't know the full story of her ordeal. At that time no one did, not even Paulette.

A few years later, after I wrote a series of stories about the organization for a newspaper in Los Angeles, I started to receive emails encouraging me to stay on the subject from someone whose email address contained a familiar name – it was Paulette herself. She had settled the last of her lawsuits with the Church of Scientology in 1985, and had kept mostly under the radar since then. I was thrilled to receive her messages and at the same time a little perplexed about why she was secretly reaching out to an unknown writer on the other side of the country to give him a pat on the back. I supposed that in her way she was still fighting Scientology, which had targeted her so tenaciously in the past.

For a few years I continued to receive those encouraging notes. Then, in 2008, when I'd moved to New York and was editing *The Village Voice*, Scientology exploded as a news story. Thanks to Tom Cruise, the Anonymous movement, and to a revealing video made by a character actor named Jason Beghe, there was a new and voracious public clamoring for fresh information about Scientology. Like me, Paulette was stunned at what was happening, and at the intensity of the interest in her from reporters who still cited her as the most notorious example of Scientology's retaliatory "Fair Game" policy.

In 2011, I proposed that we work together on a lengthy story that would revisit her ordeal. And that's when I noticed that what existed online about it was a mess. There were contradictions and gaps in the record, and plenty of questions that had never been answered. Some sources, for example, claimed that Paulette had been born in the Auschwitz Nazi death camp, which wasn't true. But at that point, even Paulette herself wasn't sure what had happened in Belgium, where she'd actually been born, and how she had survived the Holocaust. It was one of the first things we set out to investigate together, and the results surprised us both.

As with the other areas we began to explore, each supposedly settled fact turned out to be more complicated, and if anything more outrageous than we first thought. It was an encouraging sign as our project grew and we set out to learn the entire story of what Paulette had survived – not only from what she remembered, but by talking to other people who had been around her at the time, as well as through documents and other sources of information that brought the period into sharp focus.

The passage of time tends to flatten things, and events that were actually separated by several years can look contemporaneous from a distance. In Paulette's case, accounts of her harassment tend to conflate her bomb threat indictment with a later scheme that never really got going. But Paulette was actually subjected to a series of elaborate plots over many years, and she only gradually became aware of some of them as they were happening. (A couple of the schemes she never knew about at all until they came up in the writing of this book.) She was often in the dark about where the next attack was coming from, or who was going to slap her with a lawsuit. We've tried to convey that feeling in *The Unbreakable Miss Lovely*, telling the story as it unfolded in order to capture what it was like to be Paulette Cooper and become ensnared in Scientology's traps time and again.

Today, interest in Scientology has never been greater, thanks most recently to a documentary by Oscar-winning filmmaker Alex Gibney which set out, in part, to understand the appeal of Scientology to its members. In 1968, Paulette Cooper set out to do the same thing, taking a class at her local Scientology "org" in order to find out why people were joining. What she found almost immediately was that some of the people who had taken courses were being targeted for mistreatment. That interested Paulette much more than the distant possibility of going "Clear," and so she set out to discover more about Scientology and the people who ran it for a magazine article and then a book.

In the end she got far more than she bargained for.

Tony Ortega
New York, May 2015

PROLOGUE
Antwerp, 1942

R uchla Minkowski Bucholc couldn't wait any longer. Several days had passed since her cousin last came with new supplies, and Ruchla had no way of knowing if the girl would ever come again. She might have been arrested, or worse. What she did know was that she and her own two little girls, one of them just three months old, urgently needed fresh food and milk. And with no one bringing her those things, she had no option other than to go into the street and buy them herself.

Ruchla was painfully aware of how much of a risk that was. Since her husband was arrested more than two months before, she had been in hiding with the girls in an upstairs apartment, relying on family to bring them food and other necessities. If she was arrested too, she was terrified by what might happen to her children. But she had no choice. They needed to eat.

Hungry and tired, but more worried about the state of her girls, Ruchla waited until the little ones had settled down for a nap before she got ready to leave. Before she left, she wrote them a short note in case she didn't make it back and left it where it wouldn't be missed. Then she put on her coat, the one with the yellow star. She went to the door, took one look back at her girls, and then walked down the stairs to the street.

Some time later, on the streets of Antwerp, Ruchla was stopped and asked to produce papers that would prove that she was a Belgian Jew and not an immigrant. She didn't have the papers they wanted to see, and so she was arrested.

Ruchla and her husband Chaim Bucholc had arrived in Antwerp in the late 1920s, earlier than most of the Polish Jews who would come to Belgium, and then found themselves trapped when the small nation fell to the German Army in the spring of 1940 after just 18 days of fighting. Chaim was a talented leatherworker, and he had fallen in with a group of close friends – a journalist and a local bureaucrat among them. But they could do nothing for him as the Nazi occupiers tacked on indignity after indignity to the lives of the Jews living in the city.

By 1942, leaving the house meant wearing clothing emblazoned with a yellow Star of David, and as summer came on, arrests picked up. Increasingly, soldiers were randomly rousting Antwerp's Jews and demanding proof that they were Belgian citizens. If they couldn't come up with any, they were taken away and not heard from again. Ruchla, meanwhile, was getting ready to deliver her second child. Sarah had come in 1940 and had turned two years old as Ruchla's due date neared in July.

Then, on July 22, 1942, Chaim was taken off a train and arrested. He was a Polish Jew living in Antwerp under occupation, and that was enough to seal his fate. Four days later, Ruchla gave birth. Her husband never laid eyes on his second daughter.

After his arrest, Chaim was taken to the Breendonk concentration camp about halfway between Antwerp and Brussels, where a Nazi overseer known for his cruelty named Philip Schmitt was starving prisoners and subjecting them to daily beatings. Schmitt was also put in charge of a new transport center in the nearby town of Mechelen, where an old barracks was being turned into a holding center for Jews who would be put on trains bound for Poland. Chaim Bucholc was among the first set of prisoners moved from Breendonk into the new Mechelen transport center to await shipment to the east.

In August, the Nazi soldiers in Antwerp moved from snatching a few foreign Jews to making mass arrests. They rounded up hundreds of people, and then demanded to see proof of citizenship. Those who couldn't produce documentation were taken to the Mechelen center. At this point Belgian Jews were immune from being rounded up, but this would change a few months later.

Ruchla went into hiding with her two girls. She couldn't afford to be out on the street at all now. And she had no idea what had happened to her husband. She was unaware that on September 10, Chaim was rousted out of the Dossin barracks by Schmitt's soldiers to be put on a train with 1,047 other passengers. Designated Transport VIII, the train moved out of Mechelen and arrived three days later at Auschwitz-Birkenau in

Nazi-controlled Poland, where the men were separated from the women, children, and the infirm, who were gassed right away. Sometime later, Chaim Bucholc was led into the gas chambers himself. He was 38 years old.

In October, nearly three months after Chaim had been arrested and her youngest was born, Ruchla was arrested. She was taken to Mechelen, where she was herded with the next group to be put on a train.

Ruchla Minkowski Bucholc, prisoner 950, was put on Transport XIV, one of 995 Jews who left for Auschwitz on October 24, 1942 to their deaths. She was 31 years old.

After Ruchla's arrest, her daughters were cared for by Chaim's family, and it was her brother who found the note Ruchla had scribbled to the girls before she was taken away. "Play and be happy," it read. She had left behind a two-year-old daughter named Sarah, and an infant girl she had named Paula, but who was so small she would always be known as Paulette.

***

New York, 1973

The bottle of valium Paulette had been saving up for killing herself suddenly looked like her best option. Not, as she'd previously planned, to be taken in a few months' time, but right now. Today. This horrible, awful, wretched evening of July 26, 1973. Her 31st birthday.

If she could stand to drink more of the vodka she'd been pouring down her throat all day, Paulette figured she would have the courage to choke down enough of the pills for her to just bliss out and never wake up. Then, finally, it would be all over.

Why wait, she asked herself. Why not right now, right here? She had nothing left to live for. Everyone she knew thought she was a liar. About everything. Even her best friends. Even her parents. Even her goddamned lawyers. Especially her goddamned lawyers.

A year ago – just a year ago – her career was unstoppable. Three books out by the age of 30. Major articles showing up regularly in the biggest, most important publications in the world, from the London *Sunday Times* to the *Washington Post* to the *New York Times*.

And even after all the trouble started, she was well into the best book of her life, the one about forensic crime scene investigations that her agent thought could turn into television shows and movies. It was the book that was going to pull her out of the nightmare that had taken over her life since last December.

But then the first review had come out in that morning's paper, and it was a pan. She'd felt sick as she realized that the new book wasn't going to rescue her from the living hell that her life had become. And it was only going to get worse as October neared.

October meant federal court. A trial chamber packed with reporters. *THE UNITED STATES OF AMERICA V. PAULETTE MARCIA COOPER*. Having to explain again how she didn't have anything to do with those bomb threats typed in illiterate phrases while no one believed her denials.

Paulette's hands trembled as she held the vodka and the bottle of valium. She was sick of arguing with herself over whether it was better to wait and see what happened or end it now. Why wait for October? Why not just do it now and save herself all that pain? Yes, she decided, she would do it now.

And at that moment, her telephone rang.

Almost as a reflex, Paulette picked up the phone. She recognized the voice at the other end of the line – it was an old college friend, calling to wish her a happy birthday. An old friend who had heard nothing about her troubles. Who had no idea what a wreck her life had become, or that she was facing a federal trial. An old friend who just wanted to catch up.

For a moment, the haze of Paulette's suicidal depression lifted, and she began to remember the good times with her friend, and then she thought of what had happened to bring her to this desperate point, the traumas she'd been through and how close she was to being totally destroyed.

Paulette thought of how close she had come to ending her life, and she felt herself pull back from the brink. Something deep inside her said no, that will not happen now. I am not finished yet. I will fight on, because I am telling the truth.

1

The man who thought
he was God
New York, 1968

Paulette thought Bill was strange. Maybe even dangerous. But she let him come over to her apartment anyway, even though she was unsure what he was so worked up about. She was still dealing with the news that Robert F. Kennedy had died in Los Angeles that morning, after being shot the day before, and she thought that might have upset Bill too.

While she watched the TV reports in her Manhattan apartment, she thought about Jack Kennedy's assassination five years earlier and couldn't believe it had happened again. On Tuesday – June 4, 1968 – RFK had won the California Democratic presidential primary over Minnesota Senator Eugene McCarthy and then, just after midnight, he was shot while walking through a kitchen passageway at the Ambassador Hotel. He lived for a little more than a day after the shooting.

Paulette felt shaky, like things were coming undone in the world. But then Bill had called out of the blue and said he wanted to see her. They had worked together a couple of years earlier as copywriters at BBDO, the giant advertising agency on Madison Avenue. Bill was strange then, too. He had been going through a breakup and he wrestled with depression, which was made worse by his heavy drinking. But he'd never forgotten that Paulette had befriended him when others kept their distance, and they'd kept in touch after she left the agency.

Now he was at her door, carrying a flowerpot. In the soil of the flowerpot he had stuck a Eugene McCarthy button, his idea of a joke, she supposed. She asked him to sit down on her couch and poured him a drink.

Paulette lived in a narrow five-story townhouse at 16 East 80th Street, off Fifth Avenue. Because her apartment was on the ground floor, she fought a constant battle with cockroaches and silverfish. This time, however, Bill was anxious to talk and didn't give a thought to Paulette's creative ideas about housecleaning. When she asked him what was so important, he asked her to sit on his lap.

They were friends, not lovers. But this was 1968, so she sat in his lap. Bill then told her that he had come to the realization that he was the reincarnation of Jesus Christ. Trying not to look too surprised, Paulette asked him when he'd come to that conclusion. Since he had joined Scientology, Bill answered.

Paulette had heard of it. In fact, she was hearing a lot about Scientology, because it seemed to be turning into something of a fad. She'd even read about its founder, L. Ron Hubbard, and knew that he claimed to produce superhuman followers he called "Clears." But she didn't know Hubbard could turn a man like Bill into a major deity.

She told Bill he was too conservative for something as outlandish as Scientology. But he'd been helped by it, he said. Under Scientology processing, it was possible to go into the past and learn about your former lives. It had convinced him that he was the creator of the universe. His life had improved immensely, and it was all because of L. Ron Hubbard.

Paulette scoffed, telling him that anything can be helpful, at least for a short time, as long as you believe in it strongly enough.

"You're wrong," he said. "And just to prove to you that Scientology has really helped me, look how much I've changed. All I used to care about was making money. Now all I care about is helping people. I've given $700 away this week to people standing on the street corner who looked like they needed to be helped. Look," he said, and pulled out a list of names on crumpled sheets of paper. He'd written down the telephone numbers and occupations of everyone he'd met lately on street corners in Greenwich Village.

"What are you going to do with those?" Paulette asked.

"Help them, too."

"How?"

"By keeping the mafia away from them."

"But the mafia isn't *after* them."

Bill smiled. "That's because I wrote down their names."

13

Paulette nodded, wondering how the man had become so delusional. He prattled on about his abilities to change the world now that he was immortal. He seemed happy and genuinely excited about his new life, but in his eyes, Paulette saw something else. Her training from working years earlier with very ill mental patients kicked in. She understood the situation.

And then Bill wrapped his arms tightly around her and said, "God has decided to rape you." Paulette struggled against his grip and had the presence of mind to keep him talking about Scientology. How did it work? What did he hope to do with it? It distracted him enough that she was able to slip from his arms and then move him, little by little, to the door.

"Just look what it's done for me," he said, still going on about how Scientology had changed his life.

It was a relief when Paulette finally got him to leave.

After Bill was gone, Paulette looked for a phone number. She wanted to talk to Roger, a former boyfriend, someone she had worked with at BBDO. She knew that Roger had also dabbled in Scientology, and thought he might be able to make sense of what just happened.

She first noticed Roger when she went for a job interview at BBDO's offices on Madison Avenue in 1966. She spotted him on her way past some cubicles – he was the handsome, dark-haired man giving her the once over. She already knew another man in the office. Barry was an old grade school classmate, and he was excited to see her. He had been hired a few weeks earlier, also as a junior copywriter, and he hoped she could get work there too. Paulette wanted it badly. Not only for the creative opportunity and a decent starting salary, but because there were few women in copywriting and she liked the challenge of breaking into the field. She passed the interview and got the position. (And soon found that Barry was making $500 more in salary for the same job, which irked her.)

On her first day of work, she stopped at Barry's cubicle to say hello, and she wondered if the good looking man was also still there. When he saw her, Roger stopped typing and stood up. He was tall, which she liked. He shook her hand and said he hoped he'd be seeing her around. After work, Roger asked her for a drink, and soon they were dating.

At BBDO, Paulette mostly worked on the Campbell's Soup account, and she got noticed when she came up with a campaign that encouraged customers to mix soups ("One Plus One Equals New!"). It even got her written up with praise in the industry bible, *Madison Avenue* magazine.

The copywriters at BBDO worked in groups, and lunches were the three-Martini type. After work they would hit the bar downstairs at the 383 Madison Avenue building where they drank some more. On Friday afternoons all but one of Paulette's co-workers ditched their cubicles to spend the afternoon in the bar, leaving behind one designated non-drinker to keep an eye out for bosses. Most of her co-workers were men, and Paulette tried to keep up with their heavy drinking, and sometimes the next morning she had only a hazy memory of what had gone on.

After one night of prodigious consumption, she recalled the next morning in a haze that she'd let Roger take a Polaroid photograph of her wearing a sheer nightgown that showed her silhouette underneath. She had some worries about it, but did nothing at the time.

Her fling with Roger didn't last long, and by 1967 she was poached by another ad agency that offered her $17,000 a year, almost triple what BBDO was paying her. At the new agency, she remained friends with Roger, and that's how she knew that he'd become interested in Scientology.

Roger had stumbled onto it while pursuing a waitress who kept putting him off because every evening she had to go to some kind of night school. "How about the weekend?" he asked her, but she went to classes then, too.

What was this place that took up so much of her time? He decided to find out, and it turned out to be the Scientology "org" at the Hotel Martinique on Greeley Square, a block from the Empire State Building. Thinking it might help him get in with the waitress, Roger agreed to take Scientology's introductory class, its "Communication Course." But the waitress was soon forgotten because he became hooked on Scientology. Roger then began to tell his friends about it. Including Bill, his colleague at BBDO.

Bill was gifted and smart, but the break-up of his marriage and his heavy drinking had him fighting despair. Others thought he was eccentric, but he didn't mind that. He enjoyed the shock value of walking around the city in a black cape and black hood, like something out of an Ingmar Bergman film. With his penchant for weirdness and his emotional state after his break-up, perhaps anything could have sent him over the edge. But it was Scientology that had clearly unhinged him.

Bill never forgot that while others thought he was weird, Paulette had befriended him, trying to help him snap out of his funk. So when things had gotten truly strange, he had looked her up. After she convinced Bill to leave her apartment that day after RFK was assassinated, Paulette called up Roger and told him what had happened, that Scientology had convinced Bill that he was Jesus incarnate.

Roger's answer stunned her. "Maybe he really is," he said.

Maybe he really is? The words stuck in her mind, and made her wonder about Scientology – what about it could have attracted these two men she had known in such a cauldron of talent and smarts as BBDO, and made them consider, even for a moment, something so bizarre?

By this time, she'd ditched advertising altogether and was trying to make it as a magazine writer. Paulette began to wonder if she'd found her next big story subject. Maybe it was time to find out how Scientology was attracting people like Roger and Bill. How did it work? And was Bill's experience a warning that there was something off, maybe even something dangerous about Scientology?

She started looking into taking a course at the local church.

The Scientology "org" at the Hotel Martinique on Broadway at

32nd Street was a hive of activity. The Beaux Arts hotel had been constructed between 1897 and 1911 and became a glamorous attraction. The Professional Golf Association of America – the PGA – was created during a meeting there in 1916. But by the 1960s the hotel had faded, and Scientology took over its large ballroom and a collection of offices for workers who ran the org.

In 1968, the ballroom was regularly filled with young people taking courses, day and night. Leonard Cohen was known for showing up with his two girlfriends for some auditing. John McMaster, the world's first "Clear," stopped through on his frequent trips around the world as Scientology's ambassador. Jim Dincalci, who would become L. Ron Hubbard's personal medical aide, made his first forays into Scientology there and liked it so much he ditched medical school so he could spend more time on his courses.

People were flowing in and out at all hours, and all under the watchful gaze of a large black and white photograph of Hubbard. Some of the seekers had been attracted to the place after seeing stickers that someone had placed in the bathrooms of just about every bar in the city: "After drugs comes Scientology."

The movement was in one of its growth spurts, attracting young people who had come to Manhattan looking for the counterculture, but wanting more than an acid trip. Scientologists told anyone who would listen that they were having out-of-body experiences without any drugs, and that taking courses would unleash their true potential. For those who gave it a try, they soon found themselves in the Hotel Martinique's ballroom, watching people shout and scream at each other. Part of L. Ron Hubbard's training involved something called "bullbaiting." It required one person to hold perfectly still, without flinching or even blinking, while his partner screamed obscenities or tried to find an insult or tease that caused the subject to react.

Jim Dincalci was shocked when he saw how rough it could get. Men were not only shouting at women during bullbaiting, but also touching them in an attempt to get them to react. Some of it would have been offensive in another context. But this was Scientology. And it was what Paulette walked into one weekend as she began her investigation into the church.

She had signed up for Scientology's introductory course using a pseudonym – Paula Madison – which she'd borrowed from the famous avenue near her apartment. The course, "Success through Communications," involved a series of different exercises that would take place over two days. The first exercise had her sitting across from another person, staring into his eyes and daring not to blink. After suppressing an urge to laugh, Paulette soon found the experience almost unbearable. She itched. Her muscles twitched. Her vision began to blur and her mind lost focus, but she had to keep staring without moving or she'd hear "FLUNK!" screamed at her.

If that happened, she had to start all over again. As the hours went by, her vision increasingly played tricks on her as the face of the man she stared at went through ugly transformations. She was hallucinating, which was the point.

Like other movements of the time, Scientology offered

mind-bending trips into an alternative reality. New recruits were told that L. Ron Hubbard had discovered the true nature of the human mind, and through his training routines, they could explore a universe inside themselves. That exploration could take them into their past lives and could eventually bring them "total freedom"—an attractive promise, if a vague one. And to begin that journey, their career as Scientologists began with hours-long staring contests. From the outside, it looked like a cheap carnival trick that produced a mild trance state, but to Scientologists it was deadly serious. Especially when it got to the exercise on the second day—bullbaiting.

For this, Paulette had to hold perfectly still as a Scientologist yelled things at her to get her to flinch. Watching how others had done it, she expected that the man facing her would pick on her appearance. The trick seemed to be to find the "button" that would make someone react by saying something about the shape of their nose, the blemishes on their skin, or their taste in clothes. But with Paulette, the men who took turns testing her went for something else. They tried to outdo each other with obscene talk. "You know what I'm going to do to you?" they'd ask. And then they'd watch her face closely as they described the most vivid perversions they could think of.

Paulette was disgusted, but managed to take it. Like most single women in New York, she'd been through her share of dirty telephone calls. She'd just never had one in person before. She really only got uncomfortable when a senior official walked over to take a turn with her. Holding rock steady, she kept staring ahead as he began talking to her, discussing nothing important. Then, suddenly, he lunged forward until his nose was nearly touching hers. Staring into her eyes, he said, "We've been watching you since you first came in here. We think you're really a writer."

She blanched, but held still. He interrogated her roughly, trying to get her to flinch. All she could do was stare straight at him, letting her eyes out of focus a little. And then she hit on a strategy to keep her mind off of what he was yelling at her. She thought about kissing him. It revolted her, and she knew that her face must have shown it, but not enough to get the dreaded "Flunk!" shouted at her. She wasn't allowed to flinch, or move, or say anything. She just kept her look of distaste while he kept accusing her of spying.

Before the bullbaiting, when she was between other sessions, Paulette had wandered around the place, asking questions. At one point, she'd even lifted several documents from one office, some of which had lists of Scientology students who had been designated something called "suppressive." She tried to do some other poking around in the few minutes she had before another exercise started up. But after the senior official had accused her of being a writer, she wondered if they really were on to her.

Finally, he changed the subject and, like the others, started up with the sex talk. But he was obviously an old pro, and his dirty talk was levels of magnitude more disgusting than what the other men had come up with. And after all that, he finished with an invitation. "Why don't you come over and join in the some of the great orgies we have over here on Tuesday nights?"

21

When the bullbaiting was done, a woman told her that she was wanted by the "ethics officer" upstairs. Paulette didn't know what that was, but it didn't sound good. She was taken to a waiting area and was asked to take a seat. But she'd hardly arrived when the name "Paula Madison" was called out. She was directed into an office by a young woman. Paulette said she'd go in a minute, after she went to the bathroom. "No, you need to go in here now," the woman insisted.

Paulette didn't like the sound of that. She repeated that she had to go to the bathroom, and nervously watched as other Scientologists gathered around. The woman insisted again that she see the ethics officer, whoever that was.

"I have to go to the bathroom, and if you don't let me go, I will pee right here on your rug," Paulette said.

The woman, defeated, nodded to the bathroom, and Paulette went to it quickly. She stayed in there for a while, waiting for an opportunity to escape, and then made for the door.

Once she was out, she never went back.

Even before her trip to the org, Paulette already knew more than most members of the public about Scientology. She had first learned about its founder, L. Ron Hubbard, when she read a book by Martin Gardner, *Fads and Fallacies in the Name of Science*. Gardner eviscerated Hubbard's book *Dianetics*, lumping the science fiction writer in with dozens of other people he considered "cranks."

A revised version of Gardner's book had come out in 1957,

and that's when Paulette had read it, when she was 15. She had always been a voracious reader. At Mamaroneck High School, in the Westchester County town where Paulette's adopted parents had moved from Manhattan's Upper West Side when she was 12, she would arrive a half hour early in the mornings to study Greek. She figured it was a good way to supplement the Latin she was learning later in the day.

Paulette wanted badly to get into Wellesley, the prestigious Massachusetts women's liberal arts college, but even though her grades were good enough, she failed an important test during an interview with the school's dean of women. When she was asked what she'd been reading lately, Paulette answered that she'd just finished *Crime and Punishment*. "By Tolstoy," the dean said. "No, by Dostoyevsky," Paulette answered. The dean repeated her error twice, but Paulette didn't back down, insisting that she was correct.

She realized later that the proper response to the dean should have been, "I thought it was Dostoyevsky, and I'll look it up when I get home." In 1960, that's how a Wellesley woman handled such a situation. It dawned on her years later that that she'd been too insistent that she was right. She was feisty, and she knew it.

Paulette was tiny, just slightly over five feet tall. She was petite and a brunette with a great figure, but her city smarts made as much of a good first impression as her good looks. She was formidable and ambitious, anyone could see that. But if she wasn't Wellesley material, it was fine with Paulette's parents, who wanted her to go to Brandeis anyway.

Named after Louis D. Brandeis, the Supreme Court's first Jewish justice, the Waltham, Massachusetts liberal arts college had been founded in 1948 by Jewish immigrants who were trying to create a sort of Harvard for Jews. Soon enough, Jewish students were breaking barriers and getting into Ivy League schools on their own. Still, Brandeis remained a prestigious destination for a Jewish girl from New York.

Paulette graduated from Brandeis in January 1964, taking a degree in psychology with honors after only three years (including a semester off for an appendix operation and a summer at Harvard studying comparative religion). After graduating, she worked for several months at Harvard's medical school in a study on schizophrenia. It was there that she learned to read the warning signs which appear when a patient is about to blow a gasket.

When her internship was over, she moved to Manhattan, getting a tiny place at 15 Charles Street in the Village, and began absorbing the life of a city going through a cultural upheaval. Paulette began taking graduate courses at Columbia University's Teachers College, but soon realized it wasn't a good fit for her. She finished a master's degree at City College while she worked at a job in a research firm during the day.

The job had her psychoanalyzing television commercials, and it put Paulette in contact with people at BBDO, eventually resulting in an interview for a position. And that's when she walked in for the first time and spotted Roger, and later made friends with Bill.

After she was poached a year later by a second ad agency

– Norman, Craig, & Kummel – she began to wonder if she'd made the right decision to leave BBDO when she found herself day after day storyboarding ads for Ajax, the window cleaner. By then Paulette had moved out of the Village to the East 60's, first in a place on 63rd Street, then into one of the first condominium buildings in the city at 64th Street and 2nd Avenue. Just months before, down the block at 1st Avenue, Warner LeRoy, son of *Wizard of Oz* producer Mervyn LeRoy, had opened the city's new hot spot, Maxwell's Plum, which combined a movie theater with an upscale hamburger café that attracted a thriving singles scene.

Paulette would look out her window on the third floor to see if she could spot good-looking men heading to Maxwell's Plum, and if she spied some, she'd go for a drink. Downstairs in her own building – the 34-story St. Tropez – was Frank Valenza's booming restaurant, Proof of the Pudding, which introduced cherry tomatoes to trendy eaters. The smell of garlic coming from the place drove Paulette nuts, especially because her meager freelance budget often had her skipping meals. "One day, if I work hard enough, I'll be successful enough to eat there every night," she vowed.

She shared the cramped quarters with a couple of roommates. The apartment was owned by a woman Paulette knew through her father Ted's jewelry business. The summer before, Paulette had spent a month working in his office when the woman who would become her landlord sold several pieces to finance a diamond engagement ring for herself. Later, after the woman had paid for the piece, Ted Cooper caught a glimpse of a flaw in the diamond that was only barely perceptible. Paulette was stunned when her father refunded the woman $16,000.

"She would never have known. Why would you do that?" Paulette asked her dad.

"Because *I* knew," he said.

Until that summer, she'd thought of her father as a hen-pecked man who simply did what her mother told him. But working for him, she could see that people respected him, and he was savvier than she had given him credit for. That same summer, when she brought home a man she liked for dinner, she knew her parents were uncomfortable simply because the man wasn't Jewish. But her father handled it well.

"I'm not going to tell you to break up with him, because then you'll be even more anxious to date him," he told her. "But I will mention that there was only a 20 percent chance of rain this evening, and he wore galoshes. Given your personality, would you ever really be happy with someone like that?"

Ted Cooper knew his thrill-seeking, ambitious daughter well.

By 1967, when she lived at the St. Tropez, Paulette knew that what she really wanted to do was write for magazines. She asked how long she had to work on the Ajax account at Norman, Craig, & Kummel before she qualified for unemployment. Five months, she was told. So at four-and-a-half months, she gave two weeks' notice.

Living on unemployment, she started looking for splashy story subjects that would get her noticed. For an example, she didn't have to look farther than her friend Albert Podell. In a city of outsized characters, Podell stood out. He was an attorney in the Village who had recently returned from a 19-month drive around the world. He and a friend had motored a four-wheel drive vehicle to the most remote ends of the planet, and then had written a book about it. While promoting the book early in 1968, Podell appeared on the Alan Burke television show – one of the earliest shows that featured a host who insulted the audience as he barked about politics and the news of the day. After the show, Podell invited the entire staff of the show back to his Sullivan Street apartment for a party.

He also invited Paulette. She was surprised to see that one of her old classmates from Brandeis, Sheila Rabb, was there. Sheila was an associate producer at the television show, and she introduced Paulette to her boss, the show's producer. His name was Paul Noble.

Paul had grown up in Forest Hills, Queens, and had gone to Forest Hills High School, Cornell University, and then Boston University for a master's degree. He got a job at WGBH in Boston and helped produce *Prospects of Mankind*, one of the earliest public affairs shows on television, hosted by Eleanor Roosevelt. Some episodes of the show had been taped at Brandeis while Paulette was a student there, but the two had never met.

One of Mrs. Roosevelt's guests was John F. Kennedy, and Paul explained how he'd literally given JFK the shirt off his back when it turned out the new president had worn a white shirt, which drove the TV cameras of the time crazy. Paul gave him a blue shirt and then mailed JFK's white J. Crew shirt to him. Paulette liked that detail – she could tell that Paul Noble was a man of integrity.

Paulette was 25, Paul was 32. She was impressed that he was in television and had met such important people, producing shows for Eleanor Roosevelt and Bishop Fulton Sheen. She told him about her graduate work in psychology, studying early childhood memory. But now she was trying to make it as a writer. Like her friend Albert, she wanted to write books that got noticed.

After Podell's party, Paul and Paulette went on a couple of dates. They liked each other's company, but nothing romantic developed. They had made strong impressions on each other, but went their separate ways.

Several months later, around the time Bill told Paulette he was Jesus Christ, and after she'd moved uptown to a place of her own, the cockroach-infested ground-floor apartment on East 80th Street, she began having success landing stories in magazines. For *TV Guide*, she advised readers how to get their pets into commercials, and for *Cosmopolitan* she wrote "A Girl's Guide to Diamonds," which came easy, with her father in the business.

Ted Cooper had worked in a well-known and prestigious diamond import business started by his father-in-law, Solomon Toepfer, before he opened his own concern. And it was diamonds that kept Ted and Stella Cooper making regular trips to Antwerp, the industry's world headquarters. The Coopers preferred to go to Europe by sea and Paulette got used to the life aboard cruise ships at an early age.

When she was only 18, in 1960, Paulette spent one cruise from Europe to New York dodging a Marine major-general who insisted on dining with her parents several times. He'd find excuses to talk to Paulette alone, and kept telling her that he wanted to be her first sexual experience. She wasn't tempted. But that same cruise, she did have a heavy crush on a California man named Robert Smith who had been living in Italy as an opera singer, and who called himself "Roberto Smittini." She made the mistake of writing about what they got up to together in her trip diary, and when her mother read it, Stella and Ted had meltdowns.

Paulette gave Smith her address, and they exchanged a few letters before the connection faded, probably hastened by Ted's threats to go after him if he ever contacted Paulette again. And despite her father's worst fears, Paulette's virginity was still intact. (She saved that for one of her Brandeis professors.)

She was accustomed to older men approaching her during ocean cruises. In 1968, aboard the *S.S. France*, she was picked up by a 55-year-old man who threw his back out when he lifted her during a dance. He was CBS news anchor Eric Sevareid. For the next couple of years, Sevareid would stop in to see Paulette every few months when he was in town. They'd hole up in the Stanhope Hotel and take in the Bobby Short show.

That year, in September 1968, when the *Washington Post* wanted to understand a new trend in the cruise business, it bought a story by Paulette that explained the marvel of the *S.S. Independence*. The ship was breaking with tradition, asking

29

extremely low rates for passage, but charging for all meals—an unheard-of practice in the stuffy, custom-laden world of class-conscious cruising. "Whether it was the attractive ship, the informal style, or the 'bargain' that attracted them, there is no doubt that the passengers sailing were very different from the conservative, elderly, well-traveled crowd who were there last year," Paulette wrote with the experience to know the difference. Not everyone was happy with the change. She quoted a crew member who complained about "people who don't know how to tip, don't know fore from aft, a bow from their elbow, and keep calling the damned ship a 'boat'."

For Paulette, the story was validation that her career was going in the right direction. She was 26 years old and had three stories published, and all three were in major publications—*TV Guide*, *Cosmopolitan*, and the *Washington Post*.

2

'Have you ever practiced cannibalism?'

P aulette knew she wouldn't get much more information from the Scientology org itself. She needed to talk to people who had more experience with the church and she was fortunate to find a few people who proved very helpful. Two years earlier, a man named Ray Buckingham had spoken out about his experiences in Scientology on a New York radio program. He was a voice teacher who had spent some time in the church and had helped get several of his students into it, but then he had found himself the target of Scientology's program of "ethics".

Reacting to breakaway groups that had threatened to undermine his authority, in 1965 L. Ron Hubbard had put in place strict new security measures which included labeling Scientology's perceived enemies as "Suppressive Persons." Once the ethics apparatus of Scientology labeled a person an "SP," everyone who wanted to remain in good standing with the church had to "disconnect" from that person entirely.

Buckingham was stunned when his star pupil, a young Broadway singer, announced that she was disconnecting from him because he'd been labeled suppressive. He'd invested about $30,000 in her career and had several parts lined up for her that she walked away from. Suddenly no one in the church would talk to him, which is how he learned he'd been branded an enemy of Scientology.

Paulette heard about Buckingham and tracked him down. He was a very useful source, giving her an insider's view of the church and connecting her with other people who had run afoul of the organization. He was also the first person who told Paulette that he had received death threats and was literally afraid for his life because of his involvement with Scientology.

Through Buckingham, Paulette met other ex-church members, and she started hearing other troubling stories about interrogations and control. She learned that high-level Scientologists were regularly put through humiliating "security checks," which were lists of questions asked by ethics officers as a subject is holding onto an "E-meter." A device that measures skin galvanism (only one-quarter of the operations of a polygraph, which also measures respiration, blood pressure, and heartbeat), the machine reacts in a way that Scientologists were convinced would show when they were hiding something. Under that kind of pressure, they were asked questions from a list Paulette obtained:

Have you ever raped anyone?

Have you ever been raped?

Have you ever been involved in an abortion?

Have you ever assisted in an abortion?

Have you ever practiced cannibalism?

Have you ever committed adultery?

Have you ever practiced sex with animals?

Have you ever exhibited yourself in public?

Have you ever had intercourse with a member of your family?

Have you ever slept with a member of a race of another color?

Have you practiced sex with children?

Have you ever taken money for giving anyone sexual intercourse?

Have you ever been a voyeur?

Have you ever masturbated?

And there were many more. Another document that unnerved Paulette was one she had managed to pick up during her weekend at the org. It was an official announcement that a woman had been declared a suppressive person – in effect, it was the woman's excommunication order. The document accused the woman of outrageous (and hard to believe) crimes. She had supposedly pushed five men down a flight of stairs, for example. When Paulette tried to locate the woman, she turned out to have an unlisted number, which in those days was unusual. Paulette couldn't help wondering if the woman was being harassed. And she also wondered if Buckingham really wasn't exaggerating about being afraid for his life.

As Paulette continued to gather information, she used some creative methods she'd learned from other reporters. There was the way she learned more about L. Ron Hubbard's family, for example. She knew that Hubbard's father was supposed to be a naval commander living in the Midwest, and the pulp fiction writer had referred to his father as Commander H. L. Hubbard. Paulette managed to find a listing for a Harry Hubbard, and when she called and he asked who she was, she quickly made up a name.

"Paula Hubbard. I wonder if we're related," she said.

That got the old man talking. He went through the entire family tree, and told her birth dates and locations and marriage details, all in an attempt to figure out if "Paula" was a member of the family. She later made extensive use of the details he gave her. Paulette also scheduled a train trip down to Washington D.C., where she knew there was a mother lode of documents on the church.

In 1958, concerned about the health claims being made by Hubbard, the Food and Drug Administration had infiltrated Scientology's "Founding Church" in Washington D.C. (Hubbard had actually incorporated his first church in Camden, New Jersey in December, 1953, and then some of his followers opened what would come to be known as the "mother church" in Los Angeles in February, 1954. Hubbard didn't create the "Founding Church of Scientology" in D.C. until July 1955.) For several years, the FDA quietly gathered information about the way Scientologists used "E-meters" and made claims about their ability to heal ailments.

Then, on January 4, 1963, the FDA, with the help of the Capitol Police, raided the church, seizing more than a hundred of the devices and thousands of pages of documents. The ensuing court case descended into years of squabbling about the devices and the church's First Amendment religious rights. After the matter had been appealed and returned to district court, a settlement was reached in 1971 that required Scientology to label every E-meter with a warning, sort of like on a cigarette pack. It read: "The device known as a Hubbard Electrometer, or E-meter, used in auditing, a process of Scientology and Dianetics, is not medically or scientifically useful for the diagnosis, treatment, or prevention of any disease. It is not medically or scientifically capable of improving the health or bodily functions of anyone."

Paulette was less interested in the court fight over the E-meters than getting a look at the piles of documents the raid had snared. For days, at the Justice Department, she pored over them, gaining valuable insight into Hubbard and Scientology's history.

Someone who noticed how hard Paulette was working was a Justice employee named Michael Sanders and he helped get her hands on a copy of the scathing 1965 investigation of Scientology by Australia's state of Victoria. One of the harshest denunciations of the church ever produced by a government body, the probe had been launched in 1963, and after hearing from both current and former church members, its author, Queens Counsel Kevin Victor Anderson, recommended that legislators banish Scientology in no uncertain terms.

"If there should be detected in this Report a note of unrelieved denunciation of Scientology, it is because the evidence has shown its theories to be fantastic and impossible, its principles perverted and ill-founded, and its techniques debased and harmful," Anderson wrote. "While making an appeal to the public as a worthy system whereby ability, intelligence, and personality may be improved, it employs techniques which further its real purpose of securing domination over and mental enslavement of its adherents. It involves the administration by persons without any training in medicine or psychology of quasi-psychological treatment, which is harmful medically, morally and socially."

After her trip to Washington resulted in her reading so many key documents, Paulette knew she had sufficient material for her story. But she was also aware that she had competition, because if the crowds of young people down at the Hotel Martinique demonstrated Scientology's growing popularity, it was also becoming popular as a subject for journalists.

In November 1968, *LIFE* magazine printed a major article which featured a sidebar by a man named Alan Levy who had gone through quite a few levels of Scientology training in order to write about it. In April 1969, a hip New York publication, *EYE*, ran a lengthy and smart piece by a writer named George Malko. While its criticism of Hubbard's ideas was cutting, Malko was impressed by the church's popularity with the young. In June, a much more harshly critical story showed up in *Parents* magazine by a married couple, Arlene and Howard Eisenberg, under the title "The Dangerous New Cult of Scientology."

Paulette knew she had no time to waste. She finished her article and her agent, Ted Chichak, looked for a magazine that would run it. They both soon found that Scientology already had a litigious reputation, and most outlets weren't anxious to take it on. One of the magazines that rejected the piece was one of the most popular magazines in the United Kingdom, *Queen*. But *Queen*, at least, let Paulette know that it was interested in her as a correspondent, and asked her to send a writing sample for future assignments. In a cheeky move, Paulette sent them the Scientology article draft as her writing sample. They then sent her a check for $240 and scheduled it for a future issue.

Originally *The Queen*, a society magazine, the publication had changed hands in the 60's and then began catering to younger readers fascinated with swinging London's moneyed set at play. In 1968, it had been sold again, to its rival, *Harper's Bazaar*, and it had only a few more issues left under its old name.

Paulette didn't know when her story would appear. Then, one day, she got two telephone calls from men she didn't know. Each of them threatened to kill her if she kept writing about Scientology. She called Ted, her agent, and asked what the hell was going on. He checked, and sure enough, the December 1969 issue of *Queen* had come out – the very last issue that would come out under that name – and it contained a story by Paulette Cooper, "The Tragi-farce of Scientology."

Things would never be the same.

Paulette Cooper's story on Scientology in *Queen* was not the first, not the longest, and not the most damning thing that had been written about the odd organization. Like others, she described Scientology's emphasis on bringing in money and the increasing prices members paid as they went higher and higher on Hubbard's scheme of courses. She was also not the first to point out that Hubbard had claimed to be a nuclear physicist but flunked the only class he took at George Washington University in molecular and atomic physics, and left school without a degree in his sophomore year.

But Paulette's *Queen* story was the first to highlight the sexual improprieties auditors tended to get into with their subjects (known as "preclears" in Scientology jargon). The relationship between auditor and preclear could be intensely personal, and some auditors took advantage of it. Church members who felt abused found themselves being harassed if they spoke up. And when some of them asked for refunds, they hit a brick wall. More than previous writers, Paulette focused on the harassment of those who dared to speak up about Scientology, whether they'd been in the church or not.

Queen's editors had saddled the story with an unwieldy full title that Paulette didn't see until it was published: "The cringer, the bully, the necromancer, the con-man are all typical figures in the Gothic comedy. All play their part in *THE TRAGI-FARCE OF SCIENTOLOGY*"

And at the bottom of the first page of the article there was a short notation:

THIS MATERIAL IS TAKEN FROM THE SCANDAL OF SCI-

*ENTOLOGY, BY PAULETTE COOPER, WHICH IS TO BE PUB-
LISHED NEXT YEAR.*

Paulette didn't have a publisher yet, but she already knew
that she wanted to turn all the material she'd been gathering into
a book.

That wasn't Paulette's only idea for raising her profile. She
figured she had to do something flashy to get noticed, just like
her friend who had driven around the world had done. And so,
she decided to become the world's first female stowaway. In the
winter of 1970, Paulette boarded the *Leonardo Da Vinci* cruise
ship in New York harbor without a ticket.

For the next seven days, as the *Leonardo* headed for the Caribbean and back, Paulette pretended to drink like a sailor in one
of the ship's bars, the only place she could loiter all day without raising suspicions that she didn't actually have a cabin. In
a piano, she hid a small attaché case, in which she'd stuffed two
blouses, four evening dresses, and a long evening gown.

Over the next several days, she had to fend off one proposi-
tion after another by men who found her an irresistible target –
not only was she an attractive single woman traveling alone, but
at the pool she wore a bikini, swimwear which was still somewhat
uncommon for the cruising set. On the first night, the ship's
doctor insisted on taking her back to her cabin, and she thought
the game was up. But she managed to find an unoccupied cabin
by pure luck, and kept him out of it by pretending that she was
coming down with the flu. After he left, she hurried to a hiding spot in an out-of-the way lounge. She then had to make up

more excuses the next morning when the doctor called the room where he'd left her and the man who was actually staying there answered the phone.

The idea to stow away was something Paulette had been thinking about for years. She'd read a book that described various stories of stowing away through history and it had struck her that they were all stories about men. Then, on a cruise with her parents, a young man had been arrested when he was found hiding somewhere in the ship. Paulette told her friends about it, pointing out that the stowaway's mistake was trying to stay hidden. She said the only way to succeed was to remain out in the open so everyone got used to seeing you. She told her friends she was familiar enough with life aboard cruise ships that she could easily pull it off. They made her pay for that brag with a lot of teasing, and she knew she'd never live it down until she made the attempt.

Although it was her first attempt to stow away, Paulette's trip on the *Leonardo* was her fifteenth cruise. She was very familiar with the kind of people who sailed – including the randy men. After the near disaster of the first night, she became more careful about offers to see her home to her nonexistent cabin. Her strategy was to outlast the other drinkers, staying at the bar well after the midnight buffet. It left her severely sleep-deprived, but one day she allowed one man to take her to the early afternoon showing of *Bonnie & Clyde* in the ship's theater, and then another man to take her to the late afternoon showing. She slept through both. For seven days, she dodged one pass after another with similar schemes, but she always stayed in the open, knowing that her growing reputation as an odd character actually helped her chances. By the cruise's end, she was exhausted, and she was also terrified that she'd get caught at the last minute by police at the dock. Instead, two of the ship's security agents helped her get home.

Although she'd succeeded, she knew that if she wrote about the experience, there was still a chance she could be prosecuted. So she sat on the story for several months. In the meantime, Paulette kept developing her travel writing career. Just a few weeks after her *Queen* magazine story was published, she appeared in the *New York Times* for a story on a bargain three-lake cruise in Switzerland. The *Washington Post* bought another cruise story from her, this time about a computer dating gimmick on the Greek Line to Bermuda. Then, two months later, in September 1970, the *Post* ran a short account of her week as a stowaway—she'd decided enough time had passed since stealing a week on the *Leonardo da Vinci* that she could risk writing about it. Her risk paid off: Stanley Donen, director of *Singin' in the Rain*, took out an option on the story for a possible movie on her experience, and Paulette was asked to appear on radio and television shows, including an episode of *To Tell the Truth*.

Paulette craved the glamorous life of a magazine writer, and it was quickly falling into place for her. She joined the American Society of Journalists and Authors, and at one of its events she met a woman named Barbara Lewis. Barbara was tall, brunette, and stunning, and she had just written a book with the provocative title *The Sexual Power of Marijuana*. Like Paulette, she spent much of her time on travel stories for women's magazines, and with her good looks she seemed like the model of a Manhattan freelance writer at the time. The two immediately hit it off and quickly became friends.

Barbara had Paulette over to her apartment at the Churchill, a luxury 34-story building a few blocks from the United Nations at 300 E. 40th Street, and Paulette became enchanted with it. This was the kind of place where she saw herself living – a spacious apartment in a large building with an elegant front portico, mahogany lobby, and with amenities like a pool and sauna on the roof and 24-hour doormen in the lobby. She often visited Barbara at the Churchill to discuss their writing assignments and the men they were dating.

And very soon, Paulette learned that Barbara had a terrible secret. A year earlier, a man who worked in the Churchill, using a master key, stole into Barbara's room one night, then bound and raped her violently over a six to seven hour period, beating her with the butt of a handgun. In the morning, still bound, Barbara managed to crawl out to the hallway and, with her nose, rang a doorbell for help. She never saw the man, who covered up her eyes. But she knew the sound of his voice.

Later that day, a utility man didn't show up to work. He was immediately suspected, and when it turned out that he had fled to Puerto Rico, he was extradited. Police asked Barbara to identify him, telling her that they had found her radio in his apartment. They showed her a photo lineup, and then told her which one to pick out. He pleaded guilty, receiving a seven-year sentence.

Barbara admitted to Paulette that she lived in fear that he would return after getting out of prison to kill her, and it didn't help that a friend of his would call her, telling her that she'd identified the wrong man.

Even after Barbara told her about the attack, Paulette was still determined to get her own apartment at the Churchill, in part so she could remain close to her new friend.

In the spring of 1970, George Malko turned his 1969 *EYE* magazine article into a book, *Scientology: The Now Religion*. Once again, Malko had done a skillful job probing the church, and the way he took apart Hubbard's ideas with a fine-toothed comb must have taken incredible patience. He pointed out that everyone in the church seemed to agree that Scientology worked and was helping them, but none of them could really define exactly what it *was*. As in his previous article, Malko's criticisms of Hubbard's ideas were devastating, but presented in a clever, dispassionate style. Malko uncritically accepted Scientology's claim to 15 million members, which turned out to be pure fantasy (the true number at that time was probably closer to 60 or 70 thousand). He seemed impressed by the enthusiasm of young people flocking to the Hotel Martinique, and he also admitted to some admiration for Hubbard, for his bravado if nothing else. Malko's book received good reviews. *The Village Voice* in particular praised the way it took apart Hubbard's philosophy.

Paulette, meanwhile, worried that Malko's book getting to market first had reduced her own chances with a big publisher, namely Random House. In 1970, she corresponded with Random House editor Robert Loomis, who expressed an interest in her manuscript, but was wary about legal problems. She tried to ease his fears by acknowledging, in a letter, that she understood that the final edit would have to be "more objective, weaker, and greatly watered down." She wasn't married to her writing, she said, and was more than willing to take out some of the more sensational passages—particularly those based on foreign newspaper articles that would be harder to shore up with additional research. She also tried to sway Loomis by telling him that the book would get support from the American Medical Association and the American Psychiatric Association.

One of Scientology's original touchstones was that L. Ron Hubbard published *Dianetics* in 1950 because the AMA and APA had scoffed when he tried a couple of years earlier to give them the "technology" that he had discovered which could heal the human mind. Since then, Hubbard and Scientology had demonized the medical and psychiatric establishments, which Hubbard claimed were out to destroy him. The truth was that doctors and psychiatrists mostly ignored Scientology, and when they thought about Scientology at all, they were annoyed by the unscientific claims made by the organization. Paulette knew that various medical journals would review and promote a book that debunked Hubbard's claims.

She was also hoping to get the support of the National Association for Mental Health in Great Britain, a relationship which she believed could pay off in new material to bolster the book and address Loomis's legal concerns.

The NAMH had been at the center of a growing debate about Scientology in the UK. In 1968, locals had grown impatient with the large numbers of Americans, Europeans, Australians, and South Africans who were coming to Scientology's headquarters in East Grinstead, England for courses, and there was increasing talk about kicking them out. (Hubbard himself had abandoned East Grinstead a couple of years earlier and at the time was running Scientology from a small armada of ships in the Mediterranean and Atlantic.)

Some of the Scientologists blamed the NAMH for stirring up opposition to them and for chasing Hubbard out of England. Then, in 1969, they attempted to take over the organization by flooding it with new members and electing new board members, including Scientology's UK spokesman, David Gaiman, who was nominated for chairman. When the organization fought back and expelled the Scientologists, they were taken to England's High Court in a well-publicized action, but the court found for the NAMH.

Paulette believed that in the court case, the NAMH had been able to pry "an extensive file of interesting and…supportable material" from Scientology that could help her book. She had contacted the organization and sent it four chapters of her manuscript, hoping to get access to its documents. She told Loomis that a "prestigious British psychiatrist" was willing to give her access to the court file, and the psychiatrist also planned to introduce her to Sir John Foster, who was then leading a government

45

investigation into Scientology.

The NAMH's files, Paulette wrote Loomis, "will easily run more than the 20-30 pages lost from the [foreign] newspaper pieces and will be legally defensible, I suspect exciting material that has never appeared in print before."

She also told Loomis that a Scientology spy at the NAMH had managed to copy her four chapters and got them to David Gaiman, who had been sending her aggressive letters. "At the advice of my attorney (who has been working with me right along on this book), I turned around and asked David to help me on the book, and tell me the Scientologists' side of the story."

She had then received a "chummy" letter from Gaiman, saying that he was delighted with the offer and hoped to "vet" the rest of her book. Paulette laughed off that offer, but she did send him questions and ultimately included his answers as an appendix to the book.

Besides the legal questions, Paulette was also worried that Loomis might be having second thoughts about her manuscript because Malko's book had not set the world on fire. But she suggested that Malko's book had not been bold enough, and that it was important for a writer and publisher to "stick their necks out a little" and publish "exciting, interesting, unknown, controversial material."

Despite her pitch, Loomis ultimately passed on the book. She had better luck with Harry Shorten and his paperback house, Tower Publications, Inc. Shorten was a cartoonist from the Golden Age of comics – he'd helped work on *Archie* comics and had started a longtime newspaper cartoon feature, "There Oughta Be a Law," in the early 1940s. In the late 1950s, he started a paperback line to go along with Tower Comics.

Tower Books looked for legitimate subjects that could be sold with a little sizzle. In 1970, for example, when Paulette was looking for a deal, Shorten had put out a lawyer's examination of the way political prisoners were being treated in Athens – it had the catchy title *Barbarism in Greece.*

Shorten paid Paulette a $1,500 advance, and scheduled *The Scandal of Scientology* for the spring of 1971. Scientology soon found out about the deal, and began sending Shorten increasingly threatening letters as the publishing date neared, vowing to sue him if the book came out. What neither Paulette or Shorten realized was that as the spring of 1971 loomed, they had already come under intense surveillance by a shadowy group that had decided Paulette posed a serious threat.

L. Ron Hubbard had long told friends that he had visions of a guardian angel. He would see her in odd places – even, he told one friend, on the wing of his glider as he flew it in the 1930s. She had wings, and fiery red hair, and he referred to her as his "Empress."

Hubbard received plenty of encouragement about his visions. In 1945 and 1946, after the war, he had lived with John Whiteside "Jack" Parsons, a Caltech rocket scientist who, along with Hubbard, studied the arcane ideas of English occultist Aleister Crowley. Among Crowley's ideas was that each person has a "Holy

Guardian Angel." Years later, after Scientology had come under attack, Hubbard once again turned to his Empress, his guardian angel.

In 1966, Hubbard created a new intelligence-gathering and covert operations unit in Scientology and called it the Office of the Guardian. He put in charge of it his third wife, Mary Sue, and she came to be known as the Guardian. She had fiery red hair and a steely temperament to match. Within a few years, the Guardian's Office became as sophisticated a spy network and intelligence-gathering outfit as any in the world, matching or exceeding the resources of many nations. It would even make fools, for years, of the most sophisticated government on earth.

In 1971, Mary Sue Hubbard still oversaw the Guardian's Office, but the person who ran it day to day from the headquarters in England was another formidable figure: a tall, dark-haired woman with an intimidating manner whose name was Jane Kember. She could make men shake with fear, and part of her mystique came from her accent, which people had a hard time placing. (She had grown up in Rhodesia.)

It was Jane Kember's job to run a worldwide spy network that was tasked with informing Hubbard and Mary Sue about threats before they fully materialized, and to eliminate those threats immediately, often with stunning cruelty. Guardian's Office records showed that by early 1971, it was surveilling Paulette Cooper with intense scrutiny.

On March 11, 1971, Paulette received a telephone call from someone she spoke freely to about her upcoming plans. A short description of that call ended up in a Guardian's Office internal document, suggesting that Paulette didn't realize that a trusted friend was feeding Scientology information about her. Or, alternatively, the description could have been written in a manner to hide that the call was listened to through a wiretap.

Paulette told the caller that she was flying to Scotland on March 31 for a travel story. And if previously she had told Robert Loomis that she was planning to visit the NAMH and its document trove, she now said that her friend Russell Barton—a psychiatrist who ran the Rochester State Hospital—told her not to waste her time. Despite the court case of the year before, the NAMH was still infiltrated by Scientologists, he told her. Paulette also said in the telephone conversation that her book was scheduled to be released on June 1.

Scientology now had the date of publication, and stepped up its efforts to stop it from happening.

Twelve days later, on March 23, an editor at Tower Publications received a letter from Joel Kreiner, representing the Church of Scientology of California—Scientology's "mother church." The letter was a threat to sue if Paulette's book was published, and claimed, falsely, that "Miss Cooper's manuscript was refused publication in the UK due to its libelous content."

On the night of March 31, Paulette flew on BOAC, the British airline, and arrived on the morning of April 1 at Edinburgh airport. Not realizing that her plans were being so carefully watched, she assumed that no one but her parents knew exactly when she was traveling. She didn't expect to be met at the airport. But there, waiting for her, was David Gaiman. A tall, somewhat gangly man with a doughy face, Gaiman had risen to be both the chief spokesman of Scientology in the United Kingdom as well as a top operative worldwide in the Guardian's Office.

He walked up to her, smiling, and handed her some papers. He informed her that they were writs for libel, and that she was being sued for her *Queen* magazine article, which had come out more than a year earlier. Her heart raced as she tried to understand what was happening. Later, she learned that his papers were a hoax. (She wouldn't be served with an actual lawsuit about the magazine story for several more months.)

Gaiman was the man who had cheerily offered previously to help her with the church's side of things in her book, and now he'd accosted her in what seemed to be an obvious intimidation attempt.

When Paulette checked into her hotel in Edinburgh, the front desk began getting peppered by phone calls from people who didn't identify themselves but wanted to know her room number. Gaiman showed up and also asked for her room number, claiming he wanted to interview her for a "scientific publication."

Paulette found numerous people outside the hotel staring at her and following her movements. She told hotel officials about it, and the police were called—and the people, probably church members organized by Gaiman, quickly scattered. A freelance photographer who worked for the *Sunday Dispatch* later told her that he'd been hired by Gaiman to get a shot of her for Scientology's propaganda magazine, *Freedom*, but he'd had a tough time getting a good angle because she wore a scarf and dark glasses when she went outside. Gaiman was unhappy with the result and tried to bargain down what he'd promised to pay. The photographer also said that when the police had been called, Gaiman quickly got out of Scotland.

Two weeks later, the New York offices of Tower Publications got a visit from Reverend Arthur J. Maren, "Minister of Public Relations" to the U.S. Churches of Scientology. According to a Guardian's Office document, Arte Maren's visit was "badly received."

Then, in May, with just weeks to go before the release of the book, Tower received a flurry of messages from various Scientology churches, threatening the company with lawsuits if Paulette's book actually came out. From attorneys representing the Church of Scientology of Hawaii, a telegram arrived, warning Tower that its author had not been telling the publisher everything about herself: "*BE ADVISED OF MY CLIENTS INTENTION TO PURSUE MAXIMUM LEGAL RECOURSE SUGGEST YOU PRIZE YOURSELF OF COOPER LIBEL ATTEMPT BOTH HERE AND ABROAD OF WHICH SHE HAS BEEN CAREFUL NOT TO INFORM YOU.*"

Joel Kreiner, the attorney for the mother church in California, sent a similar telegram: "*THIS WILL ADVISE YOU ON BEHALF OF MY CLIENTS THAT PREPARATION IS NOW UNDERWAY ON COMPLAINT TO BE FILED IN THE EVENT YOU PUBLISH THE MANUSCRIPT ON SCIENTOLOGY SUBMITTED TO YOU BY PAULETTE COOPER...*"

An attorney for the New York church informed Tower that publication of the book would result in an immediate lawsuit for libel. And on May 24, a week before publication, Kreiner sent another letter: "...a complaint for libel is under preparation and will be filed immediately upon the publication of the Cooper manuscript...I have been advised by the Church to proceed with legal action immediately..."

A notation in a Guardian's Office document shows that with just days to go, the same unnamed person who had called Paulette in March phoned her again, and got her to confirm that June 1 was still the date for the book to come out. Paulette also revealed that she was well into her next project: the first book for the layman about forensic crime scene investigation (still a new idea then) that she planned to call "The Medical Detectives."

Then, on May 30, just two days before *The Scandal of Scientology* was to be released, the Guardian's Office began a new strategy. A notation in a GO document showed that on that day, one of its operatives met with Roger, Paulette's old BBDO boyfriend.

After a flurry of intense activity by the church had failed to stop the publication of the book, Scientology was shifting to a new strategy: it wanted to learn about Paulette's sexual history

3

The Scandal of Scientology

There was nothing subtle about *The Scandal of Scientology*. From almost the first page, Paulette set out to warn the world about Scientology's real aims, its track record for legal battles, and its potential for harm. After a brief caveat in her foreword that Scientology might be able to clean up its act and someday become a mainstream religion, her book was an unrelenting, 22-chapter indictment of Hubbard and his creation.

Paulette's book was a paperback intended for a mass audience, and it was consciously more harsh than previous books – in the cover's subtitle, it even carried a subtle reference to Malko's more positive hardcover that had preceded it:

A chilling examination of the nature, beliefs, and practices of the "now religion"

Paulette also referred to Malko's book inside, noting that *Scien-*

tology: The Now Religion had been sued by Scientology in September 1970. After a judge refused to grant summary judgment to the defense, Malko's publisher settled with the church, paying $7,500 and putting out a statement of "regret for any misstatements which may have been made in the book," and pulled the book off the market. Malko learned about the capitulation while he was on assignment on another story in Australia. He seemed to have little interest in continuing to cover the story or in speaking out further.

Paulette's book, on the other hand, was immediately in great demand. In fact, suspiciously so. Dropping by the New York Public Library on Fifth Avenue one day, Paulette checked to see how many copies had been ordered. But when she looked for the book in the card catalog, she found that "Book Missing" had been written on the relevant card, and not by a librarian. When she asked about it, she was told that the library had ordered 50 copies, but all of them were stolen hours after they had been stocked. She could guess who had done it.

She heard similar stories around the country. (Years later, in Los Angeles, a librarian told her that *The Scandal of Scientology* was kept under lock and key, and if a patron wanted to read a copy, it had to be within sight of the staff because there had been so many attempts to steal them.) But the paperback was a great success despite the attempts at sabotage. Some 50,000 copies were printed because it was packed with so much surprising information about an organization that had received so little coverage in the past.

54

In the book, Paulette warned readers about the way members were mined for extremely private information which was then stored and shared among Scientology officials. Even L. Ron Hubbard might see the most private confessions made by a "preclear" in the process of auditing. She noted that Hubbard's foundational text, *Dianetics*, had an obsession with marital violence and abortions: "In the case studies of his first book, you discover that most fathers spent a good portion of their marital lives giving engrams to their unborn children by beating their wives while they were pregnant."

She told how the prenatal obsessions of *Dianetics*, written in 1950, were supplanted two years later by Scientology's interests in past lives, and seeing how far back in the past one could "remember" living in another solar system or galaxy. "One Scientologist claims he fell out of a spaceship 55,000,000,000,000,000,000 years ago and became a manta ray fish after having been killed by one."

At the time, in 1971, Hubbard was somewhere on the ship *Apollo*, running Scientology from sea, and was surrounded by followers who had signed billion-year contracts, even children under the age of ten, some of whom had been made to walk the plank and plunge into the Aegean, which Paulette also wrote about.

She described how Scientology responded to criticism by attacking the critic. This was a policy that Hubbard very clearly spelled out: "We do not want Scientology to be reported in the press anywhere else but on the religion page of newspapers. It is destructive of word of mouth to permit the public press to express their biased and badly reported sensationalism. Therefore we should be very alert to sue for slander at the slightest chance so as to discourage the public press from mentioning Scientology." Their real hatred was reserved not for outsiders but for Scientologists who had turned away from the organization—dubbed "suppressive persons."

Paulette dug up the divorce complaint of Hubbard's second wife, Sara Northrup, which revealed that Hubbard had not divorced his first wife, Margaret Grubb, before marrying Northrup in 1946. Paulette's publication of this fact was the first since 1951, when newspapers first reported Northrup's revelation of Hubbard's bigamy.

Her book detailed how Hubbard was particularly interested in attracting children and celebrities to Scientology. A Scientology Celebrity Centre in Hollywood had opened up, and Scientology had managed to attract Tennessee Williams, Mama Cass Elliot, Jim Morrison, and William Burroughs. (Burroughs had left by the time Paulette's book appeared.) Scientology had also captured the imagination of Charles Manson, who had first encountered it in prison. "After his release, *The [New York] Times* reported, he went to Los Angeles where he was said to have met local Scientologists and attended several parties for movie stars, possibly the July 18 dedication of the Celebrity Centre. Scientology literature was also said to be found at the ranch when Manson and his family were captured. But for reasons unknown, it is claimed that Manson may have been made a 'suppressive person' by the Scientologists, and there have also been hints that he may have joined the Process, the sex and Satan group which originally broke away from Scientology."

Paulette discussed Scientology's attempts to get tax-exempt status and recognition as a church, and its (mostly failed) attempts at political influence. "Scientology is perhaps a religion, is probably a philosophy, is definitely a business, is potentially a political force, and is also a form of therapy, or as they call it now, pastoral counseling. Most people do not realize this, since the Scientologists draw attention only to the idea that they are a religion and a philosophy. Thus, they have been able to keep the public in the dark about what is happening -- and they have also been largely able to avoid public outcry." It was an astonishing read by any era's standards.

Three days after the book came out, a woman showed up at Paulette's East 80th Street apartment to serve her legal papers. Just as she had been threatened previously, Paulette was being sued for libel. But this lawsuit was for damages resulting from her *Queen* magazine article that had come out a year and a half before, not her book which was fresh from the printing press. (Paulette was dismayed when she realized the church objected most strongly to the article's strange headline about "necromancers" and a "con-man"—words that the editors of *Queen* had put on the article without her knowledge.)

She tried not to let the lawsuit get her down—things were actually looking very good in her life. With her first published book in demand, on July 26, Paulette turned 29 years old. She had several more books in the works, and she was still developing her travel-writing career.

In one travel assignment, she even had another strange religious order to investigate. That summer, she traveled to the Netherlands to the town of Staphorst, which was becoming famous for the odd behavior of its residents. Located about 120 miles from Amsterdam in the state of Overijssel, the insular town was home to about 10,000 people "described as more Calvinist than Calvin," Paulette wrote for the *New York Times* in a story that appeared in October. Wearing drab clothes and practicing such medieval customs as bathing only once a week and only then in a tub that had a covering so no flesh could be glimpsed by others, the Staphorsters took their religion very seriously.

Their suspicion of outsiders was so consuming, however, inbreeding was not only producing noticeable affects in their appearance, it was also bringing sterility. Bans on pre-marital sex had been lifted: Paulette noted that a couple had to prove that they could get pregnant before they could marry. Paulette had wanted to title the story "Bewitched, Bothered, and Be-Guildered," but her editors settled on "Getting Stoned (by the Natives) in Staphorst," a reference to the way the Staphorsters had pelted Paulette's rental car with rocks when she first pulled into town. "Paulette Cooper, a freelance who lives in New York City, is the author of *The Scandal of Scientology*," noted the lengthy story, which also carried photos of the Staphorsters in their medieval garb while wearing scowls on their faces.

In July, she'd had an even bigger spread in the magazine of

the *Sunday Times of London* – a 6,000-word account of her week as a cruise ship stowaway, including a glamorous shot of her in a bikini, splashed across two pages.

Paulette was getting key placement in the world's most important publications, she was becoming an expert in off-beat religions, and she even looked the part of an attractive, high-flying magazine writer. Three more books on completely different subjects were underway. Her career was taking off like a rocket. Even her legal problems seemed to be going away: In November, the lawsuit over the *Queen* magazine article was settled. *Harper's Bazaar*, which had taken over *Queen*, paid a nominal amount after putting out an innocuous statement about the article.

But then, in December, as promised, Scientology filed a lawsuit against Paulette's book, asking for $1.5 million in damages for "untrue, libelous, and defamatory statements about the Church." It was a public act by a church that was becoming known for using the courts to punish its critics. Cooper didn't know, however, that Scientology was also still engaged in a very different, and very private, campaign to ruin her.

On February 29, 1972, Jane Kember wrote a memo to one of her underlings, a man named Terry Milner, whose title was Deputy Guardian, Information, United States (DG Info US). "Re Paulette Cooper," it began. "We need to know the following as she is an unhandled attacker of Scientology." Kember asked Milner to find out when and why Paulette had begun her book. She asked him to find out how she had met some of the people she had relied on for information – Michael Sanders, the Justice Dept. employee, *LIFE* magazine writer Alan Levy and several former church members.

"Who is Paulette connected to?" Kember asked in the memo, and complained that Paulette seemed to be so current on important information. Until they knew more about her, Kember griped, they couldn't hit her back.

"She has done an excellent smear job [of] Scientology, and we have no data with [which] to handle her!" Kember concluded.

Milner understood what that meant. He immediately put out word to the operatives working for him: They were to continue their surveillance of Paulette, learn about her past and her associations, and then to begin spreading slander about her – particularly about her sex life. The Guardian's Office and its spy division—Branch One of the Information Branch or "B-I"— used highly professional methods to place informants and gather information. But it could also use very crude methods to get what it wanted.

The ensuing flood of obscene calls from men was a hassle, if not very creative. Even though she was listed in the phone book, until this time Paulette had only rarely received obscene calls. Now, suddenly, they were plentiful. One man admitted that he was calling from Cincinnati, and wanted to know when the second printing of her book was coming out. A long-distance literate obscene phone call – it made little sense. Some calls were more ominous.

"We're gonna push you under a subway car when we catch

you at the station," was one, while another went, "We're gonna give you the .44 treatment."

That one rung a bell. Hubbard, at one point, had talked about "exteriorizing" from the body with the use of the "R2-45" method, and he'd fired a .45-caliber pistol while on stage. (Documents show that Hubbard later used the prospect of the "R2-45" method to intimidate church members who got out of line.)

Other calls were comical. "This is President Nixon and I just want to make something perfectly clear," and, "This is Flo Zieg-field and we've got a great part for you in the Follies. Call me at the Waldorf."

Others were blunt, such as one message left on her machine which said, "I want to fuck your cunt and suck your titties. Call me." In another prank, someone mailed her pornographic maga-zines from Canada by way of her publisher, Tower Books. (In a notation in Guardian's Office records, putting Paulette on two pornographic mailing lists had resulted in "nil results.")

Many of the men who called pretended to be interested in dating her. They would say, for example, that they had met her at a publisher's party. (She rarely went to such events, so she would know right away that the call was phony.) They tended to ask what she was writing about next, pumping her for information at the same time that they were asking her out on a date. Paulette would usually ask them the same question: "If you met me, what do I look like?" They tended to get her hair correct – long and brown – but usually guessed wrong on her height and assumed she was tall.

On February 18, 1972, Paulette was asked to speak at a MENSA meeting, and when she was walking to it someone jumped out of a car and handed her a summons related to the December lawsuit. It unnerved her, and she noticed that someone else from the church sat in the first row at the meeting itself, taping her talk.

More worrisome were the threatening phone calls, and that some of the men who called her seemed to know what she had been doing and where she had been. It was becoming obvious that people were keeping a close eye on her, and Paulette couldn't help but wonder if her phone had been tapped. She called the phone company and asked that a serviceman come out to look at her setup. After a short examination, the serviceman asked Paulette to follow her into the building's basement so he could show her something. Her telephone line, he said, had been tampered with. The technician showed her that the lines that went only to her apartment had been frayed, as if alligator clamps had been put on them so someone could listen in. The lines for the other apartments appeared to be untouched.

Paulette was livid. For months, she'd been putting up with prankish interruptions in her life. But now, things were getting out of hand. It was one thing to try to shake her up at a public speaking event. But to tap her phone?

Paulette decided to act fast, thinking that the church wasn't used to getting a taste of its own medicine. If she could just get off a shot across its bow, perhaps Scientology would back off. She called up Paul Rheingold, the attorney who had represented Ralph

Nader against General Motors in a similar harassment lawsuit a couple of years earlier. They quickly put together a 15-page complaint they knew would make news and that they both thought would scare the church off. On March 30, they filed a $15.4 million suit against the Church of Scientology of New York. Paulette was sure the lawsuit would end the harassment – she still thought it was only the New York org that was hassling her.

To ensure that result, she sought as much publicity as she could about her harassment to give her lawsuit more impact. In February, the influential Reverend Lester Kinsolving responded to her request by writing about Paulette for his nationally syndicated column. "Churches have been generally reluctant to engage in the expense and acrimony of lawsuits," he wrote, "But an organization called 'the church of Scientology' appears to have taken just the opposite course."

He praised Paulette's book, and quoted her saying that she had spent two years researching it, and lawyers had vetted every word. She told Kinsolving, "They are suing me in England as well as the US. When I arrived in Edinburgh last April, they met the plane and hired a photographer to bug me for days. One hundred of them surrounded the hotel, and so many phone calls were received asking for my room number that the C.I.D. (police) had to come in." In all, she said, Scientology was pursuing 58 lawsuits for libel against other people that she was aware of. Some were truly bizarre. The previous year, satirist and prankster Paul Krassner had promoted the upcoming 13th anniversary issue of *The Realist* by saying it would include an article titled "The Rise of Sirhan Sirhan in the Scientology Hierarchy." Krassner had meant it as a joke – the article didn't exist – but Scientology filed a libel suit against Krassner anyway, asking for $750,000.

Rev. Kinsolving pointed out that two years earlier, he had written about Scientology for the first time, and quoted Hubbard describing his invention, Dianetics, as "a milestone for man, comparable to his discovery of fire, and superior to his invention of the wheel and the arch." Scientologists then threatened to sue Kinsolving, demanding a retraction. But the reverend owned a copy of *Dianetics: The Modern Science of Mental Health*, and he pointed out that the statement is practically the first one Hubbard makes in it.

Paulette was thrilled with Kinsolving's story, and sent out copies of it to other prominent writers, hoping to get even more support. On April 5, 1972, she heard back from one of L. Ron Hubbard's old colleagues, the science fiction writer L. Sprague de Camp. "I saw the piece in last Saturday's paper about your countersuit. That's socking it to 'em," he wrote.

He pointed to a statement James Meisler, the Scientology reverend, had made, expressing surprise that Paulette was suing the church after, he assumed, she had "sort of faded away." Meisler's statement, de Camp wrote, "seems to me a virtual admission that the [church's] suit was meant to harass and that the Scientologists had been engaged in the offense of barratry. You might ask Mr. Rheingold whether barratry is a criminal offense in New York State."

Ten days before she sued the Church of Scientology, Paulette was sent a letter that helps explain why L. Ron Hubbard and his wife Mary Sue considered her such a threat. The letter was from Hubbard's second wife – the wife he had tried to erase from existence.

Hubbard met Sara Elizabeth Northrup in 1945, when he'd been demobilized from the Navy following the war. His wanderings in California had taken him to the large, notorious Pasadena house of rocket scientist Jack Parsons, an amateur occultist who only rented rooms to other eccentrics. Northrup was Parsons's girlfriend, but soon after Hubbard moved in and joined Parsons in his occult activities, he stole Northrup away. Parsons didn't seem too put out by it. By that time, Hubbard had separated from his first wife, Margaret "Polly" Grubb, but he was still legally married to her when he proposed to Northrup. They were married in Maryland in 1946.

Northrup reportedly wrote some of Hubbard's published stories, perhaps helping to explain his prodigious output, and she was with him when, in 1950, he published *Dianetics: The Modern Science of Mental Health*, the popular book that sparked a brief craze. (Their daughter Alexis arrived just a few weeks before the book did.) By 1951, however, the craze had subsided, Hubbard was broke, and his marriage was a shambles. Things got so bad, at one point Hubbard absconded with Alexis to Cuba, while Sara went to the press with damning allegations about the state of her husband's mind. She also accused him of torture.

A few months later, Sara got custody of her daughter when

she signed a retraction of her previous statements about Hubbard, and the marriage was legally ended. But then Hubbard began a long campaign to erase any mention of her and to pretend that he'd never married her and even that Alexis wasn't his daughter.

In 1968, Hubbard gave an interview to the UK television program, *Granada*. By then, he'd had four children with his third wife, Mary Sue Whipp. The interview included this exchange:

Hubbard: *How many times have I been married? I've been married twice. And I'm very happily married just now. I have a lovely wife, and I have four children. My first wife is dead.*
Interviewer: *What happened to your second wife?*
Hubbard: *I never had a second wife.*

It was a nonsensical answer that made obvious how badly Hubbard wanted to erase from his life his bigamous marriage to Sara Northrup, and his fathering of her child, Alexis.

By the time Paulette's book came out in the spring of 1971, Alexis Hollister was in college. (She had taken the last name of the man Sara had married after Hubbard, Miles Hollister.) While she was researching the book, Paulette had contacted Sara Hollister in Hawaii. They had exchanged some letters. After the book came out, Alexis also reached out to Paulette. She said she wanted to visit Paulette in New York.

Paulette was wary, suspecting that it might be a hoax. But she gave Alexis directions for how to find her at 16 E. 80th Street, and the young woman came down from Smith College in Massachusetts. As Paulette waited for her to show up, she thought about all the forms of identification she was going to ask for. This woman was going to have to do a lot to convince Paulette that she really was the daughter of L. Ron Hubbard.

And then there was a knock at the door. Paulette opened it, and all of her doubts melted away. It was L. Ron Hubbard's daughter all right. There was no mistaking it. Alexis was 22, she had the characteristic red hair, and she even had some of his facial features. Paulette was convinced. Alexis explained her reason for wanting to see Paulette, and it made her wince. Alexis wanted to know how Paulette had been convinced that her father had committed bigamy. Because if it were true, Alexis said, it made her a bastard.

Paulette's heart sank. In the early 1970s, the notion of "illegitimacy" was still a serious social stigma. Paulette didn't know what to say.

"Don't worry. I'd rather know the truth. I can take it," Alexis told her.

Paulette showed her the documents which proved that Hubbard had still been married to his first wife, Polly Grubb, when he married Sara Northrup in 1946. Even though the divorce with Polly was final by the next year, 1947, and Alexis wasn't born until 1950, the fact that her mother's marriage had been bigamous when it started was enough to convince Alexis that her birth wasn't legitimate. She thanked Paulette.

Then, on March 20, Sara sent Paulette a lengthy letter from

67

Maui. She said that in the fall – in the months after Paulette's book came out – a couple of men had come to visit her. "They were very pale – wore cheap black suits, white shirts, dark ties," Sara wrote. They claimed to be "agents," but wouldn't tell her what agency they worked for. They asked her a lot of questions, and then warned her that reporters – or people posing as reporters – would be coming around to ask about Hubbard. They told her not to say anything. When Sara said she wouldn't answer any of their questions unless they properly identified themselves, the men left, saying they were going to check with "headquarters." They never returned.

Sara wrote that Alexis had also been approached by Hubbard's agents, and they had delivered her a note at college that said Sara had been a prostitute, that she'd worked during the war as a Nazi spy, and that Alexis was an illegitimate child. The men who read it to her told her the note was written by FBI director J. Edgar Hoover.

But Alexis didn't buy it. She knew they weren't FBI agents. She understood who had written the note. "She was both angry and shocked that Ron could do such a thing," Sara wrote to Paulette.

In June 1951, Sara had signed a retraction of her earlier claims about Hubbard in order to get custody of Alexis and to finalize the divorce. But her 1972 letter to Paulette showed that in fact, she hadn't changed her mind at all. And if Sara went public with such thoughts, it could be the nightmare of 1951 all over again for Hubbard.

But he and Mary Sue, if they knew about Paulette's interactions with Sara and Alexis, had even more reason to be alarmed as the summer of 1972 came on. Because it was then that Paulette began working directly with another member of the family.

4

Nibs

While she was finishing up the manuscript of her book in 1970, Paulette was approached by a man named Robert Kaufman, who had written a book of his own about his experiences inside Scientology. Kaufman was a musician living in New York, a pianist who had played in major Broadway productions and had some success in solo concerts. In 1966, Kaufman had been brought into Scientology by friends on the Upper West Side. Extremely skeptical at first, Kaufman had eventually become so dedicated to Scientology he stopped working and went to England to complete the "Saint Hill Special Briefing Course" so he could go "Clear." As he went Clear and beyond with additional courses in Scotland, however, he became increasingly frustrated with what he considered inconsistent and capricious instructions by counselors (some of whom were only teenagers). And the interruptions always ended up costing him more money. Finally fed up, Kaufman came back to New York, suffered a mental breakdown, and hospitalized himself. Then, to help get through his recovery, he'd written down his experiences.

By 1969 he had a completed manuscript, but he'd spent more than a year in a failing attempt to find a publisher. Then, about the time he got to know Paulette, his fortunes changed as he gained the interest of a man who saw in Kaufman's inside account of Scientology the possible answer to his company's decline.

Maurice Girodias was a remarkable publisher. At 15, he'd drawn the cover image for the original edition of Henry Miller's *Tropic of Cancer*, which was published by his father Jack Kahane's Paris company, Obelisk Press. After his father's death in 1939, Girodias inherited Obelisk, nursed it through the war, and then founded his own imprint, Olympia Press. In its familiar green covers, Vladimir Nabokov's *Lolita* was published in 1955, and William Burroughs' *Naked Lunch* in 1959 (about the time Burroughs was starting his own involvement in Scientology). By 1971, Girodias had left Paris and was working out of New York and London, and his company was in decline. To Girodias, Kaufman's book looked like what he needed to turn things around. It promised to be explosive. Kaufman planned to reveal, for the first time, the secrets to Scientology's upper-level teachings in a book written not by a journalist, but by someone who had been inside the organization.

Like Ray Buckingham, Kaufman told Paulette that he literally feared for his life, and he urged her to be cautious. Kaufman's book, *Inside Scientology: How I Joined Scientology and Became Superhuman* came out in June 1972. And by the time it hit bookstores it was already being sued. The church had filed suit in March, naming 18 defendants, including Paulette, who was accused of convincing Kaufman to write his book in a conspiracy – even though she didn't actually meet him until after he'd completed his manuscript. There was subsequently an attempt to serve her the lawsuit at her apartment at 2:30 in the morning. Just what she needed – a knock on the door in the middle of the night while living alone and already spending time and money on her other legal issues cutting into her ability to make a living.

But *Inside Scientology*'s publication had another surprising result: Girodias soon heard from an unlikely person who said he wanted to help promote the book: L. Ron Hubbard, Jr. Called "Nibs" by the family, he was one of two children Hubbard had by his first wife, Polly. Like his father, Nibs was fair skinned and red-haired. But unlike his father, Nibs was uncomfortable in front of a crowd and seemed to have inherited few of the traits that made his father a leader of men. During Scientology's early years, Nibs had tried to be his father's lieutenant. But he walked away from the church multiple times, struggled to raise his own family, and would come crawling back, looking for his father's forgiveness. He was in and out of Hubbard's good graces multiple times, but now, in 1972, he claimed to be finished with Scientology and his father. In fact, he was looking to cause trouble for the organization.

Kaufman told Paulette about Nibs wanting to get involved, and he asked her to help Nibs write a foreword for another edition of his book. Kaufman told her that Girodias was planning both a paperback and a German translation of *Inside Scientology*.

In the summer of 1972, Paulette had left her apartment in New York and was staying with her parents in Mamaroneck. So Nibs took the train each day from the city, and Stella Cooper, Paulette's mother, picked him up at the station and brought him to the house so he and Paulette could hammer out the new foreword for Kaufman's book.

Paulette was staying with her parents because she was recovering from surgery. She'd had benign uterine fibroid tumors removed, and although it was a routine procedure, it left her with serious pain and lingering effects. "I hurt, I hurt," Paulette would mutter as the pain from her surgery kept recurring, and her mother did what she could to help alleviate it.

Paulette was unusually sensitive to what Ted and Stella Cooper thought of her. She knew that much of her own motivation for becoming a writer was simply to give her parents something to be proud of. And now, a year after her first book, the second was coming out. It was a short book, published by Arbor Press, with the title *Growing Up Puerto Rican*. Paulette had interviewed 19 Puerto Rican children growing up in New York. The unrelenting stories of poverty and discrimination prompted the *Hartford Courant* to call it a "sad book" that "should be read by whites." *Publisher's Weekly* compared it favorably to another work that had won the National Book Award. Another slim volume by Paulette, this one for young children, was coming out in a few months: *Let's Find Out About Halloween*, was its title. Three books published and she was only 30. She knew her parents were impressed.

But she also struggled in her relationship with Ted and Stella. Maybe it wasn't unusual for a young woman – and especially during the Sexual Revolution – to have deep-seated issues with her parents. Her differences with them had come on when she was a teenager, which was also not unusual. Being adopted also contributed – Paulette was tiny, and both of her parents were tall, and sometimes people asked about it. Ted had even spent a year before he was married as a semi-pro basketball player in a Michigan league of trade teams. His team was sponsored by a dentist, and Ted was paid $40 a week to cover his salary and expenses as he barnstormed around the state. But things did not always run smoothly, because on at least one occasion, he had to sit out a game when a town wouldn't let a Jew play its local squad.

Paulette loved his stories about his time as "Shorty" Cooper, semi-pro ballplayer, his time as a margin clerk working the a frantic floor the day of the 1929 stock market crash, the time he met Harry Houdini, the time he saw a rollercoaster go off the rails and people were killed...she hung onto his every word.

Paulette's differences with Stella were, on the one hand, the typical sort. Stella wanted her daughter to be a more observant Jew, to get married and give her grandkids. But Paulette sometimes pushed the boundaries with her mother. She would drive on Yom Kippur and go for Chinese food, for example, on a day when her mother was fasting and driving was forbidden.

While Paulette recuperated from her surgery in the summer of 1972, however, there was something of a truce in the Cooper household, especially now that they had such an illustrious guest.

Nibs was glad to accept the hospitality of Ted and Stella Cooper. He told Paulette that he loved her mother's cooking, and he had rarely lived so comfortably.

She enjoyed working with Nibs. He was clearly a tortured soul, the son of the Great Man who was trying to save humanity. They focused on getting down memories of his father for the short piece. A couple of times late that summer, when she felt well enough to go home, Nibs also visited Paulette in her Manhattan apartment on East 80th Street, where they worked on the document, sometimes taking turns on her typewriter. They talked about his memories of his father, and together they produced a 63-page manuscript titled "A Look Into Scientology, or 1/10 of 1 percent of Scientology."

At the outset of the lengthy essay, Nibs wrote that he wasn't out to "crucify" his father, but in the ensuing pages, L. Ron Hubbard and Scientology took a serious beating.

"The night before I was born on May 7, 1934, 8:05 am, the two of them had a vicious fight after a party, and although my mother was approximately five months pregnant, he beat her up. She went into premature labor and I was born," Nibs wrote about Hubbard and his mother, Margaret "Polly" Grubb.

Polly and Hubbard had met in 1933 on a field while waiting to fly gliders. She was an aviator and five years his senior, but she was taken by the 22-year-old redhead with a strong singing voice and a flair for the dramatic. They were married on April 13. As her pregnancy with their first child developed, Hubbard's father, Harry Hubbard, would ask Polly, "How is my Nibs?" The name stuck.

At the time he became a father, L. Ron Hubbard was struggling to make a living as a writer. "He wrote pulp adventure for men's magazines on the level of the Arabian-Prince-who-saves-the-kingdom and later Dad often wrote that Scientology would save the world. He also wrote westerns, science fiction (he was best-known for this), screen plays, and confession magazine stories as if he were a woman. He was capable of writing in so many styles that he told me on two occasions he wrote every story in one magazine as if he were a different author. He wrote no outlines in advance, made no preparations, and he could write a novelette in one night with no rewrites. It helped that he typed 97 words a minute which was amazing since he only used 4 fingers."

Hubbard and Polly had a second child, Katherine. But by the end of the war, they were living apart. Nibs wrote that in 1947, his father told him he was thinking of marrying for the second time, to Sara Northrup. Nibs later found out that his father had already married Sara in 1946, about a year before his divorce with Polly was final. (Hubbard's third wife, Mary Sue Whipp, he met at a Dianetics Center in Wichita. They were married in 1952.)

Nibs wrote that his father actually lived a fascinating life and had several legitimate claims to fame – he had met a president (Calvin Coolidge), became an eagle scout at a very young age, and had set a glider record – but instead, his father made up a lot of untrue stories about himself to create a mythical background that didn't exist. And that included myths about the work he was most famous for. Nibs wrote that his father claimed to have been working on what would become Dianetics and Scientology as early as 1938, but the first time Nibs heard anything about the new "mental science" from his father was in 1947.

In *Dianetics: The Modern Science of Mental Health*, which was published in 1950, Hubbard claimed to have worked with hundreds of test subjects in what sounded like years of research. But he later admitted to his son that he'd thrown it together in about three months. As for those hundreds of cases, Nibs suspected that his father was really just describing his own neuroses. Hubbard, for example, claimed that abortion attempts were more common than people realized. In *Dianetics*, Hubbard made it sound as if every American woman made dozens of abortion attempts during a typical pregnancy. But Nibs wrote that it was his father who was obsessed with abortion, and related seeing his father sitting on his mother's stomach at their Bremerton, Washington home in 1941, causing her to have an abortion. Later, his mother told him that Hubbard "had forced her to have two abortions during their marriage." (Hubbard himself, in a letter he wrote to Veterans Affairs, claimed that Polly experienced "five spontaneous abortions.")

After the spectacular success of *Dianetics* in the summer of 1950, the craze it created gradually died down, and by the next year, Hubbard was bankrupt and had lost the right to use the word "Dianetics" to a creditor. In 1952, he regrouped, went to Phoenix, Arizona, and started over, this time calling his movement "Scientology." He asked his son to join him there to become an instructor and help him rise from the ashes. Nibs, only 18 and not yet graduated from high school, was thrilled. He found himself thrust into the role of prince to his father the king, and he could not have been happier. Nibs had students, he had money, and he was getting laid.

In December 1952, he went with his father to Philadelphia, where Hubbard put on a special set of lectures he called a "congress" (Nibs said his father would do this whenever he needed extra cash), and was on hand when federal marshals showed up to serve Hubbard with a subpoena. His followers got into a scuffle with the marshals, and the incident only fed Hubbard's growing paranoia about government agents and being drawn into litigation or criminal prosecutions.

The next year, Nibs wrote, his father began thinking seriously of a strategy that he believed would insulate him and Scientology from such meddling. "I have always found it interesting that my father turned Scientology into a religion, for I had never known him to be a religious man, attend a Church or even talk of God....What I think really interested Dad...was that calling his group a religion gave him more latitude in regard to corporate structure, made it harder for people and groups to try to get him to curb his activities and gave him tax exemption."

"Perhaps we could call it a Spiritual Guidance Center," L. Ron Hubbard wrote to one of his most loyal followers, a woman named Helen O'Brien, in a letter dated April 10, 1953. Admitting that Scientology "couldn't get worse public opinion," and as a result, fewer customers, Hubbard figured it was time to start a new direction. "I await your reaction on the religion angle."

On December 18, 1953 in Camden, New Jersey, Nibs, his

wife, his father, and a few others signed the papers to create three corporate entities: The Church of Scientology, the Church of American Science, and the Church of Spiritual Engineering. Hubbard said that he had specifically chosen the word "church" and its Christian connotation for recruiting purposes. In February, another Church of Scientology was founded in Los Angeles, and soon became the mother church of the organization. Religion was good for business, and Nibs watched his father become a rich man. By 1972, he estimated, his father had $7 million stashed away, much of it in greenbacks in shoe boxes because his father didn't trust banks.

Nibs himself was making less and less money. As Scientology grew, his father put in more controls so that more money flowed to the top, but there was less for others. His income dropped to about $20 a week, not enough to support his own growing family.

On November 23, 1959, Nibs walked away from the DC org while his father was in Melbourne. After a few months, Nibs started getting threatening messages, including, "*NIBS THE FOUNDING CHURCH IS ISSUING A WARRANT FOR YOUR ARREST...YOU HAD BETTER GET A LAYWER QUICK. DR. HUBBARD.*" For the next three years, Nibs made money doing private Scientology auditing—it was the only "profession" he knew.

Nibs described an L. Ron Hubbard who came off as a con man cynically manipulating people who were gullible enough to fall for ideas about past lives and mental science he had tossed off without much consideration or research: "I remember when I was 7 to 10 years old, Dad used to tell Katy and I long bedtime stories which he obviously made up on the spur of the moment. These same stories with little variation later emerged in various books and writings of his as facts about our past lives or present situations."

In 1952, Nibs said, he helped work on the bizarre book *A History of Man*, which supposedly described the 76-trillion-year evolution of human beings. "He just wrote the book off the top of his head as he had done in his earlier science fiction and other stories," Nibs wrote.

But over time, he said, as Scientology grew, his father actually came to believe in his creation. "I don't think it's the money that keeps him in Scientology now. He is totally dedicated to his stated goals. I think he completely believes in himself, what he's doing, and where he's going."

Nibs himself was finished with his father's invention. After giving up auditing in 1962, he had helped the FDA and the IRS with their investigations, and had testified in litigation. And now he'd written his father's story with one of his father's biggest enemies, Paulette Cooper.

Besides working on "A Look Inside Scientology" together, Paulette and Nibs also talked about Robert Kaufman, who wasn't handling things well. Months earlier, when Maurice Girodias first announced in the trade press that he was going to publish Kaufman's book *Inside Scientology*, a man named James Meisler from the local Scientology office – the org at the Hotel Martinique – called Kaufman, saying he was "a reverend" in the church and he demanded to see Kaufman's manuscript. (A couple of years earlier, Scientology staff members had suddenly started wearing clerical collars and crosses as Hubbard tried to get the church recognized as such for tax reasons and so Scientology staff, as 'ministers,' could avoid being depleted by the draft.) Meisler told Kaufman that he wanted to make corrections to the manuscript before it was published. Kaufman refused, and Meisler responded ominously, "It's your neck. We've got you covered on all fronts."

Soon after that, Kaufman was approached by a man named Larry Tepper who said he was thinking of leaving Scientology and could Kaufman help him make up his mind? Kaufman somehow decided it was a good idea to loan Tepper the first hundred pages or so of his unpublished book. Days later, photocopied versions of the pages – with marked changes – showed up at Olympia Press, mailed from Scientology's Los Angeles offices. (Later, the rest of the pages were stolen from Olympia's offices, and also were returned with "corrections.")

Kaufman's guard was down in part because he was concentrating so hard on a piano recital he was giving that spring at Little Carnegie Playhouse, next door to the great hall itself. The day before the recital, someone identifying himself as Robert Kaufman called the Little Carnegie and cancelled the performance, saying that he had a funeral to attend. When the audience arrived for Kaufman's show, they found the doors locked and no one in the box office. Many went home. When Kaufman arrived, he got someone from Carnegie Hall next door to open up the doors.

Angry at the prank, Kaufman still gave his performance, but a critic with the *New York Times* noted that he played too "aggressively."

Paulette was alarmed by the recital incident. She knew that Kaufman had been hospitalized when he first returned from England. She knew how much the recital meant to him as he tried to get his musical career back to what it had been. If the church was behind the prank – could it really be that cruel?

By now, she was even more determined to get word out about Scientology's practices and the way it retaliated against critics. Over the late summer and into the fall of 1972, she, Nibs, Kaufman, and a man named Bernie Green made multiple appearances on local radio and television shows.

Bernard and Barbara Green lived on the Upper West Side, and in their West End Avenue apartment they had run something they called the "International Awareness Center." Bernie Green had joined Scientology in 1953, and his center was a licensed franchise that introduced people to Scientology before sending them on to the Hotel Martinique for additional training. But then in 1969, the church had cut off Green's license and, he claimed, had spread libelous information about him. He sued with the help of a former Scientologist and attorney named John Seffern, who Paulette was also getting to know well.

The Greens lost their libel suit, but they were now helping to spread information about Scientology, and Bernie gladly joined Paulette and Kaufman in their media rounds. During one local television show on October 25, Scientology's minister James

Meisler was also a guest with Paulette and Green and Kaufman. When Paulette was asked a question, Meisler shouted, "Are you going to plug your book again, Paulette?"

It embarrassed her, and she not only didn't mention her book but didn't even say her own name. She did refer to "Mr. Meisler's snide comments."

But Kaufman spoke up when she was finished. "By the way, that was Paulette Cooper, author of *The Scandal of Scientology*, and although she's only five-foot-two and 90 pounds, she's holy terror to the Scientologists, who are absolutely petrified of her."

It was a satisfying moment, and she felt good as they walked out of the building after the program had finished.

But outside, the Guardian's Office was waiting.

While Paulette continued to warn the public about Scientology, the church stepped up its harassment campaign against her. In the summer and fall of 1972, journalists received phone calls from Scientologists, saying they had "shocking" information about Paulette that was going to ruin her lawsuit against the church. Paulette knew that L. Ron Hubbard had written instructions for how to smear an enemy, and pretending to have "shocking" news about them was one of its main tenets.

In a 1966 "executive letter" Hubbard had published for Scientologists, he laid out How to Do a Noisy Investigation: "You find out where he or she works...and say, 'I am investigating Mr/ Mrs...for criminal activities as he/she has been trying to prevent Man's freedom and is restricting my religious freedom and that of my friends and children,' etc.…You say now and then, 'I have already got some *astounding* facts,' etc.…It doesn't matter if you don't get much info. Just be *NOISY*…"

A man that Paulette had figured out was hiding his affiliation with the church called her repeatedly, peppering her with questions. For some reason, he was particularly curious if she had any pets. In fact, Paulette had a Yorkie she called Tiki and a Chinchilla Persian cat named Bubby. When Bob Kaufman came over and went with her on a trip to the pet store, they realized they were being followed.

A few days later, a man who worked at a mental health hospital contacted Paulette after reading her book. They met to talk, and as she left a restaurant she spotted a man making a very bad job of trying to hide the fact that he was tailing her.

Paulette was surprised when one day she heard from James Meisler, the minister at the New York org, who called and left a message. When she called him back, he told her "I just wanted to know what Paulette Cooper was really like." He offered to meet, but she told him it was a ridiculous idea. She couldn't stand him and she knew he felt the same way. He told her that he didn't want to meet because of the lawsuits that had already been filed.

"I just want to know what made you write your book," he said.

Sure he did, Paulette thought. In their libel suit, the church needed to prove that she had "malice," for the church. Anything she said to Meisler the church might use against her. She turned down his offer to meet, and instead laid into him for harassing

Robert Kaufman. He denied it. "You trapped him in a restaurant, threatened him, stole his manuscript, tried to injunct it in Boston, you're injuncting it now in New York, and you've sued him, and you don't call that harassment?" she said.

"That's our legal department. We didn't harass him," Meisler told her.

He asked her if she'd ever taken courses in Scientology in New York or Washington. She told him that she'd never hidden the fact that she'd taken a weekend class at the New York org. Based on other things that Paulette had written, Meisler told her they had something in common: a dislike for what went on in mental hospitals. But she still refused when he asked to meet. Signing off, he said, "Thanks for the info."

That didn't sit well with her. She wondered for days if she'd said something she shouldn't have.

A few weeks later, someone claiming to be from a credit bureau called the superintendent of her building and asked, "Who pays Paulette Cooper's rent? And how is it paid?" (Paulette had not applied for any new credit in about a year.) When the superintendent refused to answer, Paulette's landlord then received a call from someone claiming to be from a credit bureau who wanted to know if Paulette's rent was paid by her father. Ted Cooper, the person lied, had been writing bad checks and they wanted to warn the landlord.

Paulette also heard from Bill, the guy who, four years earlier, had told her he was Jesus Christ and set her on her exploration of Scientology. He called and said he'd been contacted by a man name Maren who wanted to know if he realized he was featured in Paulette's book. (In the introduction to *The Scandal of Scientology*, she had described the scene when Bill told her he was God, but she hadn't named him.) He was sent copies of the pages from the book where the story appeared, apparently to soften him up.

Bill said "Maren"—presumably Arte Maren, the church's public relations man—called again, and read him a list of questions about Paulette's private habits, including her sexual preferences. Bill refused to answer, and then told Paulette about it.

On September 7, 1972, Deputy Guardian Terry Milner wrote an update of his activities to Mo Budlong, another high-ranking executive in the Guardian's Office who worked directly under Jane Kember.

"SITUATION: Michael Sanders, ex-IRS Attorney in attack against Church, connected with Kaufman, Cooper and Nibs in PT [present time]," the memo began. Sanders was the Justice Department employee who had helped Paulette search through Scientology documents seized in the 1964 FDA investigation. Milner's memo indicated that two Scientology agents had infiltrated Sanders' office so copies of the church documents could be obtained.

"SITUATION: Paulette Cooper still at large."

Milner noted that the GO was now looking into a local prosecutor that Paulette had been dating, a man named Bob Straus. The operatives had obtained a Dunn & Bradstreet report about him. Milner had also obtained Paulette's transcript from City College, where she'd done her master's degree, and was looking to get information about her brief time at Columbia University's Teachers College. The memo indicated that transcripts of two of the radio shows Paulette had been on with Nibs had already been sent to WorldWide – GO headquarters in Los Angeles.

A month later, on October 10, Milner sent Budlong another report about Paulette, stating that "Paulette Cooper still actively attacking Scientology." Under the heading "Why," it offered the explanation that her "continuing existance [sic] can be traced back to ineffective Bureau IV actions to handle early on."

The Guardian's Office Bureau IV handled legal matters – Milner was explaining that by now, the lawsuit against Paulette should have "handled" her and made her go away. Since that hadn't worked, Milner now said he was directing New York personnel to "attack her in as many ways as possible." The first attack – exposing her sex life – had not worked. So now, Milner's spies were investigating and "attempting commitment procedures in line with the targets on Operation Dynamite." The effort against Paulette Cooper now had a name – Operation Dynamite – and its aim was to have her committed. Committed to what, the memo didn't say.

Milner's memo also indicated that the Guardian's Office knew that Michael Sanders had called Paulette twice since May – and didn't say whether one or both phones were tapped – but the operatives who had infiltrated Sanders' office had been unable to find a file on Paulette. They weren't giving up yet, the memo said.

But neither was Paulette. Another Milner memo, from November 6, showed that the Guardian's Office was getting fairly frantic as Paulette continued to make media appearances with Nibs and Kaufman. "Paulette Cooper continues as a source of trouble for the church," Milner wrote. "Right pressure has not been brought to bear on her."

Milner suggested they might try an operation that would spread negative information about a diamond buyer's exchange used by her father and her uncle, Joe Cooper (his name was actually Lou). "Plans are to leak information about diamond syndicate in such a fashion that leak traces back from Joe Cooper to Ted Cooper to Paulette, thus cutting one of P.C.'s financial supports," the memo said. If they could ruin Ted Cooper, they could stop his daughter.

Milner indicated that a Guardian's Office operative had also tried to get Ted Cooper in trouble with the IRS by saying that the jeweler was not reporting thousands of dollars in income. Milner also reported that on October 25, a GO employee had managed to fluster Paulette by taking photographs of her outside a television studio after she and Kaufman and Bernie Green had taped the show mentioned earlier. When Paulette asked the man if he worked for the church and he didn't answer, she yelled out "He is one of them!" Green then put a magazine in front of the man's camera and Paulette told him, "When the pictures come out in *Freedom* you'll be sued for invasion of privacy." (*Freedom* was the name of Scientology's propaganda magazine.)

"Such a big effect for so little work," Milner wanly noted.

The memo indicated that the Guardian's Office had even gone so far as to have some of Paulette's handwriting analyzed. "For use in future operations," it said.

But Milner's November 6 memo also showed that the Guardian's Office was becoming just as concerned about Nibs. In a cryptic note, Milner indicated that three boxes of "material" had been received from Nibs, and that "Nibs has never gotten the motivator he sought." The language was subtle, but the memo hinted that Nibs had switched sides or had been working as a double agent all along.

The day after Milner's memo was written, on November 7, 1972, Nibs made a videotaped deposition, recanting previous testimony that he'd given in a lawsuit between the IRS and the Church of Scientology. After spending the summer writing with Paulette Cooper, visiting her at her apartment, and appearing on television and radio shows with her, Nibs now said he'd been wrong to criticize his father and the church.

"I felt it was about time that I quit fooling around and being a child and quit messing about and lay the facts on the line and say what I have been doing is a whole lot of lying, a whole lot of damage to a lot of people that I value highly," he said.

Nibs was back in Scientology's camp.

Later that month, he sent a letter to Ted and Stella Cooper, whose hospitality he had enjoyed so much just a few months earlier. The note urged the Coopers that their daughter should keep her wits about her. It was a subtle and odd warning, but one that didn't seem out of place – Paulette and Nibs had been antago-

Tony Ortega

nizing Scientology all summer. Nibs merely seemed to be giving friendly advice.

What the Coopers didn't know was that their daughter was being targeted for even worse harassment. It was time for Operation Dynamite to enter its next phase. It was time to get Paulette Cooper committed.

5

Joy

In the fall of 1972, Paulette was running her own subterfuge operation. She was helping her second cousin Joy Heller keep her parents from freaking out about her sleeping arrangements. Joy was seven years younger and a few inches taller than Paulette, but in other ways they were very much alike. Both were petite young women living in swinging Manhattan and had parents from a generation which didn't fully grasp the opportunities that presented themselves in such a bustling environment.

Paulette was taking full advantage of the glamour her writing career made available. She was attracted to powerful, intellectual men. After meeting Eric Sevareid during a 1968 cruise, she'd seen him occasionally over the next couple of years. Paulette was a local dalliance – neither of them took it very seriously. But after that had faded away, Paulette started dating an assistant district attorney in Brooklyn. His name was Bob Straus. He was smart, he made her laugh, and he wanted to have lots of kids.

They argued about it, playfully, through 1972. It was the closest Paulette had come to the thought of marriage.

She was concerned enough about her future with Bob – who she thought might have political ambitions – that she contacted her old boyfriend, Roger, and persuaded him to return to her the photograph he had taken of her in her sheer nightgown. She was relieved when he agreed and turned it over.

Paulette's parents adored Bob, and when he came to visit her that summer when she was staying in Mamaroneck after her surgery, she had to keep him away because he made her laugh so hard her pain flared up awful and she feared her stitches would come loose. Bob lived in Brooklyn, and when Paulette was back in Manhattan, he'd drive over with his giant dog Virgil and they'd invade Paulette's apartment. Paulette was always a little nervous of Virgil (she'd been spooked by a large dog as a child) but he'd jump on her playfully and sloshed around on her waterbed, nearly causing a rupture. Bob would bring his legal work over, and made her laugh by the way he'd read court transcripts aloud. Or they'd go out with his lawyer friends, and they'd talk not about the law but about their dogs.

Joy, on the other hand, had fallen hard for a law student who lived just two blocks from Paulette, and both women understood what hell there would be to pay if Joy's parents knew she was spending just about every night at his apartment.

Paulette proposed a solution: Put some of your things here in my apartment and we'll tell your parents that you've moved in with me. It was a relief for Joy. She liked hanging out with her cousin anyway, and she dug the 16 E 80th Street apartment – she thought Paulette had great taste, with everything in black and white and red like in the best magazines. And the centerpiece was a glass kidney-shaped Noguchi coffee table. At night, when Joy stayed over, she slept in the small living room, and then shoved her things next to the couch so they were out of the way.

Meanwhile, the harassment had seemed to die down over the summer. But in the fall it started to pick up again. The obscene calls, the calls for dates. Also, there were more pranks. While Paulette was away on a travel story, someone called the phone company claiming to be Paulette and asked that her phone be disconnected. It was, and so was her father's when someone claiming to be Ted Cooper called the phone company and asked that his phone be shut off. Paulette had to work for a few days without a telephone until it was reconnected. For her father, who relied on calls from customers, it was a bigger problem.

Another time, a friend told Paulette that she was on a bus and noticed something startling on a newspaper another rider was reading. She said she was certain that she was seeing a photo that featured Paulette's face on a naked body. Paulette was sure it was a composite image, but she was never able to find out where the image had appeared.

Then there was also a scandal sheet that suddenly appeared. It was supposedly put out by a group called "Christians and Jews Against Pornography," and it was hand-distributed to various places around town. It claimed that Paulette Cooper had started out writing porn. (She'd once written an article about *Eros* magazine publisher Ralph Ginzburg, but hadn't written erotica herself.) It called her a pathological liar, a shoplifter, and said she achieve sexual satisfaction only through being whipped, which the leaflet said was something that she had been taught by a rabbi. It said she was spying for the Attorney General's office, that she worked as a part-time prostitute, and that she'd been fired from BBDO for corrupting the morals of her bosses.

The sheet also complained about two other authors, but they were pen names used by writers employed by Maurice Girodias. Clearly, Paulette was the real target, and the claims were based on things that her old boyfriend Roger had told the church, twisted for effect. At 15 years old she had stolen something from a shop, for example, something she never tried to hide. And before Roger, she had at one time dated a rabbi, which she mentioned to him. The rest of it was pure invention. The leaflet enraged Paulette, and she turned over a copy of it to her attorney, Paul Rheingold, as another example of harassment to cite in her lawsuit against the New York church.

And there was more fodder for the lawsuit: It was becoming harder for Paulette to make a living. The harassment and her legal issues were making it tough to do certain stories. In September, for example, she had traveled to Las Vegas for a unique story: She'd heard about the "loser's bus," which drove to Los Angeles late at night for those who had lost so much at the gaming tables they didn't have money for rooms. The bus stopped in Baker, California, in the middle of the desert, where Paulette recorded a wild scene in the predawn hours. Editors at the *New York Times* told her they loved the story and scheduled it for publication, but under Rheingold's orders, Paulette withdrew it – they were afraid that publishing the story would give the church an excuse to claim legal jurisdiction in California for their lawsuit (which eventually happened anyway).

On Monday, December 4, 1972, Paulette typed up the final page of a document she'd been putting together for several months. It was a diary of harassment that Rheingold had asked her to put together to bolster her claims in the March lawsuit.

Paulette was alleging that Scientology had tapped her phone and put her through constant harassment since the publication of her *Queen* magazine article and *The Scandal of Scientology*. Rheingold asked Paulette to write down a record of the obscene phone calls, the pranks, the smear sheet from "Christians and Jews Against Pornography," and the times she found herself being followed.

Just that morning a man had called and told her, "I don't want to upset you, Paulette, but I think you should know about the terrible things that have been written about you on a bathroom wall. Did you know there was something on a bathroom wall about you?"

"Obviously," she wrote in her diary, "the Scientologists didn't feel they got the message through [yet]."

Not only was her harassment continuing, she worried that Nibs had changed camps. She wasn't aware that the month before, he had given testimony for his father. "I'm beginning to suspect he may have gone over to the Scientologist's side and is playing both of us against the middle," she wrote, but she wondered if he had only recently had a change of heart. "I think he was OK while he was here this summer."

On that same Monday when Paulette finished up her diary of harassment for her attorney, three men checked into a Howard Johnson's motel in Manhattan under the names Frank Morris, Don Shannon, and Lawrence Harris. They had just arrived from JFK airport after a long flight from Lisbon, and they were still recovering from a shock. At the airport, a customs official had pulled "Larry" aside, and questioned him about the $100,000 he was carrying in various currencies, including Portuguese escudos, British pounds and Moroccan dirhams.

The other two barely concealed their panic, figuring they were all about to be slapped into custody. But Larry emerged from the encounter unscathed, if looking somewhat stunned, and the three grabbed a cab for the city. In the taxi, Larry explained that the customs official recognized him for who he really was – L. Ron Hubbard – but it turned out the federal agent happened to be a fan of Hubbard's science fiction, and he'd let him go without further questioning. "Frank Morris" was actually Jim Dincalci, Hubbard's medical officer, and "Don Shannon" was Paul Preston, their bodyguard.

Dincalci worried that news would spread of Hubbard's return to America after the airport incident. But Hubbard didn't seem concerned. Dincalci went out to buy them lunch and new clothes, and the next day he went to search for an apartment. The three were in New York because things in Morocco and Portugal had gotten too hot for Hubbard. Since 1967, he had been at sea, the "commodore" of his own small navy consisting of three ships, the flagship *Apollo*, the *Athena*, and the sloop *Diana*, which was not only the name of a Greek goddess but also the name of one of Hubbard's daughters.

One country after another had proved to be unfriendly to Scientology, and Hubbard was running out of safe ports. He had left the US for England in 1959, had tried to establish a presence in (and had hopes of taking over) Rhodesia in 1966, and then had launched his navy. In turn, governments in Greece and North Africa had chased out the aging science fiction writer and his crew of several hundred young followers.

In 1972, after more than five years at sea, the *Apollo* needed serious repairs and was in dry dock in Lisbon. For several months, Hubbard, his wife Mary Sue, and some of their crew had lived in Morocco and had become involved in political intrigue there. But then they received intelligence that French agents were moving in to arrest Hubbard on fraud charges. Hubbard, Mary Sue, and the rest of the crew packed quickly and headed for Lisbon on May 3. Finding that it wasn't safe there, the next day Hubbard had flown with Dincalci and Preston, bound for Chicago with a layover at JFK. After the incident with the customs agent at the airport, they decided to stay put in New York. Now, accompanied by just Dincalci and Preston, and with his wife and the rest of the crew back in Lisbon, Hubbard decided to wait things out for a while.

Dincalci soon found a sizable place in a 13-story building in Forest Hills, Queens on 112 Street, called "Executive House." Hubbard, who had not been in the US for 13 years, seemed mesmerized by how much the country had changed since 1959 and sat for hours at a time, watching television.

Joy Heller was slightly in awe of her older cousin. She was impressed that Paulette was a published author. Joy stopped by the apartment each day after working in sales at Bergdorf Goodman, in part to keep up the fiction that she was living there, but also because she liked hanging out at the apartment when she wasn't seeing her boyfriend. Which is why she was there with Paulette on December 6, 1972, when someone knocked at the door.

It was a young woman, bundled up against the chill outside, and Joy wondered how she had managed to get through the building's front door and into the vestibule outside their apartment. The woman had long black hair under a hat, and she wore a dark pea coat and gloves. She introduced herself as Margie Shepherd to Joy and Paulette, who invited her in. Margie didn't take off her coat, but went directly into her spiel, that she was gathering signatures for a petition and donations to support Cesar Chavez, the human rights activist, and the United Farm Workers. Paulette generously offered to help, and went looking for her checkbook. Margie asked for a glass of water, and Joy and Paulette went into the kitchen to fetch her one, leaving Margie alone briefly in the living room.

When they came back, and Paulette began writing out a check, Joy couldn't help noticing that Margie had not only kept her coat on, she also hadn't taken off her gloves. Joy thought it was slightly odd – the weather outside might have been cold, but in the ground floor apartment the temperature was warm. Paulette gave Margie the check and took the petition, which was on a clipboard, and signed it. Joy signed it as well. Then Margie went on her way.

Soon, Paulette and Joy had nearly forgotten about Margie's visit.

On December 8, 1972, two days after Margie Shepherd visited Paulette's apartment, the Church of Scientology offices at the Hotel Martinique received a very strange letter. Incoherent, badly spelled, and vague, the short note contained the words "I'll bomb you."

Five days later, a second letter arrived, this one just as badly put together, but it began with the word "James," apparently a reference to James Meisler, the "reverend" who was the org's spokesman. This second letter also contained a vague threat: "I'll give you one week before scientology is a exploding volcano."

Meisler contacted the FBI. He told the agency that the notes were clearly bomb threats, and he had two main suspects in mind for who might have sent them: Paulette Cooper and Robert Kaufman.

Paulette had no idea that the FBI was beginning an investigation of her. On December 15, two days after the Scientology org received the second threat letter, she made a move in the night to a new apartment.

After dreaming about it for two years, she was finally moving into the Churchill, at 300 E. 40th Street. Barbara Lewis had notified her when an apartment opened up underneath her own place – Barbara was in 5H, and Paulette moved into 3H. She would now have a 24-hour doorman, and an apartment that wasn't on the ground floor which made her feel much safer. Joy agreed to stay in the apartment on 80th Street as Paulette moved her stuff into the new place in the Churchill.

Four days later, Joy heard a buzz at the front door of the townhouse. The building on 80th Street had a very distinctive red front door, and on either side of it were narrow windows. Joy could see through those windows that on the other side of the door was a light-skinned black man with a large afro. He was very well dressed in a camel hair coat, and he was holding a bouquet of roses in his gloved hands. Her boyfriend had just recently sent her flowers, and she assumed he'd done it again. She opened the door to let the man in.

He handed her a card which had her last name on it, but the first initial was wrong. Joy didn't really have time to think about it, because the man suddenly pulled a revolver out of the flowers, and grabbed her, putting the barrel of the gun against the back of her neck. Paralyzed with fear, Joy had no time to react. But he held her only for a moment. Then he pushed her away and went into her apartment. He was only inside briefly, and she watched in terror as he walked back out of the apartment, passed by her, and then fled the building.

Joy screamed her head off until other people came and called the police. As soon as she had her wits about her, she called her boyfriend, who came running from his apartment two blocks away. She told him what had happened – the details about the flowers, the card, the gun to her neck, and that he'd pushed into the apartment, apparently looking for something but not finding it.

They called Paulette, and all three of them immediately came to the same conclusion – this was meant to intimidate her. Joy's boyfriend asked Paulette, "Does the church know that you moved? You have to tell them."

Paulette said that she would. But the incident left her shaken. What if the man had found her in the apartment? Is that what he was looking for?

Paulette didn't have much time to puzzle it over because within a few days, she was surprised by a visit by two FBI agents. One of them, Special Agent Bruce Brotman, told her that they just wanted to ask her a few questions and said perhaps she could help them out on a case.

What a coincidence, Paulette thought. She happened to be working on her fourth book, the longest of her books so far, which would be called *The Medical Detectives*. Decades before *CSI* became a hit on television, Paulette was exploring the way science was changing the way police handled crime scene investigation. And now the FBI wanted her advice? Tell me how I can help, she told them.

Brotman said that James Meisler, the public relations man at the Scientology org at the Hotel Martinique, had reported two bomb threats that had been received at the church.

Meisler. She frowned. She was already tired of the man's name. Not only had he tried to intimidate Bob Kaufman over his book, but she had noticed that when he was interviewed by the press, he tended to be hit with quotes from her book. When that happened, Meisler would accuse her and Kaufman of bigotry for investigating the church.

The agents told Paulette that they were trying to figure out who might have sent the anonymous bomb threats. And they told her that when they asked Meisler who might have done it, he had named her.

She laughed.

"I was going to say Meisler was behind it," she told them. "If he said I did it, then it's a phony letter. They have a lot of real enemies they would have named if they'd received a real letter."

She told him it was just the latest form of harassment that she'd been enduring. She explained how Scientology was given to pranks and dirty tricks – she'd sued the church earlier in the year after she found evidence that her telephone had been tapped. Of course such an organization would be capable of sending *itself* fake bomb threats, she pointed out. The whole thing was so ridiculous, she thought. And when the agents asked her to be fingerprinted, she readily agreed.

She had nothing to hide, after all.

About a month later, in January 1973, agent Brotman was back. In the ensuing weeks, things had seemed to calm down. The dirty phone calls and threats had fallen off, to Paulette's relief. She assumed that her change in address to the Churchill had bought her some time before the church realized that she'd moved. (At this point, she simply didn't grasp the breadth of the Guardian's Office surveillance operation. The church in fact knew immediately where she had moved and when.)

She was surprised to see Brotman, but welcomed him into her apartment again. He was still looking into the bomb threats, he told her. And now her stomach started doing flips as he told her that he had interviewed her boyfriend, Bob Straus, as well as Joy's boyfriend. They had each told Brotman that Paulette was not the type to send bomb threats through the mail.

Well, that was some reassurance, she thought. But why was the FBI even considering Meisler's nonsense that she might have done something as ridiculous as threaten to blow up a church of Scientology? Brotman left after she said she had nothing else to tell him.

It still didn't occur to her to hire an attorney and put the FBI on the spot about its investigation, possibly because she had other things occupying her mind. She had *The Medical Detectives* to finish up. It was turning into her best book, and her agent Ted told her he thought it could be a bestseller. Deeply researched, it really had no precedent, and would bring to light dramatic new ways of solving crimes. It had the potential to turn into television or movie projects. She bore down to get it done, but also managed a trip to the Caribbean, still developing her travel writing career.

Then, on February 4, Barbara Lewis came downstairs to her apartment. The two visited with each other a few times a day, so Barbara's knock on the door didn't come as a surprise. But the ashen look on Barbara's face did.

She had in her hands a piece of paper with some typing on it, with words in all capitals, like it had been created on an IBM Selectric typewriter.

"What is it?" Paulette asked. Then, when she saw what it was, she wanted to vomit.

"They're all over the building," Barbara said.

DEAR FELLOW TENANT:

THERE IS A WOMAN OF VERY BAD CHARACTER WHO HAS RECENTLY TAKEN RESIDENCE IN OUR BUILDING. MR. FREDRICKSON, OUR MANAGER, HAS PERMITTED THIS. PERHAPS MR. FREDRICKSON DID NOT KNOW OF HER PAST HISTORY, BUT I DO.

SHE HAS RECENTLY BEEN FORCED TO MOVE OUT OF TWO APARTMENTS FOR ILLICIT PARTIES AND SEXUAL PERVERSIONS. AS A MATTER OF FACT, HER LAST EXCURSION TO EUROPE PROVED QUITE EMBARRASSING, AS SHE WAS CAUGHT, BY OFFICIALS, TRYING TO SEXUALLY ABUSE A 2 YEAR OLD BABY GIRL.

I AM APPALLED THAT SUCH A DEGENERATE BE PERMITTED TO LIVE AND WORK AMONG DECENT PEOPLE SUCH AS OURSELVES. IT'S TRUE THAT WE'RE NOT PERFECT, BUT

*THIS 30 YR OLD SICK CHILD IS AN EXAMPLE OF WHAT THE
SCUM OF THIS SOCIETY IS CAPABLE OF.*

*YOU DON'T HAVE TO TAKE MY WORD FOR IT. IT'S EASY
TO SEE FOR YOURSELF. SHE'S 30 YEARS OLD, WITH THE
BUILD OF A 10 YEAR OLD CHILD. HER NOSE IS VERY LARGE,
AND NOT UNLIKE THAT OF A "HALLOWEEN WITCH." HER
TONGUE IS NOTICABLY SWOLLEN FROM AN ATTACK OF
VENEREAL DISEASE IN THE PAST.*

*SHE IS A TENANT IN APARTMENT 3 H. HER NAME IS MISS
PAULETTE COOPER.*

*I ASK YOU TO PLEASE CONTACT MR. FREDRICKSON,
AND HELP ME TO HAVE THIS WOMAN REMOVED FROM OUR
RESIDENCE, AND, IF POSSIBLE, PUT UNDER APPROPRIATE
PSYCHIATRIC CARE.*

A CONCERNED NEIGHBOR

Hundreds of the letters reached the residents of the Churchill.

None of it was true, except for her age – and even that bothered her. She was in the habit of keeping her age unknown, for
reasons that were even more obvious in 1972.

It was Scientology, she knew. But she wondered at some of
the details. The mention of the swollen tongue was odd, and she
thought it could have come from only one source: Roger, her
old boyfriend from BBDO. He had known that her tongue was
slightly unusual. He noticed it for the first time when she was eating an ice cream cone, and asked her about it. She explained that
she had what doctors called "geographic tongue," which resulted

in slight striations, possibly because of a vitamin deficiency in her childhood. It wasn't something others would notice. Could Roger be working to help them with her harassment?

The letter's reference to the two-year old girl also confirmed to Paulette that the smear had to come from Scientology. In her book, she had written about a church auditor who had molested a child. She withheld from the book that the child was only two years old. But the church knew. And now they were accusing her of the same thing. The letter also said she had just returned from Europe. She thought it was an odd mistake. She'd actually just come back from the Caribbean, but that they knew she'd traveled at all suggested they were keeping tabs on her.

She was still puzzling over the letter when there was another knock at her door. It was Margie Shepherd, the young woman who had visited Paulette at her E. 80th Street apartment two months earlier, when she was canvassing for the United Farm Workers. Margie was standing there with another young woman she introduced as Paula Tyler. Margie said she'd thought of Paulette when Paula told her she needed help finding a place to live.

Paulette invited them in, and they talked about what a great place the Churchill building was. She might have stopped to wonder how Margie had known that she'd moved since the last time she saw her. She also might have thought it curious that Margie had looked her up to do her a favor when their only previous encounter was the short time it took for Paulette to give her a check and a signature for Cesar Chavez.

But Paulette's head was still spinning over the smear letter.

She was extremely trusting, and felt flattered that she'd be called upon for her ability to help Paula, who was hoping she could also get an apartment in the Churchill. Paula told a distressing tale of how she'd come to need Paulette's help. She had come out from California, hitch-hiking all the way, and during her trip, she'd been raped. Now she was in New York without a place to stay and not knowing anyone. She had money, and could afford an apartment at the Churchill, and could Paulette help her get a place?

In fact, Paulette did know about an apartment that was coming open on the 16th floor. Pleased to have put them together, Margie Shepherd told Paulette that she needed to get going. She was headed to Boston, she said, and took her leave. Paulette never saw her or heard of her again.

Paulette did help Paula Tyler get into an apartment, and also introduced her to Barbara Lewis. After she moved in, Paula began joining Paulette and Barbara in Paulette's third floor apartment almost every day to spend time with them.

A couple of weeks after Margie and Paula's visit, Paulette was subpoenaed to appear at a federal grand jury. She felt flattered, and was excited to appear. Expecting that she would be consulted as an authority on Scientology, she went alone to the proceedings – without a lawyer – thinking that the grand jury needed her expertise to make sense of James Meisler, his church, and the phony "bomb threats."

Meisler was there, at the federal courthouse, wearing a long black robe and an oversized cross. Paulette rolled her eyes. Meisler looked ridiculous – at least, to someone who understood that L. Ron Hubbard had sold Scientology as an "exact science" for more than 20 years, but had only recently asked that some "ministers" adopt clerical garb. It was a show for tax reasons, she thought, and she looked forward to explaining that to the large number of grand jurors in the sizeable chambers.

The night before, her boyfriend, Bob Straus, the assistant district attorney, warned her that she might be on dangerous ground. Don't open your mouth, he told her, until you're sure that you're not the target of the investigation. He wrote up for her a short script to keep with her when she was asked to testify. He told her to ask, "Am I the target of this investigation?"

She was alarmed, but Bob told her not to worry. He told her the prosecutor, assistant US Attorney John D. Gordon III, would surely tell her that she was not the subject of the investigation. But just in case, Bob wrote down what she should say next, depending on how Gordon answered.

When the time came, and she was standing before the grand jury after Gordon had called her, she asked the question from the piece of paper Bob had written for her.

"Am I the target of this investigation?" she read.

Gordon told her that yes, she was.

Paulette was stunned, but she looked at the piece of paper again, and read what Bob had written down in case that was Gordon's answer.

"May I return with a lawyer?" she asked.

Gordon said yes, and Paulette went back to her apartment with her stomach in her throat.

After she told Bob what had happened, he told her to get an attorney, and fast. But as she began calling around, she was told she'd need to come up with at least $5,000 cash for a retainer – and on her measly freelancing income, that was out of the question.

One attorney she consulted said he would call Gordon to get a sense of how serious the prosecutor was. He then called her back and said Gordon had told him the government had physical evidence against Paulette, but he wouldn't explain what it was. The attorney told her an indictment was very likely, and she'd need to pay premium prices.

Shaken, she decided if she was going to have to pay so much, she might as well have an attorney with a strong reputation. She hired Charles A. Stillman, who was becoming known for defending high-profile clients after previously working as a federal prosecutor.

She managed to come up with $5,000 when her parents agreed to pay half of it. And telling them why – well, she couldn't bring herself to tell the entire story yet. She just told them she was in trouble and needed help.

Stillman and his younger colleague, Jay Zelermyer, told Paulette they didn't know what evidence the prosecutor, Gordon, believed that he had. Stillman told her he wanted to get an initial question out of the way first: Did she do it? Paulette was gutted. She had to convince her own attorney that she hadn't sent bomb threats to a church?

She asked if taking a polygraph exam might help, and they

agreed to set one up. She assumed the tests were infallible and that taking one would make the whole problem go away. They sent her to be examined by Nat Lorendi, a police department examiner who was known for getting confessions out of suspects. Paulette didn't like his coarse, *dees*-and-*dose* style, and she was surprised when he yelled some of the questions at her. Lorendi told her attorneys that the results were inconclusive, but indicated heavy stress, which correlated with lying. His conclusion – which she knew he'd give in court – was that she was probably guilty.

Alarmed, Paulette and her attorneys then turned to polygraph expert Richard O. Arther's firm, but the results were also inconclusive – Paulette failed the control questions, suggesting that she was not someone who should be tested on the machines. When she was asked if a pink piece of paper with a blue border was pink, she said yes – but the machine indicated that she was "lying." Paulette was told that as a professional writer, her sensitivity to the multiple meanings of words made her a bad subject for a polygraph.

On March 14, 1973, Mo Budlong of the Guardian's Office received a report which suggested that Paulette Cooper was still under heavy surveillance, and that her apartment or her attorney's office may have been broken into. "Dear Mo: These are Paulette's notes. They are headed accordingly by herself. It has given us insight into how they may proceed in Rheingold's legal case," the document said, referring to Paulette's 1972 harassment lawsuit against the New York org.

The next day the GO in New York sent out another report about what had now come to be known as "Operation Lovely." The opening lines of the memo, addressed to Terry Milner, made it clear that Scientology's spy network was closely watching Paulette's prosecution over the bomb threats. "As you well know, Op. Lovely is getting much hotter on this end, but is nevertheless moving along quite nicely. The decision on Miss Lovely's court trip should be coming down any day now."

The memo went on to say that the GO had discovered a "large amount" of additional "enemy connections" to Paulette, in part through – somehow – getting 458 pages of copies of her correspondence to other people, including Nibs.

6

'you people are always watching me'

While her legal situation was getting dicier by the day, Paulette by now had an unlikely new ally—a Toronto grandmother. The previous fall, Nan McLean and her family had decided to defect from Scientology after three years of enthusiastic participation. After joining in 1969, by the next year Nan was regularly making the 100-mile round trip drive to the Toronto org from her home north of the city. Her son, John, had quit high school to join the "Sea Org" crew on the yacht *Apollo*, where L. Ron Hubbard was running Scientology from the Mediterranean and Atlantic.

But then the McLeans soured on Scientology. Nan had tried to report problems she saw at the Toronto facility, but soon found that following the church's rules about submitting complaints only made her a target for harassment. By the fall of 1972, the entire family was out, and they wanted the public to know what they had experienced.

Nan McLean became a vocal critic of Scientology, and after she made a television appearance early in 1973, she got a call from Paulette Cooper. The two rapidly became good friends. After 11 pm, when the long distance rates went down, Paulette would call Nan and they would talk for hours almost daily. Paulette soon made a trip to Canada to meet the family.

The two women had little in common except that they were both being followed and harassed by agents of Scientology and were both determined to tell the world about it. At that time, there was almost no one in the U.S. and Canada but Paulette Cooper and Nan McLean who was willing to talk publicly about Hubbard's church and its controversies.

Nan soon understood every detail of Paulette's history and the legal problems she faced. They talked into the night about what Paulette's attorneys were doing to help her. They shared research they had done on the church, swapping documents and notes. And Nan was one of the few people who understood just how Paulette's legal troubles were affecting her.

As Paulette waited for her next date with the federal grand jury, she dragged through each day out of her mind with worry, chain-smoking Marlboro cigarettes, eating little, and drinking a lot of cheap vodka. Her weight, already low, plunged.

Paula Tyler, the woman she'd helped get a place in the building, worried about Paulette's weight loss – she would go from 98 pounds down to only 83 by the summer – and Paula also worried about Paulette's state of mind.

Paulette was practically living in the same pink terry cloth bathrobe, unable to put on real clothes as she waited for the next call from her attorneys. She couldn't even bring herself to leave the building for the funeral of Malcolm McTear Davis, the editor of *Travel* magazine, one of her closest friends, and a man who had helped her get her start in the business. She was becoming a wreck.

The night before her next grand jury appearance, Paulette finally got to see photocopies of the two bomb threat letters that had been sent to the Scientology org. She couldn't believe how comical they appeared, and nothing like the way she wrote. The first one was badly spelled, the spacing was odd, and the threat was vague...

These damn books they are closingin on me
I know you're all around me everywhere. My tongue is
swollen --- i hurt---- my operation----YOU did it to me--
you people are always watching me-Ill get you
you' re like the Nazis or thex Arabs--- I'll bomb you
i'll kill you!
I forget sometimes But I'll get you
If my Friends dont do it then Ill do it!!!

There was that reference to her tongue being swollen again, which she assumed came from Roger, her old BBDO boyfriend. But the next reference "I hurt – my operation," surprised her.

She thought about the previous summer, when she and Nibs had worked together at her parents' house in Mamaroneck.

"I hurt, I hurt," she'd moan to her mother when the pain of her operation flared up. Nibs had heard her say that. Could *Nibs* have had something to do with the letters?

The second letter, mailed five days after the first, appeared to be addressed to James Meisler, spokesman for the New York Scientology org...

> *JAMES*
> *This is the last time i am warning you*
> *I don't know why I'm doing this but you are all out*
> *to get me i'm sick of this*
> *Hitler -Hubbard-Meisler   must b e destroyed*
> *You no longer will look down on me*
> *I give you one week before scientology is a*
> *exploding volcano*
> *I will knock you out if my friends wont*

The reference to an "exploding volcano" was a puzzling one. An erupting volcano would eventually become a familiar symbol for Scientology on the cover of newer editions of *Dianetics*, its founding book. But in 1973, not many people knew that volcanoes were part of the church's upper-level teachings.

Paulette's lawyers started asking her about Robert Kaufman, whose book *Inside Scientology* was the first to reveal what was in those teachings. Kaufman wrote that high-level members pay large amounts to learn bizarre things about the history of the galaxy, including a dictator named Xenu who lived 75 million years ago. Xenu had detonated nuclear bombs in Earth's volcanoes to vaporize and cluster together billions of surplus beings, according to Hubbard.

It seemed incredible, but could Kaufman have been involved in the bomb threats? Paulette told her lawyers she didn't think so. She'd become good friends with him, and although he'd been under nearly as much harassment as her – and hadn't handled it very well – she didn't see him getting involved with the church to harass her.

When Gordon turned over copies of the letters, her attorneys had talked with him. They told Paulette that Gordon believed she had purposefully written the letters in an illiterate style to camouflage her involvement.

Paulette was stunned. Not only did she feel insulted that anyone would think she was capable of writing anything so illiterate as these letters, but how did Gordon explain that the same phrase – about her swollen tongue – was in one of the bomb threat letters *and* the smear letter that had been sent to the residents of the Churchill? Had Paulette smeared *herself* by sending that revolting letter to her neighbors?

Her attorneys had pointed that out, they said. And they insisted that Paulette had no motive to cause such trouble – her career was going well, she had books coming out, why would she bother? But they said Gordon believed that a disturbed person could act in irrational ways. He thought it was possible that she could have written the smear letter to the residents of the Churchill in order to camouflage her involvement in the bomb threats.

It made no sense to Paulette, and she still didn't know what physical evidence Gordon believed he had, besides the ridiculous letters themselves.

Paulette would be questioned the next day before the grand jury, and they wondered what made Gordon so sure she had typed the letters. Had Gordon somehow obtained other letters or manuscripts that Paulette had typed, and compared them to the bomb threats? Did Gordon believe they'd had all been created on the same typewriter?

Paulette had forgotten that Nibs had had access to her machine the previous summer. Robert Kaufman had also come over on occasion. And so had other people. Her lawyers hired their own expert to examine her typewriter. Was it the key to the case?

The next day, while she waited outside the grand jury room for the session to begin, Paulette saw James Meisler, presumably waiting to testify against her. She also noticed FBI agent Brotman come out of the room. He avoided her stare. (Brotman was commended for his work investigating Paulette. He later boasted about his success in the case and showed off his commendation to an old college roommate, not realizing that he happened to be Paulette's cousin.)

Paulette told herself she could get through this. She only needed to tell the truth, and she'd be fine. She hadn't typed or sent the silly bomb threat letters, and as long as she told the truth, they couldn't charge her with a crime.

Gordon began asking her questions, soliciting basic information about her background and what she did for a living. Then he presented her the letters, and she had the first opportunity to see them and their envelopes in their original form. They were on two kinds of stationery. The first letter was on typical stationery, but the second one was on paper that was lightweight airmail paper, which surprised her. If you were going to send a letter from one address in New York City to another, you wouldn't use that kind of paper. Gordon started asking her about the letters, about the stationery, about the words.

She calmly answered what she knew. She had never seen the letters until she had seen copies of them the previous day at her attorney's office. She didn't know where the stationery came from. She didn't recognize the writing in them.

Gordon pressed her, asking her if she'd touched the letters.

They weren't mine. So I didn't touch them, she said.

Did you type them?

No.

If you didn't write them, who do you think did?

I would assume Mr. Meisler knows the answer to that question, she answered.

For what seemed like hours, Gordon, who had a nervous habit of shaking his leg, went around the same territory, asking her about the same things. Finally, he ended the questioning and asked her to leave the room.

A short time later, he asked her to come back in.

Something was different. He was no longer asking her accusatory questions. Now, he calmly asked for her Social Security number. He asked if she was on any medications or drugs. He asked if she was aware of her current circumstances.

What was he getting at? She told him of course she knew what was happening and why she was there. She noticed that his leg was shaking even more.

At that point, Gordon leaned in and lowered his sight at her. "Well, then, could you explain how your *fingerprint* got on the second letter?"

Paulette felt faint as the blood rushed from her face. She thought she was going to collapse. She managed to keep her outward composure, but the room felt like it was spinning.

Gordon told her that besides her fingerprint on one of the letters, the government had hired a document expert who had compared samples of other things Paulette had typed, and the expert concluded that her machine had been used to type up the two bomb threat letters.

Paulette didn't know why her fingerprint would be on one of the letters, but she suspected that L. Ron Hubbard Jr. – Nibs – had some involvement because of the wording in them. She pointed out that he had worked with her the previous summer, and he'd had access to her apartment.

By the time she got done talking about Nibs, she was feeling better. She'd spent the whole day telling the truth. And telling the truth would convince the jurors that she had nothing to do with the threats.

The next day, her attorney phoned. Though it was Charles Stillman she had hired because of his reputation as a former prosecutor, it was Stillman's younger colleague, Jay Zelermyer, who was doing most of the leg work on her case. Just a few years out of law school, Zelermyer actually had extensive contacts in New York's prosecutor circles, through Stillman, and he had called Gordon to find out the result of the grand jury proceedings.

Paulette assumed everything was going to turn out fine. So she was stunned when he told her that Gordon planned to indict her on two counts for the bomb threats, and a third count for perjury. Gordon believed she had lied to the grand jury.

She felt unsteady on her feet. She couldn't assimilate the news – she saw her life falling apart, her career over. She would have to go through a very public trial. She might even go to prison. Her lawyers said that details about her private life would be presented by the prosecution to build a case intended to show that she was capable of sending bomb threats. That she'd smoked pot. That she'd slept with several men and had never been married. It might have been the Sexual Revolution, but she knew what the newspapers would do with that kind of information, and her parents would have to be exposed to it.

Barbara came down and tried to console her, but it was hopeless. She was crying. And drinking. And smoking like a fiend. Paula Tyler came over to hear what had happened. She seemed shocked and horrified by the news. And then Paulette had to call and tell her parents.

She told her father that she was going to be indicted. Ted Cooper tried to console her but she was almost incoherent. When she mentioned that the trial was going to cost a lot of money, he said he was prepared to back her up financially, whatever she had done.

"But just out of curiosity," he said, "did you do it?"

Paulette couldn't believe it.

"Dad, I've lied to you about a few things in the past, like what time I really came home some nights. But this is important, so I wouldn't lie to you about it," she said. "I didn't do it."

Paula Tyler could hear the emotion in Paulette's voice, and her own eyes began to water as Paulette began to cry at what her father said.

"Mom and I wouldn't want you to perjure yourself before a grand jury and admit to a crime you didn't do just to save us money," he said. "And if we have to sell the house to defend you, we'll do it."

Paulette could hear that her father was holding back tears. Hearing him almost crying made her start up again and then Paula could no longer control herself. She and Paula and Barbara wept and wept.

Six miles away, on the second floor of a house in the Elmhurst neighborhood of Queens, L. Ron Hubbard was sitting at a small desk, tapping away at a typewriter on a project that had taken up much of the winter and early spring.

After a bleak Christmas in Forest Hills, Hubbard and Jim

Dincalci and Paul Preston had moved about two miles west to a two-story walkup in the middle of the block on a short street named Codwise Place. Dincalci and Preston told the family living downstairs that Hubbard was their uncle.

Hubbard made a few forays into the neighborhood, but mostly he stayed in the apartment and watched a lot of television. Dincalci prepared meals, and Preston decoded messages coming from the *Apollo*. They used a dictionary for the cipher, with a number like "155/9" referring to the ninth word on page 155 of the *American Heritage Dictionary*. Preston converted numbers into words and words into numbers, and relayed messages on a payphone down the street.

Their first couple of months in New York, Hubbard complained of various ailments, and his teeth were rotting in his head. One tooth actually fell out, and Dincalci tried to get Hubbard to see a dentist. A large sebaceous cyst had developed on Hubbard's forehead, and he forbade Dincalci from doing anything about it. But Dincalci did get him into Manhattan to see a chiropractor and started him on a regimen of allergy shots. Gradually, over the winter, Hubbard began to feel better.

As his health improved, Hubbard began to take more interest in the communications going back and forth to the *Apollo*, and also to consider where things with Scientology might be headed.

For the last few years, his armada had been kicked out of one country after another, and now they were running out of available ports. If something wasn't done about it, what kind of future could Scientology have?

In 1967, the Freedom of Information Act had gone into effect after being signed into law the year before by President Lyndon Johnson. Scientology had been one of the first to make extensive use of it, ordering its attorneys to find out how much information government agencies had about Hubbard in their files (it turned out to be a great deal).

While he sat in the apartment in Queens, Hubbard worked out an ambitious plan that he thought might take care of all these problems at the same time. If the negative information about Scientology could be retrieved and expunged from files in major countries like the United States and the United Kingdom, it would stop the damaging reports going to smaller countries like Greece and Morocco and Portugal that were turning away Hubbard and his ships.

On April 28, 1973, after much back and forth with the Guardian's Office, Hubbard finalized plans for the new project—numbered GO 732—which would target documents in 17 countries. Hubbard called it the "Snow White Program."

"A gradual reduction of available countries occurring since 1967, trend DANGER," the Guardian's Order read. "Recent exposures of official records have brought about the possession of data showing that England and the US have in the past spread false reports in several other countries which have caused trouble."

The plan to counter those reports was to expose them and, through litigation, get them destroyed.

In the detailed April 28 report, different countries were considered separate "Snow White Operating Targets," or SWOTs. SWOT 4, for example was Portugal, and was also known as "Project Mirror." SWOT 9 was Belgium (Project Bashful), and SWOT 11 was Italy (Project Dopey). Project Hunter would target the United States, while Project Witch and Project Stepmother each would operate in the United Kingdom. (Hubbard had sent Jim Dincalci to the library to look up names from the fairy tale for him to use in the project.)

The document talked about "legally" expunging files, but in its details, it talked about suing psychiatrists for genocide, "clearing" files in countries around the world, and obtaining documents "by any means."

Hubbard had given his worldwide espionage organization an audacious new goal. By any means, his operatives had been instructed to infiltrate every government organization on Earth that might harbor negative information about him—and destroy it.

In Queens that spring, however, the scene hardly resembled a spy thriller. After Dincalci prepared dinner, Hubbard would regale him with yarns about his past. About how the press was wrong that he'd never finished college, and that he had been one of the first casualties of the Second World War. (His war record didn't reflect it, however.) He told Dincalci that the cyst on his forehead was filled with shrapnel from that injury, but Dincalci had it X-rayed and didn't find any shrapnel in it.

Hubbard also went into the wild exploits of his past lives on other planets. When he went into these tales, Hubbard looked off into space, and Dincalci noticed that the 62-year-old man went into a kind of reverie while he spoke. Then, after a lengthy narrative, he'd come out of it, blinking his eyes and smacking his lips while he looked around, like he was trying to remember where he was. Dincalci thought it was odd.

On May 17, 1973, Paulette was indicted. The three counts – two for the bomb threats, one for perjury for lying to the grand jury – each carried penalties of 5 years in federal prison and a fine of $5,000, for a total of 15 years and $15,000.

The intervening days were more torture. Each time she went to the Churchill's lobby, she was afraid she would see police arriving to take her away. Her lawyers arranged for her to turn herself in.

On May 27, she went to the federal courthouse to be arraigned. She found herself in a room of people eyeing her curiously and wondering what she was doing there. Her attorneys were with her, as well as her parents and her father's lawyer, Irving Gruber, whom she had known her entire life.

She was embarrassed that Irving was there to witness her humiliation. Her lawyers had suggested that her mother wear her finest – and Stella was there wearing a mink coat and her diamonds. They wanted to give the magistrate the right impression. But her mother just looked out of place (in fact they all did), and Paulette couldn't help noticing the covetous looks aimed her mother's way by the other suspects awaiting arraignment.

Paulette was then marched downstairs to be fingerprinted

and have her mug shot taken. She tried to make a few jokes, but she wasn't laughing inside. She was fortunate that no reporters were hanging around. They were in another courtroom, where one of the Watergate figures was in a hearing, and so far, word of Paulette's indictment had not become news.

Leaving the courtroom, she opened the envelope she'd been given to look at the indictment inside. The title on it horrified her.

The United States of America vs. Paulette Marcia Cooper

She felt like 200 million people – the entire country – had just declared itself to be against her. The United States vs. me, she thought, shaking her head.

As a condition of her indictment, she could not leave the state of New York. That alone was going to be a headache, she thought. She had good friends in New Jersey and Connecticut who were just minutes away. But now they might as well be on the moon.

Jay Zelermyer, her attorney, talked over with her the very real consequences she was facing. He had hired a document examiner of his own at Paulette's expense, and she had also concluded that Paulette's machine was used to type the bomb threat letters. Paulette's chances for conviction were very real. But Zelermyer told her she might get only a few years in federal prison because of her lack of a criminal record.

"Only a few years," she thought. And she wondered how she'd survive prison.

Every day, Paulette was sure her story would hit the press. And if it did, she knew her life as a writer was over. She could see the headline on the cover of the *New York Post*: "Woman Writer Threatens to Blow Up Church" or something similarly sensational. The readers of a paper like the *Post* – in fact, the readers of just about any publication – would not understand the difference between an indictment and a conviction. And with Scientology still a mystery to most people, all that mattered was that she'd supposedly endangered a religious facility.

Even if she weren't convicted, what editor would hire a writer who had been accused of trying to blow up the subject of one of her books?

The likelihood of ruinous publicity weighed on her as much as the coming trial, which was scheduled for October 31 – Halloween, appropriately enough. If the trial happened, then she knew the publicity would come. The thought of what her parents might have to endure if that happened wore her down.

Then, also in May, she learned that it was already worse than she thought: Her parents had been targeted. She only now found out that two months earlier another smear letter had arrived at her parents' home in Mamaroneck. Again, the allegations were outlandish and were intended to upset the Coopers and Paulette. The letter said Paulette couldn't write, and that she'd had perverted sex with the Coopers' rabbi. Ted and Stella Cooper were religious Jews, and the accusation, as groundless as it was, was upsetting to all of them.

The letter also suggested that the real people behind her

ongoing harassment were Bernie and Barbara Green. The thought that the Greens were behind her harassment – even with their affinity for Scientology's underlying ideas – struck Paulette as just another bad joke by Scientology and an attempt to pull them into the mess.

It was clear to her that the letter was another ham-fisted attempt to hurt her. But the thought of her parents reading it felt like a knife stabbing into her.

She was so sensitive to what they thought of her – the previous summer, she'd felt elated by their praise at her books coming out. But now, they had to read filth about her screwing their rabbi. And their daughter had been indicted and faced fifteen years in prison. They told Paulette they had warned their close friends to expect to see some unpleasant stories about their daughter in the newspapers, even though she was completely innocent of the charges. She hated that her parents felt compelled to say something to their friends.

Paulette was beginning to despair, and with that came desperate thoughts.

7

Jerry

At least Paulette had her friends at the Churchill. Barbara visited multiple times each day and was always willing to listen to her troubles. Paula Tyler was not only coming by nearly every day to check up on her, but she also started bringing around a guy she knew. His name was Jerry Levin.

Jerry was a little below average height, a little stocky, and being a redhead didn't look like a "Jerry Levin." He said he had grown up in Wappinger Falls in Duchess County, north of the city and that he had seen combat flying helicopters in Vietnam. On weekends he drove a car for a living and they wouldn't see him. But during the week he'd stay with Paula Tyler, and the two of them came over day after day, to hang out with Paulette and Barbara.

Paulette also had developed a deepening friendship with John Seffern, the attorney who had handled a lawsuit for the Greens. Seffern had been a Scientologist and had amassed a large collection of the organization's magazines and newsletters.

Seffern lived in a large rent-controlled apartment on the Upper West Side, and had rooms to keep the many publications the church sent him. (And kept sending – Scientology was already well known for never taking people off its mailing lists.) He had boxes full of the stuff. And as an attorney, he knew it might come in handy at some point.

One day, Paulette found herself leafing through some of his copies of Scientology's *Freedom* magazine when she saw a photograph that made her jump.

It was a young woman who looked very much like Paula Tyler.

She showed Seffern, and they talked about what she should do with it. She returned home and went to Barbara's apartment to show it to her—she agreed that it did look like the young woman living upstairs. They discussed their next move, and then Paulette asked Jerry Levin to come over. She told him she wanted to show him something, then handed him the folded magazine so that only the photograph showed.

She asked Jerry if it looked like Paula, and he said yes, it did. What was it from?

She then unfolded the magazine to show him what it was. He looked shocked.

Paulette and Barbara went to Paula's apartment later to confront her. But when they showed the magazine to her, Paula seemed genuinely surprised.

I'm insulted, she said. It clearly wasn't her, and she said she was hurt that they would think she was a Scientologist.

Paula's reaction seemed genuine. Maybe it wasn't her, Paulette thought. She apologized.

A couple of weeks later, Paula came down to Paulette's apartment shaking and crying. She said she'd received a telegram from Europe. Her parents had been injured in a car accident, and she needed to leave right away.

Paulette never saw her again.

Thankfully, there was Jerry. He came over to her apartment nearly as often as Barbara did, helping her to take care of her apartment as well as talk long into the night about what was happening in her case. In May, he offered to move in with her. Just to keep an eye on her and help her with things, he said.

Jerry seemed harmless. At least, she had no interest in sleeping with him. But a companion did seem like a good idea. Her boyfriend, Bob, even encouraged it – he could see Jerry was no threat, and besides, Paulette was already in such a poor mental state, she wasn't sleeping with Bob anyway. Jerry brought down his few things and stuffed them into a closet.

During the week, he stayed with her in apartment 3H at the Churchill. He took care of Tiki, her Yorkie, when she could barely get out of bed, and then only to wander around in her pink bathrobe. Jerry went shopping for her when she couldn't bear to leave the apartment, and he purchased the few things she ate each day, as well as her vodka. It was all she could keep down.

Barbara would come over, and the two of them would try to lighten her mood, take care of some things around the apartment, and try to get her to put something into her body besides vodka and cigarette smoke. Jerry would listen to her patiently, and said things she wanted to hear. "You have to be brave if you're going to take on those bastards," he said about Scientology.

Bob was coming around less and less. By June, Paulette knew he was starting to see someone else. She really couldn't blame him. She'd never been as into the idea of starting a family with him as Bob had. And now she didn't want anyone to touch her. Her weight was getting dangerously low and she looked terrible. All she could think about was that at any point, the press would start writing about her indictment, and then her career—and her life—would be over.

For the first time, she began to think about suicide. She could not put herself, or her parents, through the publicity and humiliation of the trial scheduled in October. It didn't matter that she hadn't sent the bomb threats. The press wouldn't care. Scientology would have accomplished what it wanted. She'd be ruined. Her parents would be humiliated and might stop supporting her – they had been paying her rent and her legal bills.

She began to have nightmares about prison. She had no real knowledge of what a federal prison for women would be like, but that only fueled her worst fears. She'd wake up in the middle of the night in a cold sweat – if, that is, she hadn't drunk herself into a stupor in a vain attempt to fall asleep.

Jerry's presence in the apartment helped. Weekends when he went driving and she was alone were especially difficult for her, but at least during the week he was around, and he was always supportive. It was getting hard not to think that everyone she knew thought privately that she had sent the letters and was lying about it. Her attorneys didn't really seem to care one way or the other, and her parents claimed that they believed her. But she couldn't help thinking that everyone doubted her and only told her what she wanted to hear. Her paranoia only got magnified by the excessive drinking and lack of sleep. As time went on, she couldn't pass out until about 6 in the morning, and then she'd wake up just a few hours later feeling like she was going to retch.

It was in the mornings when her attorney, Jay, was likely to call with bad news. She'd have a hard time getting back to sleep while she worried about the telephone ringing. But weeks would go by without any word from Stillman or Zelermyer about what they were trying to do to head off the October trial. And sometimes it was worse not to hear anything at all.

After she dragged herself out of bed, she'd force herself to eat a boiled egg or two. Then she'd have nothing until a glass of Clamato juice in the evening. The pain from her surgery the year before returned, and she had lost so much weight – down to 83 pounds – her periods stopped.

She was smoking up to four packs a day now, and the vodka wasn't enough; she started adding valium to the mix to calm her nerves and to help her sleep. She started to hoard the pills, saving up for October. She wanted to have enough valium to kill herself just before the trial, if it really came to that.

While Paulette spent much of the day during the summer of 1973 in a despondent haze, her paranoia and despair alternated with rage. She thought about what she would have to go through to prove her innocence at a trial and it made her furious. She was fed up with her attorneys, who didn't seem to take her suggestions seriously. And she went over and over the details with Barbara and Jerry. The bomb threat letters had language that pointed to her old boyfriend Roger, who had joined Scientology and, as far as she knew, was still in it. But other phrases made her suspect Nibs, L. Ron Hubbard's son, who by now had flipped and was working for the church again. Not only was there the phrase – "I hurt, my operation" – that made her think of the previous summer, when Nibs had been with her following her surgery, but the lack of punctuation, the lack of apostrophes, was how Nibs scribbled the notes she had turned into writing when they worked together.

One of the smear letters had also pointed at the Greens, and as ridiculous as that seemed, could they be a part of it, helping the church frame one of its enemies in order to get back the franchise they lost? She searched her mind for the memory: Had she touched their stationery while she was at their house?

The Greens had told her attorneys that Nibs had visited them in December, about the time the letters were mailed. But that was a strange detail. Nibs hadn't told Paulette he was in town then, and she couldn't believe that he wouldn't look her up. Could Nibs and the Greens have been working together to frame her? Could Nibs have worked with Meisler? How else could that reference to her abdominal pain have appeared on the letter? Her mind reeled.

But even more puzzling than who was behind it was the question of *how*. How had one fingerprint from the third finger on her left hand ended up on the back of the second bomb threat letter? And how had they been typed up on her machine without her knowing it? Had stationery from the apartment somehow been taken? By Nibs? By Bob Kaufman? Each of them had been in her apartment in the months leading up to the letters being sent in December. Either of them could have typed them up when she wasn't in the room. She hated to suspect Kaufman, who had been such a good friend and had helped her with her book. But he was unstable – he'd been hospitalized after leaving Scientology, and he had been under his own harassment campaign by the church.

She went around and around with it, and none of it made sense. And when she wasn't obsessed with the letters, she was imagining what her life would be like if the trial happened. As June slid into July, her black despair deepened. She stopped taking care of Tiki – and she was grateful that Jerry helped. She also needed the half of the rent payment he was supplying. She couldn't bring herself to leave the apartment, or take care of herself. The impending trial meant she couldn't leave the state of New York, but it hardly mattered – she couldn't pull herself together even to leave the Churchill.

A few times when she tried, she broke down and cried after taking only a few steps outside the building.

She didn't blame Jerry that he took long breaks upstairs at night on the pool deck, smoking. She didn't blame him for wanting a little privacy. He kept asking her to come up to the rooftop pool at night that summer. It will make you feel better to get out of the apartment and get some fresh air, he said. She went a few times at his insistence to the pool. But he would climb on the small ledge surrounding it, with nothing to keep him from falling 33 floors down. He kept needling her to climb up on the ledge with him. "Come on up! I'll take care of you," he said. "If you don't have the guts to do this small thing, how are you going to have the courage to face up to those bastards in court?"

He seemed unusually insistent about it at times. But she begged off. She knew there was a great nighttime view of the Empire State Building and the new World Trade Center towers, which had opened just that April. But the thought of the sheer drop made her nauseous. And frightened. Too frightened even to trust her good friend.

One of the few things that took her attention away from her problems were the Watergate hearings, which had been going on since May 17. Broadcast each day live on one of the three major networks, which took turns covering it, the unfolding Senate inquiry at least gave Paulette and Jerry and Barbara something to talk about besides her indictment.

The hearings had also inspired a new book project. With people talking about break-ins and surveillance, Paulette thought up a title – "Are You Bugged? How to Tell if You're Being Bugged, Followed, Tapped, or Sexually Trapped" – and looked for someone to "front" the book. She needed someone with the credentials and experience to provide information that she could write up.

She knew a young private investigator who had helped her on a case of a man whose wife had become a Scientologist. The detective's name was Anthony Pellicano, and he was thirsty for publicity. With his knowledge of surveillance and Paulette's experience of investigating a shadowy organization like Scientology, they figured they could make a good team.

On July 2, they signed a contract to produce the book together. But over time, Pellicano didn't give her the information he had promised. She gamely finished a manuscript on her own, but it was ultimately rejected for publication.

That she managed any writing at all surprised Barbara, who had done little writing of her own since her own trauma. Barbara told a friend, "Paulette can do more during a nervous breakdown than most healthy people can in a lifetime."

As her 31st birthday – July 26, 1973 – neared, there was really only one thing Paulette was looking forward to. *The Medical Detectives* was coming out, after her own attorneys had delayed its publication. When she had showed them a prepublication copy, they told her they were alarmed by a reference to a bombing on the back cover. It had nothing to do with her case, but the association was too risky. They called the publisher and told him the lines could not appear on the book. Making the change had set the book back. But in July, it was finally coming out.

The first review arrived the morning of her birthday. It was the only one that would turn out not to be positive. (She would win an "Edgar" from the Mystery Writers of America in nonfiction for the book.) She was devastated by the negative review.

Her black mood went into new depths. Meanwhile, Bob called, and said he had changed his mind about seeing her for her birthday that evening.

She couldn't blame him. She knew it was over with him – he'd hinted about meeting another woman at a family wedding. By then, Paulette hardly cared to see anyone. Jerry and Barbara tried to lift her mood, but by the evening, she was lower than she'd ever been. She could not understand how she would live through what was coming. It just seemed impossible. The stock of valium she'd been collecting looked lethal. As she drank more, she started thinking about consuming it.

Then, the telephone rang.

It was an old Brandeis friend who was now an editor at the Arts & Leisure pages of the *New York Times*. The friend had called to wish her old classmate a happy birthday, but she could tell immediately that Paulette was in trouble.

Paulette never told her friend how close she came to killing herself that night. She poured out her troubles and her friend said the right things to help Paulette calm down. For hours, the friend kept her on the phone, until Paulette finally passed out.

8

Transport XXI
Brussels, 1946

Paulette awakes in bright light and sits up, rubbing her eyes. It takes a moment to remember where she is, until the mildew smell and the coarse linens remind her.

It was a noise that woke her. There's a scene playing out at the other end of the room, over the rows of similar beds, all of them illuminated by harsh, bright electric light. The sounds and movement at the other end of the room are out of place. It's before dawn, and the lights shouldn't be on this early. She feels a tightness in the pit of her stomach even before she can make out what's going on. And then, as she becomes a little less sleepy, it becomes clear.

Tante Brunya is leaving.

Paulette knows it instantly, can sense it from the way Tante Brunya is dressed. Clearly she is going away somewhere. The woman has on an overcoat and a hat, and sturdy shoes. She's

Tony Ortega

dressed for a trip. And she's standing over a young girl with blonde curls who is tying her shoelaces and gathering her things, as if Brunya's journey can't begin until the girl is packed and ready to go with her.

Paulette understands: The young girl, DeeDee, is leaving the orphanage with Tante Brunya and they are going to America.

The shock of it hits her like a blow to the chest.

She sits there in her bed under the glaring light and watches Tante Brunya take DeeDee's things in one hand and DeeDee in the other, and they walk out, never even glancing at her. She is too shocked to make any noise or try to stop them. Instead, she pictures herself running after them, begging to be taken along. Tante – "aunt" in French – has been the closest thing to a mother she's had in the drab orphanage, and now not only is Brunya leaving, but she has chosen another girl to take with her.

Tante Brunya had not even said goodbye.

Paulette fights an urge to fall back on the bed in tears. She wipes her eyes and stands up to get dressed. She'll go find her sister and tell her what's happened. Sarah is two years older and knows more. But because of their age difference, the two girls are kept in different parts of the orphanage and don't see each other very often.

Paulette is only four years old, and has dim memories of other places where she and her sister had lived. Only one event before today had sharply stood out.

She was lying in bed at another orphanage in a large room with many other children when the droning sound of airplanes grew in the distance. The sound seemed to send everyone into a panic. Adults ran into the room, screaming about turning out the lights and pulling down window shades.

She remembered thinking she was going to die, and how awful it sounded as the other children kept screaming with the noise of the airplanes overhead. She needed to go to the bathroom, which was in the center of the large, bifurcated room, but she didn't dare move. So she wet the bed while she waited for the planes to pass.

There had been no air raids at Tante Brunya's orphanage. Paulette and her sister had been moved there about a year ago, and she had a bare grasp of the idea that the war was over but that outside, things were still very bad. Many of the children weren't even orphans. But their parents kept them there because they couldn't afford to feed and clothe them on the outside.

Things were difficult inside, too. They sometimes missed meals, or had to go without milk, or sometimes the bread or oatmeal was inedible. She was often ill, and she and her sister and just about everyone else was underweight, undersized, and suffering from other effects of malnutrition.

A few months after Tante Brunya went to America, Paulette's sister was gone too. Sarah was adopted by an aunt and went to live in Antwerp, hours away.

Now, she was on her own. On the weekends, parents and aunts and uncles would come to be reunited with their children, and they sometimes brought nice things to eat and new clothes. But her parents never came. Paulette sat on the grass on visiting days and watched the others, wondering when her parents would come for her.

Week after week, they never did. And neither Tante Brunya nor any of the other adults ever told her why.

On July 22, 1942, Leonard Alexander Rodrigues Lopes, a Dutch Jew of Portuguese descent who lived in Antwerp and worked as a reporter for the London newspaper the *Daily Express*, brought the news to his friend Sijbren de Hoo that neither of them wanted to hear. Their good companion, Chaim Bucholc, had been arrested and taken to a Nazi concentration camp.

The three men, and another named Ghislain Jules de Wulf, had been tight for more than a decade. De Hoo was an Amsterdam bureaucrat who often came to Antwerp. Bucholc was a highly skilled leatherworker who had emigrated to the Belgian city from Poland in the late 1920s with his young wife, Ruchla Minkowski.

The four young men had become confidants and looked out for each other. When De Hoo went on an arduous Arctic expedition in 1930, Bucholc fashioned some custom leather clothing for the trip. In 1938, when De Hoo was offered the opportunity to take over the Bata shoe factory in Warsaw, he planned on taking Bucholc with him and even talked with Rodrigues Lopes about joining them. But doubts about conditions in Poland convinced them not to go.

The next year, as Europe was once again plunged into war, de Hoo and Rodrigues Lopes each went through divorces; Rodrigues Lopes moved to Holland, but in 1941 he returned to Belgium as conditions for Jews in Amsterdam deteriorated more rapidly than they had in Antwerp, which fell to the Nazis in May, 1940.

Under Nazi occupation in Holland, De Hoo was put in charge of food rationing. Increasingly, he was in a difficult spot: He had to serve the Nazi occupiers, but he also wanted to help his Jewish friends, who were running out of options. And in Antwerp, things were getting increasingly dangerous for Rodrigues Lopes, and for Chaim and Ruchla Bucholc, who were in hiding with their two-year-old daughter, Sarah.

When Chaim was arrested, not only did he leave behind his young daughter, but Ruchla was very pregnant with their second child. Just four days after Chaim was taken away, on July 26, 1942, Ruchla gave birth to another daughter. She was named Paula, and Chaim never laid eyes on her.

He was likely held for only about a week at the Breendonck concentration camp before he was among some of the first Jews moved to the Dossin barracks at the new Mechelen transport center, from which Belgium's incarcerated Jews were sent to the Auschwitz extermination camp.

On September 10, 1942, Chaim Bucholc was among 1,048 prisoners on a train designated Transport VIII. This early in the war, the transport appeared to be a normal passenger train, and not the cattle trucks that would come into use later, after the Nazis became concerned about escapes. Three days later, the train arrived in Auschwitz, where Chaim was eventually executed.

Back in Belgium, Ruchla had to rely on family members to

bring her things so she and the children could remain cooped up in their second-story apartment and away from prying eyes. For three months, she and the girls stayed off the street. But eventually Ruchla had to risk a trip for supplies, and she was arrested, leaving behind the note that was discovered by her brother.

Ruchla Minkowski Bucholc, aged 31, was sent to Auschwitz on October 24, 1942.

Paula and Sarah remained in hiding for several months through the help of family friends as well as a Belgian official – Robert de Foy – who helped many other Jews stay out of the Nazi camps.

De Foy was in a tricky position. He had been head of the Belgian State Security Service before the war, and was sent to Germany as a prisoner. But the Nazis then sent him back to Belgium to help administer the country. In 1943, he had been appointed Secretary General of the Department of Justice. He was aiding the Nazis by helping to run the country, but he would posthumously be named one of the "Righteous Among the Nations" by the Yad Vashem Museum in Jerusalem for his efforts to help Jews during the war.

But even with de Foy's help, the girls were ultimately discovered by Nazi troops. On June 18, 1943, they were taken to Mechelen to await transport to Auschwitz. Paula was assigned to be the 843rd passenger on Transport XXI, the next train scheduled to leave.

It would be only the second transport to use windowless cattle cars to prevent escapes. (About 200 passengers managed to escape that April when the Belgian resistance derailed Transport XX about 6 miles after it left the camp.)

Their parents' friends – Sijbren de Hoo, Ghislain de Wulf, and Leonard Rodrigues Lopes – now began a desperate attempt to save the two children. Their one advantage, it turned out, was that the Nazi running the Dossin barracks, SS *Sturmbannführer* Philipp Schmitt, was as corrupt as he was brutal.

Leo Rodrigues Lopes had some kind of connection inside the camp—a prisoner who was being used in the camp administration, perhaps—and through that connection he hoped to sway Schmitt with a bribe.

He and De Hoo and de Wulf could do nothing when Chaim and Ruchla Bucolc were each arrested and then sent to Auschwitz. But when the girls were captured, they worked rapidly to raise cash. De Hoo used an inheritance to come up with 100,000 Dutch Guilders, and Rodrigues Lopes gathered another 10,000 of his own through friends. A wealthy man in manufacturing may also have helped contribute, as well as some Catholic organizations. Some of the cash was converted to food, bought on the black market through de Hoo's Ministry contacts, because Schmitt was apparently willing to accept a combination of such goods as well as hard cash.

Rodrigues Lopes and de Hoo had very little time for their scheme to work. Not only were the girls scheduled to leave on the next transport, but Schmitt himself was so crooked, even the Nazis considered him a disaster and soon replaced him. But that summer, Schmitt had been disciplined but not yet removed, and a bribe was raised to pay him off as well as a man named Lauterborn – who might have been the notorious Flemish Jew Hunter Felix Lauterborn.

On July 31, 1943, five days after Paula's first birthday, Transport XXI left Mechelen bound for Auschwitz with 1,553 prisoners, including 174 children, 71 of them girls.

Paula and Sarah Bucholc were not on that train. The next month, in August, a record of them appeared, showing that they had been moved to an orphanage. The bribe had worked.

Tante Brunya's orphanage was their fourth. They had been moved there, near Brussels, at some point after the war was over. Paula – more often now called Paulette for her small size – had vague memories of the previous places. But she had formed a strong impression of Brunya, who seemed to favor her.

But then Brunya had taken another girl, DeeDee, and had gone to America, and this was very difficult for Paulette to understand. She felt very alone – her sister Sarah was usually in another part of the orphanage because she was two years older, and then Sarah left entirely, taken home by their aunt, who lived in Antwerp.

Paulette knew nothing about her parents. She didn't know how lucky she was just to be alive. She had no way of knowing that her aunt couldn't afford to bring her home as well. She just knew that no one came to see her—except for one time, when they family had come for her fifth birthday, and gave her a toy ball she kept on a string.

And then, when she turned six years old, everything changed.

In the summer of 1936, Stella Toepfer went to an Adirondacks resort named Green Mansions, and she met a salesman who was there playing tennis. His name was Ted Cooper. A year later, they were married. Stella's two brothers, Abe and Dave, had inherited their father's diamond business, S. Toepfer Diamonds. After the war, during which Ted had been an X-ray technician in the Army, he joined the family firm and learned the gem trade.

Ted and Stella wanted to have children, but couldn't. Stella tried to solve their fertility problem, receiving daily injections at one point. But they suspected the problem may have been rooted in Ted's X-ray work stateside during the war – he had not received any protective clothing to use. After the war, they approached adoption agencies, but already in their late 30s, they were told they weren't ideal candidates because of their age.

One night, at a party in New York, they met a Belgian woman named Roska Fuss who asked them why they didn't have children. When they told her that they'd tried and failed, she said that her brother ran an orphanage in Belgium. Roska had one particular girl in mind. But she knew there might be a problem: Paulette Bucholc had been promised to a Philadelphia couple, both psychiatrists.

Roska decided she liked the Coopers, and sent word to have little Paulette adopted by them. But there was another hurdle: Sarah, Paulette's older sister, had already been adopted by their aunt, Chaim's sister. The aunt didn't want the two girls split up, but she couldn't afford to take in Paulette as well, so Paulette just sat in the orphanage. With the aunt refusing to budge, the Coopers were forced to wait for several months.

Ted then sent a friend to Belgium with two sets of documents that had been drawn up by his lawyer and former mess sergeant, Irving Gruber. One set of papers released Paulette from the orphanage to her aunt, the other set released her to the Coopers. The man sent by Ted Cooper stayed with the aunt and said he wasn't leaving until she signed one set of papers. Finally, she relented and signed Paulette over to the Coopers.

The aunt, however, got some measure of revenge. The day before Paulette was scheduled to fly to the United States, her aunt had her brought to her home, where Paulette's sister Sarah had been living after the aunt had adopted her. It was the first time the two girls had seen each other in two years. And before Paulette left in the morning, the aunt told them, "Kiss each other goodbye, girls, because you'll never see each other again."

The Coopers had already decided to give Paulette the middle name of Marcia, after Ted's father, Morris. Sarah, meanwhile, grew up with the name Suzy.

Nine months after the Coopers first heard about the girl in Belgium from their friend Roska – a span Stella considered highly significant – she and Ted received a telegram that a couple of days later the girl would arrive at Idlewild Airport.

On her flight to New York, Paulette was accompanied by a Belgian woman who taught her to say "I love you" in English. (Paulette, who was six, spoke only French.) During the long flight, she managed to throw up on the woman. Her only possession, besides a purple dress the orphanage had scrounged up for her, was the toy ball on a string she still took everywhere.

It was August 18, 1948, and one of the hottest days of the year when they landed at Idlewild. During the long, stifling wait for customs, the dye on Paulette's cheap purple velvet dress began to run.

Because they were coming from Belgium, the world's diamond market, the US Customs officials decided that the woman traveling with Paulette might be a smuggling risk. They were pulled aside and searched, and for some time Paulette's toy ball became the focus of their attention – were there gems inside it?

The officials were impatient, yelling at the woman and the little girl to stop acting like they only spoke French.

"We know you speak English!" they barked.

Finally, a tall man walked in and swooped Paulette up into his arms.

"I'm Ted Cooper, this is my daughter, and I'm taking her now. My lawyer is Irving Gruber. If you don't like it, call him."

It was the first time Paulette laid eyes on the man who had adopted her.

During her years in the orphanage, Paulette had never been told what happened to her biological parents. She only knew that other children had visitors, but her aunt's family was too destitute to come see her. Paulette wondered what could be so wrong with her to make her parents never come.

Now, she was in New York, and the tall man, Ted Cooper, introduced her to his wife, Stella. These were the parents who had never come, Paulette thought. And that's why the first words she spoke to her new mother were, "Why did it take you so long to get me?"

It was in French, and the Coopers didn't understand.

Underweight, malnourished, frightened, ill from the vaccinations she'd been given upon arriving, and missing her sister, Paulette Cooper's first months in the United States were a nightmare both for her and her parents. She spoke no English, and when she woke up in the night, crying and asking for her sister Suzy, her mother at first thought she was asking for a lollipop ("sucette" in French).

Stella Cooper even thought, briefly, of sending Paulette back to Belgium. But Stella's mother, who lived upstairs in the same building at 200 Pinehurst in Washington Heights, told her adoption was forever. "You couldn't return Paulette if you'd given birth to her, and you can't return her now that she's adopted," her grandmother said.

And so Stella got used to the idea of her hyperactive, undersized daughter who only gradually began to speak English.

The Coopers lived in a one-bedroom apartment. The dining room was converted into a room for Paulette. More than food, she was hungering for love and attention, something she didn't get in the series of orphanages she had lived in. She charmed adults not only because she was so small for her age, but also for her French accent, and for leaping up to kiss everyone she came in contact with, even the mailman.

In school, she struggled as she learned English, and she had a hard time sitting still. Not understanding what was being said, at times she'd just get up and wander out of the room. At home, though, she sat still and read everything she could get her hands on.

Gradually, she gained friends. Her best friend, Nora, had a very interesting aunt. Her name was Yma Sumac, and the exotic Peruvian singer with a 4-octave vocal range would come over often and sing. Paulette loved music and learned piano and could play Rachmaninoff by the time she was 10. But mostly, she loved reading.

By eight years old, she was putting out a newsletter with other children in the building. Every page was written by hand, and were then sold for a penny a page. Already, she knew that she wanted to be a writer. One of her early newsletters contained her first poem:

Whenever I am very ill, I have to swallow a big fat pill
It gives me dreams I've never seen
In Technicolor I'm a queen
I have a crown, shiny and gold
So you see it's not so bad to have a cold. Achoo.

She had seen the admiration in her father's eyes when he said that Stella had published some writing years earlier while a student at NYU. Paulette wanted badly to see that same admiration in her father's eyes, and it helped her focus on becoming a writer.

In 1950, two years after she arrived in New York, Paulette was formally adopted and given citizenship at the same time. Her parents and the family attorney, Irving Gruber, were with her while a friendly Manhattan judge asked, "Do you like your country?"

Yes, she answered.

"Do you like your parents?"

Yes.

"OK, you are now a citizen of the United States and you are adopted by the Coopers," he said.

"Aren't you going to ask me any arithmetic?" a disappointed Paulette asked.

Paulette began to excel at PS 187, where one of her classmates was Hedda Nussbaum, who would go on to become the center of a disturbing court case about the death of an adopted child with Joel Steinberg, and Hedda's testimony about being the victim of domestic violence.

At about 11, Paulette's parents began to let boys take her to the movies, with them along, and one of her earliest "dates" was with a classmate named Barry (the same Barry she would run into years later at the BBDO advertising agency).

When she turned 12, things changed as Paulette transferred to a junior high school in Mamaroneck, where the Coopers had moved, and her father, Ted, started his own business. He split away from the company that had taught him the gem business, with Stella's brothers, and founded his own firm. Stella started going to the office to work as a bookkeeper, and Paulette was home much of the time with her grandmother, who could be difficult.

Paulette was already feeling isolated at the new school, where many of the kids had known each other from feeder elementary schools. At home she felt isolated as well. But she adapted, turning always to her books. She read so avidly, she even spent hours reading the dictionary.

To her parents' dismay, she didn't have any interest in reading Hebrew. She wouldn't sit still for religious training, and she refused to be bat mitzvahed. It wasn't a religious rebellion, she just had no interest.

By 15, she was devouring books on many different subjects, but she worried that she had fallen into the wrong crowd at high school and she was developing typical frustrations about her parents which she poured into a journal. And it was then that she ran into Martin Gardner's book containing a chapter tearing apart the ideas of a man named L. Ron Hubbard.

She had no idea then, of course, how much Hubbard would become a part of her life years later.

In the summer of 1960, as she turned 18, Paulette made her first trip to Belgium on a cruise with her parents. She saw her sister Suzy for the first time since she had been adopted. At her parents' insistence, she had been corresponding with Suzy since she had arrived in the United States. The two exchanged birthday gifts – one of which was a copy of *Crime and Punishment* that Paulette received which played a role in her Wellesley interview.

She met other living relatives on the trip, and also was shown for the first time a photograph of Chaim and Ruchla Bucholc – her biological parents killed at Auschwitz. She didn't want her adoptive parents, Ted and Stella, to know it, but seeing that photo devastated her. For the first time, they became real to her. And so did their deaths – her mother's at only 31 especially haunted her. She could see her own face in theirs. Mostly that of her father's – Suzy looked more like their mother.

Her mother's sad eyes disturbed her, and stayed with her on the trip. She began to wonder about small things – had her mother liked ice cream? The color blue?

Paulette wanted to ask such questions of her father's remaining relatives in Belgium – including the aunt who had kept her in the orphanages for two years after adopting Suzy – but when she was with them the questions stuck in her throat. In some ways, she didn't want to know anything about her mother. Knowing more about how she had lived only made the thought of how she died even worse.

While they were there, the Coopers were also told that an ailing, older man had asked to see Paulette. It was Robert De Foy, the former Belgian official who had helped many Jewish children escape Nazi annihilation. Paulette had no way of knowing him, and she was slightly uncomfortable as her parents thanked the elderly man, who sat outside in the sun on a folding chair in his pajamas. He wanted Paulette to sit on his lap, perhaps as she had as an infant. He looked slightly ridiculous, with a medal or two from the war pinned to his pajamas, and Paulette was relieved when they said their goodbyes.

On their way back to the U.S., they received word on the ship in a radiogram that de Foy had died.

This was also the cruise that had a Marine major-general trying to pursue Paulette and it was the time she had engaged in heavy petting with an opera singer named Roberto Smittini.

Only weeks after the end of that cruise, she was starting her freshman year at Brandeis University, and she was experiencing a potent brew of emotions. Her trip to Belgium had still left her with complex feelings about her parents – living and dead. She was also intimidated by the environment at Brandeis, where so many smart women were planning to become writers. Paulette worried that she wouldn't be able to compete with them. She also experienced a brief fling with a flashy grad student who drove a yellow Corvette, which was as disorienting as it was fun.

And besides, she was a psych major, and figured it made sense to be in therapy. Everyone seemed to be doing it. So that fall, she sought out counseling and was referred to a man named Dr. Stanley Cath.

Over the next three years, during her Brandeis career, she continued to get therapy with Cath. She talked to him about her feelings about her parents (she found them too controlling), her worries about the future (would she make it as a writer?) her anguish over her early past, and about the events going on around her – including the assassination of John F. Kennedy, which happened during her third year of school.

After she graduated, she continued to stay in touch with Cath, sending him Christmas cards well into the 1970s. She considered him a friend, and repeatedly consulted him for advice about doctors for her physical complaints, and about her career.

She sent him copies of her books, and she dedicated her second book – *Growing up Puerto Rican* – to him. And when her life began to fall apart, she turned to Cath for help. He gave her referrals to people in New York she could talk to. But he couldn't really give her what she wanted – real help with her criminal case, which had nearly convinced her to kill herself in July 1973.

But after that low point, the lowest of her life, things slowly began to change.

In August, just a few days after Paulette's disastrous 31st birthday, a man named Roy Wallis arrived in New York to see her. He was of average height, he had curly hair and sideburns, and he wore dark specs. "Quiet" was the word that came to Paulette when she got to know him. He could sit in a group and say almost nothing during an evening, just listening to what others had to say.

Paulette eventually got out of him that he'd worked as a factory hand, a bartender, and even a gas station attendant before he'd made it to graduate school and dedicated himself to the study of Scientology at the University of Stirling in Scotland, where he was a lecturer. He'd written about Scientology as early as 1964, when he was just 19. He had then written his doctoral thesis on Hubbard's organization, and was working to expand it into a book for publication.

And like Paulette and Kaufman, he was learning the downside of writing about Scientology. Just a couple of months before his trip to New York, Wallis had written about the strange campaign of harassment he had endured since he published a paper called "The Sectarianism of Scientology," which had been based on material in his dissertation.

Wallis was a social scientist who worked as objectively as possible, so he had sent the article before publication to the church at its UK headquarters in East Grinstead, England, asking for comments that he could incorporate into it. Soon after that, a mysterious young man showed up at his university, claiming to be a student wanting to get to know Wallis. But days later Wallis found out the young man had tried to get into his house while he was away, and then he learned that none of the man's references checked out. Wallis was then subjected to a systematic smear campaign as letters were sent to university administrators claiming that Wallis was involved in a drug scandal. Other letters, clumsily forged, were supposed to be from Wallis himself, describing a homosexual affair.

"I was the subject of a concerted attempt at harassment designed to 'frighten me off' Scientology, to undermine my credibility as a commentator on their activities, or to keep me so busy handling these matters that I had little time for research," he wrote in an article that came out just before his visit to New York.

He told Paulette that he was still determined to remain as objective as possible about Scientology as he continued to gather material for his book. As she told him about her own experiences over the previous two years, he was in a better position than most to understand what she'd been through. Her indictment deeply disturbed him.

After seeing Paulette and Robert Kaufman in New York, Wallis traveled to California. He wanted to talk with Nibs – L. Ron Hubbard, Jr. – and he had no idea that Nibs had changed his mind about helping expose his father.

About a week later, Wallis returned to New York, and told Paulette that he was shocked by what Nibs had turned out to be like. He was nothing like the man who had worked with Paulette over the summer of 1972, eager to expose Scientology and hold it up to ridicule in television and radio appearances. Wallis said that Nibs had even hinted that he'd helped his father take care of his publicity problems, and over the course of their conversation, Wallis convinced Nibs to show him a couple of letters that explained what he meant. One was written by Bob Thomas, a top executive in Scientology. In his letter, Thomas rejected Nibs' plan of "double agent entrapment" of the church's "enemies." Wallis and Paulette doubted that Thomas would really reject a plan to harm Scientology's enemies, and they figured it was a letter written to cover his tracks.

Wallis showed Paulette other letters, from Nibs to his father, in which he boasted to Hubbard that he could "with one fell swoop" take care of his father's "enemies." Paulette had told Wallis that she suspected Nibs had something to do with the bomb threats. The letters that Nibs had shown Wallis didn't mention them, but they did suggest that he'd been part of some sort of campaign to neutralize someone who sounded a lot like Paulette.

Wallis told Paulette that he intended to take the letters to

John Gordon, her prosecutor. He would impress on Gordon that he was a sociologist, an academic, an objective observer who had no involvement in the case. Nibs' letters, and what Nibs had said in his interview, Wallis felt would sway Gordon that Paulette was telling the truth, and that she'd been the subject of a concerted harassment campaign – one that might even get her put in prison for a crime she didn't commit.

Wallis said he'd even fly back to New York, on his own expense, to testify at trial.

After two inconclusive polygraph examinations, Paulette turned to another lawyer for help—F. Lee Bailey. The famous defense attorney was actually disbarred at the time, but she didn't know who else to go to for help. So Paulette set aside a day to take a train up to Boston to Bailey's offices.

Waiting for her to arrive at the Back Bay Station was a young woman named Nancy Many. Nancy had joined Scientology a few years before, and while she was waiting to go to Florida to join the Sea Organization—the church's dedicated core of workers who signed billion-year contracts—she was asked to do some work for the local Guardian's Office.

Nancy's first assignment had been to infiltrate a mental health facility so she could secretly copy records of the doctors who worked in the area and deliver them to her GO superiors. She knew that similar operations were gathering information at other offices, including the Massachusetts state attorney general's office, the American Red Cross, American Cancer Society, the

YMCA, and the Better Business Bureau. That way, if someone made a complaint about Scientology to the BBB, for example, the church would know about it right away.

Nancy was told that Paulette Cooper was coming to town, and she was asked to tail Paulette to Bailey's office. Nancy didn't know how the GO's office knew Paulette was coming to Boston the next day, or how they even knew what she would be wearing – a tailored yellow suit, cream blouse, and peach scarf. But that's exactly what Paulette had on when she stepped off the train from New York.

Nancy tried to tail her without being seen, and she panicked when she suddenly lost sight of Paulette. She went into a nearby hotel to find a phone booth, but then by sheer luck Paulette also walked into the place. She then followed the petite writer to Bailey's office. Nancy never really understood why it was important to follow Paulette if the GO already knew where she was going.

Once at her destination, Paulette sat down in a large conference room, and curled up into a ball on a chair in a corner. When Frederic Joshua Barnett saw that, he decided she was innocent. If she had been guilty, he thought, she would have come right to him and started telling him how innocent she was. He sat down close to her, and began asking her about her case.

Barnett was an attorney in Bailey's firm who specialized in polygraph examinations. He believed in them deeply, and had spent years trying to get judges and courts to accept them as evidence. The summer before, in July 1972, he had testified in Washington DC, convincing the courts there to allow polygraph evidence, but an appeals court had overturned it.

Barnett had even trained to become a polygraph examiner himself so he could tell which practitioners were using the best methods. And few were as bad, he believed, as Nat Lorendi. The police department examiner wore a gun during his sessions, for example, which was supposed to be forbidden. And more than once, Lorendi had admitted to him, in front of witnesses, that he thought of a polygraph as his "rubber hose." It was so intimidating to suspects, Lorendi said, he often wouldn't even turn it on.

Barnett had once successfully testified against Lorendi in court – and he told Paulette he relished the prospect of taking him apart again.

Barnett got copies of Lorendi's charts of Paulette's examination and looked at them with the help of another expert. They were stunned to see how hard Lorendi's charts were to read. They weren't even sure what they indicated.

The data seemed to indicate, for example, that Paulette was being deceptive when she was accused of things she could not have done, things that had nothing to do with the bomb threats. Such questions can be asked to establish a subject's reaction when they must be telling the truth. In Paulette's case, she appeared to feel guilt for things she could not have done.

Barnett suspected that Paulette was a rare person that he called a "guilt reactor"—someone who responds as if she's responsible for something she had nothing to do with. He knew her background, and wondered if it had something to do with her childhood and surviving the Holocaust. Survivors are among those more likely to be guilt reactors, he explained to her. It was important that she get another examination, this time with a real expert who could account for her predispositions.

Her father, Ted, however, complained to Paulette when he found out she'd gone to Bailey's firm. Ted believed that only guilty (and usually wealthy) clients went to F. Lee Bailey to get them off on technicalities. If she hired him, jurors would assume she had committed a crime, Ted told her. So she dropped the firm, and Barnett with it. He had nothing else to do with the case.

It only ended up adding to her stress. Barnett clearly believed that she was innocent, and she liked him personally. But since her parents were paying her legal bills – Paulette had long since run out of money and couldn't continue to write much that paid in her mental state – she had to go along with their insistence that she stick with the Stillman firm, whom she was increasingly frustrated with.

Paulette heard again from Roy Wallis who, while searching through Scientology documents, came upon a 1967 policy letter written by L. Ron Hubbard. It described penalties for people that the church considered to be in "lower conditions." At the bottom of that list were people the church considered to be the "enemy." In that case, Hubbard considered them "Fair Game," and they were subject to ruination: "May be deprived of property or injured by any means by any Scientologist without any discipline of the Scientologist. May be tricked, sued or lied to or destroyed."

Paulette was stunned. She hadn't seen the document before,

but it seemed to explain what was happening to her and others – Nan McLean, and Robert Kaufman, and the Greens, for example. Here it was in black and white: Hubbard had instructed his followers to use any means necessary to destroy people the church considered "enemies."

Paulette took the document to her attorneys.

She was also encouraged when it turned out the two threat letters had some important differences. The first one contained the actual reference to an explosive device – *"I'll bomb you!"* – but the letter had no identifying information at all. It named no one as its target, and had no information about its sender. It also didn't have a fingerprint.

It was the second letter that had a fingerprint from Paulette on its back. But that second letter's threat was more vague – that Scientology would be "an exploding volcano." (And Paulette pointed out to her attorney Jay Zelermyer she was well aware that volcanoes erupt, not explode, and she wouldn't have written it that way.)

There was something else strange about the second letter: It had never been mailed.

Someone had apparently hand-delivered the second letter to the Scientology org, and technically, it hadn't been sent through the federal mail system, which put some question on Gordon's jurisdiction over it.

The first letter had been mailed, but it had no fingerprints on it.

Those details, and the discovery of the Hubbard policy which suggested that Paulette was undergoing a coordinated campaign of harassment, and the letters from Nibs that Roy Wallis had found, all added up to evidence Paulette wanted to believe that Gordon couldn't ignore.

But there were still the inconclusive polygraph examinations.

With only a couple of months to go before the scheduled trial, she and her attorneys began to talk about another risky strategy. A sodium pentothal examination – a "truth serum" test – might be enough to counter the polygraph exams. Was Paulette willing to undergo one?

She said she was, but she soon found out that it might kill her.

9

A deal offered

Encouraged that she might be building a good case, Paulette continued to search her own records and documents, looking for anything that might help as the trial neared—it was now late September, and there was only a month to go.

Paulette thought back to when the FBI had first showed up at her apartment on East 80th Street the previous December. What had been going on then? She searched through her records, looking for anything that might help refresh her memory. She went through her checkbook, skimming it until she hit December, and looked at her expenses.

And that's when she noticed it.

December 6, a check for the United Farm Workers.

That was two days before the first bomb threat letter had been received at the org.

Looking at the check stub, her dim memories of that day came rushing back. She grabbed her telephone, and dialed her

165

cousin Joy. Did she remember the day that woman – what was her name? Margie something? – came to the apartment with a petition?

Margie Shepherd, that was it.

The two women talked it over, and for the first time, they revealed that they had each noticed strange things about that short visit. Margie never took her coat or her gloves off while she was in the warm apartment, they remembered.

Could Margie have been working for Scientology? Could she have somehow lifted a piece of Joy's lightweight stationery, or in some other way obtained Paulette's fingerprint on a document?

Paulette called her attorneys, and they agreed it was a promising lead. They asked her to go through as many Scientology publications as she could, looking for Margie's name. If they could prove that someone connected to the New York org had been in her apartment just days before the bomb threats were mailed, it could be a major break.

Paulette knew where she could find a large stack of Scientology publications—at John Seffern's, the attorney for the Greens. She had gone to see him several times, valuing his advice, and she knew he had piles of church documents. He was happy to let her pore through them, and she scanned newsletters and magazines and other documents, looking for the name Margie Shepherd.

But it was another name she found that gave her a shock.

Paulette went back to the Churchill, armed with a copy of a Scientology magazine. She went to Barbara's apartment to show it to her. Then, after talking it over, the two of them went to Paulette's place.

They went in, and Paulette asked her roommate, Jerry Levin, to speak with them.

"What's up?" He asked.

Jerry had moved into the apartment in May, four months earlier. He had taken care of Tiki, Paulette's Yorkie, when Paulette was having trouble just getting herself out of bed in the morning. He had tried to get Paulette up on the sundeck on the roof for some fresh air. He had helped prepare meals. He had become a companion after Paulette's relationship with Bob Straus had ended. Unlike Bob, Jerry had been willing – even anxious – to listen to her obsessive talk about what she was going through. And what she didn't tell him directly, Barbara filled him in on.

And Jerry had been in on the long conversations with Barbara and Paulette about her legal case. Now Paulette held out the magazine to him, to show him where the name "Jerry Levin" appeared in the Scientology magazine.

"What are you saying?" He asked. "You think I'm a Scientologist because some guy has the same name?"

"Well, are you?" Paulette asked.

"No," he said. And he lit into her and Barbara for confronting him. "Jerry Levin" was a pretty common name, especially in New York, he pointed out. Was she really getting so paranoid that she thought the guy who had helped her through such a terrible time was working for the church?

"How could you accuse me of being a Scientologist?" he asked.

Barbara tried to calm them down. Paulette apologized. It did seem far-fetched. Jerry Levin was a common name. It all seemed like a replay of four months ago, when they had found the photo that looked like Paula Tyler. But this time, the evidence was even less convincing—a common name in a magazine.

Paulette muttered an apology, saying she'd been working too hard and jumped to conclusions. Jerry had offered to testify as a character witness in her trial. He'd been a friend. He'd cleaned up after her dog. It was ludicrous even to think that he was the Jerry Levin in the magazine.

It was a Friday afternoon, and after the confrontation, Jerry left for his weekend job driving a car. Paulette worried about his reaction, and she hoped Jerry had cooled off about it by the time he returned.

But he never did.

In long conversations with Jerry and Paula before they each left, and usually well into her night's supply of vodka, Paulette had poured out her doubts, her fears, even admitting that she got so drunk with her old advertising pals on a few occasions that she had blacked out and lost periods of time. She had admitted to them that she couldn't help wondering if, during one of these blackouts, she had managed to type those crazy letters and mailed them and later didn't remember doing it.

When she was sober, she realized that it was an impossibility. The first letter, at least, had been mailed, and its envelope included a Zip Code. She didn't know the Zip Code of the New

York org, and in those days, it took some effort to look it up—usually a trip down to the local post office, something she couldn't have done drunk with no memory of it.

In May, Paula had suddenly left after she got a telegram from her parents. And now, in September, Jerry was gone without a word. Had she blown his cover by confronting him about the magazine? It was too awful to think about. If Jerry had been working for the church, those late night conversations, whether they had any truth to them, would have been reported to Scientology, and Paulette couldn't bear the thought of it.

She decided it couldn't be true. Jerry had not been the "Jerry Levin" in the magazine. It was just a common name.

But it was finally dawning on her the lengths the Church of Scientology would go to ruin her. She still had no idea that the Guardian's Office had been watching her closely for more than two years, and the extent to which it had proposed and attempted numerous ways to damage her career, hurt her father's business, and smear her reputation. But even ignorant of the full program against her, Paulette had some idea of what she was up against.

She knew she had to take the truth serum test. The polygraph exams had been inconclusive. She had tried hypnotism with a prominent (and expensive) doctor, but he declared her unhypnotizable. She had even tried a voice-stress analysis test, even though she didn't believe it had any validity.

So that left truth serum. When she called a few doctors about administering the test, including her family physician, they refused, telling her that it would be dangerous for someone in poor health and weighing only 83 pounds. They told her there was a risk she might not survive it. But she told Barbara that she really had nothing to lose. If the trial actually began on October 31, she was still determined to kill herself anyway.

If her indictment hit newspapers, she believed her life wouldn't be worth living. And there had already been a close call – her mother was called for jury duty in Westchester County, and during the selection procedure, she was asked in front of the other potential jurors if any members of her family had ever been indicted for a felony. Stella Cooper didn't have it in her to lie, so she admitted that her daughter had been indicted in federal court. The judge seemed stunned, and so did the other potential jurors. Stella was immediately dismissed. She later told Paulette it had been a humiliating experience.

But no one had bothered to follow up on that startling disclosure in open court, and Paulette's secret, for now, was still safe. And her best chance of keeping it that way, the potentially fatal truth serum examination, had to happen fast, with the trial date rapidly nearing.

Len Zinberg first learned about Scientology in 1969 and in Sixties fashion: The couple that introduced him to Scientology's basic ideas, Rick and Minty Alexander, spoke to him in their Manhattan Beach, Brooklyn home from their bed, John Lennon and Yoko Ono style.

Zinberg was ripe for recruitment. He was from a secular Jewish family but had attended an Orthodox yeshiva, then James

Madison High School. Now 22, he was confused about his place in the world and was looking for something new.

The Alexanders gave him a copy of L. Ron Hubbard's *Fundamentals of Thought* and encouraged him to start taking courses at the Hotel Martinique. He got some auditing, and then scrounged up a couple of thousand dollars for a multi-course package. By 1970, he had signed a contract to work on staff.

The hours were long and the pay was very bad, only a few dollars a week. He sold plastic flowers in Times Square on Saturday nights to make enough for his food for the week. But he was in with a merry band of youngsters at the hotel who were genuinely excited about the introductory courses of Scientology and the "wins" they were getting in their communication skills.

Gradually, Len began to understand that there was a darker side to Scientology. They were engaged in a war against many enemies, and he found himself helping to do his part in that war.

His labors for the Guardian's Office started in the family home in Brooklyn. Len's father worked for the IRS, and on occasion he'd hear his father say that the agency was looking into L. Ron Hubbard and Scientology. When his father wasn't looking, Len would go through his dad's briefcase and pull out agency bulletins marked "official use only." These weren't highly classified documents, but the Guardian's Office operatives at the Hotel Martinique were happy to get them.

Then, Len met a beautiful girl at the org named Sylvia Seplowitz. They started dating, and he soon moved into her Mill Basin, Brooklyn apartment. Like Len, she was beginning to do volunteer work for the Guardian's Office. In particular, she had been asked to target a writer named Robert Kaufman.

Sylvia was told that Kaufman played piano at a dance studio in Manhattan. She went there with instructions to chat him up and convince him to take her back to his apartment, where she would then look for materials related to his upcoming book about Scientology. But despite her beauty, she found that she was all wrong for the assignment. Kaufman was playing piano, but it was a ballet studio, and she was no ballet dancer. Her advances to Kaufman were too obvious, and he didn't take the bait.

Len, meanwhile, was asked to stake out and photograph Kaufman when the writer was giving an interview near Grand Central Station. Later, Len spent several hours in a coffee shop across the street from the Churchill building, waiting for Paulette Cooper to come out so he could tail her. But she never did, and he never got the chance.

Len had been told that Paulette and Kaufman were evil "suppressives" who meant the church harm. It was all he needed to hear. Whatever he was asked to do about them, he would, which meant that in the summer of 1973, he was with three other Scientologists who broke into Kaufman's Riverside Drive apartment. It was the culmination of a complex operation run against the writer, even though his book had been out for a year and had achieved only modest sales.

An African-American Scientologist named Jerry had rented an apartment down the hall from Kaufman, and then he found a way to get introduced to the pianist through some Ghanians who also lived in the building. Jerry was himself a musician, a drummer, and before long they were regularly having breakfasts together and Kaufman got Jerry a membership at his gym.

Jerry thanked him by getting them each new combination locks for their gym lockers. He also introduced Kaufman to an attractive woman named Rosalyn and encouraged Kaufman to ask her out. Kaufman eventually did, and they went to a movie. But throughout the date, he found Rosalyn strangely distant.

Meanwhile, back at Kaufman's apartment building, Len Zinberg met Jerry with two other Scientologists. Jerry gave them a key to Kaufman's apartment, but didn't say where he had obtained it. It was obviously a copy, and a poorly made one, and one of the Scientologists had to file it down before it would work properly.

With Kaufman still on his date with Rosalyn, Len and two others went into Kaufman's apartment. They tried to disturb as little as possible, looking through papers and trying to gather information for the Guardian's Office. Len didn't think there was much in the papers of any value. If he briefly wondered why the GO was going to so much trouble to keep tabs on a man who seemed of so little importance, his training kicked in and he quickly banished the thought from his mind. Finished with their snooping, the three men left the apartment, leaving it as close as possible to how they had found it.

Kaufman never knew that his apartment had been searched.

Across town, L. Ron Hubbard and Paul Preston packed their

things and began their trip back to the yacht *Apollo*, which was still in Lisbon. Jim Dincalci followed some time later, after staying behind to pack up and clean out the Codwise Place apartment in Queens.

Hubbard had been in New York City for ten months, and his major accomplishment was putting together the Snow White Program in April, which was still kicking into gear around the world.

Hubbard and Paulette Cooper had not run into each other while he was in town.

Before he had become Paulette's lawyer, Charles Stillman had been a prosecutor at the Southern District of the US Attorney's office, working under Robert M. Morgenthau's leadership with other prominent attorneys like Bob Morvillo, who would go on to be a legendary defense attorney in his own right.

Stillman had imparted some of that experience and those connections on his younger colleague, Jay Zelermyer, who was just three years out of NYU Law School. It was Zelermyer who was doing most of the work on Paulette's case. And like Stillman, he also had made powerful connections in the US Attorney's office, including Morvillo.

At the time, Morvillo was John Gordon's boss and chief of the district's criminal division. And while Gordon was clearly enthusiastic about prosecuting Paulette Cooper in what at first had seemed a slam-dunk case, Morvillo had less to prove, Zelermyer figured.

After talking it over with Stillman, Zelermyer met with Morvillo to discuss the case.

The evidence – the fingerprint and the typewriter – did appear strong, but the motive made no sense, and Paulette insisted she had nothing to do with the letters, which were comical and didn't sound anything like Paulette's own writing. And there was plenty of evidence that the church had harassed her.

After listening to the young lawyer lay out all the lousy things about the case, Morvillo surprised Zelermyer by offering a deal. If Paulette would go back to the grand jury, admit that she had sent the letters, apologize, and promise never to do anything like it ever again, then the government would defer the prosecution. Meanwhile, records of the case would be sealed, and her confession would never be made public.

Zelermyer took the offer to Paulette, and they discussed it in his office on the 34th floor at 110 E. 59th Street. He laid out the details for her, explaining that the deal would ensure that her case wouldn't go public, which was her chief concern.

The thought of making the case go away was the first real hope Paulette had had in a long time. She told Zelermyer that the deal did seem to be a good one. She said she would take it.

"There's one hitch," Zelermyer told her.

He couldn't, ethically, have her go before the grand jury and say that she had lied previously and admit that she had actually sent the letters to the church, not if she wasn't now telling the truth.

"You have to tell me you did it. Here, now," Zelermyer said.

175

It was a test. She had been denying from the start that she had sent the letters. Now, with a deal in her grasp, would she change her story?

"I can lie to them, but I can't lie to you. I didn't do it," Paulette told him.

Zelermyer was impressed, and believed that she was telling the truth.

She had passed the test, but the deal was off.

For the truth serum examination, Zelermyer had selected David R. Coddon, a well-known neurologist at Mt. Sinai Medical Center on the Upper East Side of Manhattan.

Coddon took a serious interest in Paulette's case, talking with her and her parents and her attorneys in order to prepare numerous questions to ask her under the influence of the sodium pentothal. He encouraged her parents, Ted and Stella, to attend the test, which made Paulette uncomfortable. She had no idea what she'd say in front of them about her life as a single woman they might not know about.

She had to lie back on an operating table in a hospital gown. Coddon put a needle into the back of her hand and told her to count backwards from 10. She got to about four before falling under the drug's effect, and her last impression was that Coddon looked slightly alarmed. He later told her that it had taken longer than usual for the drug to take, but he figured it was because she had been drinking so much in recent months.

The drug relaxed her, and Coddon began to question her,

asking her if she knew how the bomb threat letters had been typed up and mailed. She said she didn't know.

He asked her how to make a bomb, and she said she had no idea.

He asked if she even knew what was in a bomb, and she said "glycerine." (Her parents laughed as Coddon explained that was what suppositories were made of.)

Who, Coddon asked her, did Paulette suspect of writing the letters? Nibs, she answered.

When the drugs wore off after the seven-hour procedure, she had no memory of the interview. Her parents told her about the funny thing about the "glycerine." Stella laughed as she said her eyes were closed and Coddon kept opening one eye and asking her who wrote the letters, and she'd say "Nibs," and then he'd open the other eye and she'd say "Nibs" again or sometimes "Meisler."

Coddon, meanwhile, was smiling. "There's not going to be a trial," he said, explaining that he was confident that she had told the truth and had no idea how the letters had been created. He would call her attorneys and stake his reputation on the results. He told her parents that he was angry that she'd been indicted, and if a trial went ahead, "I'll chain myself to the courtroom."

Paulette dared to allow herself to feel some hope.

Jay Zelermyer met again with Bob Morvillo to tell him what had happened at his office – that although Paulette Cooper had been offered a deal that Jay had told her was "costless" and that would prevent a trial and be kept sealed forever, she had turned it down because she couldn't admit to something she didn't do.

Zelermyer already knew Morvillo wasn't thrilled with the case. The Church of Scientology didn't make for a very sympathetic "victim." Word was gradually getting out about its odd ways, with tales about a strange man running things from a ship at sea, and families ripped apart by a paranoid organization.

A trial would bring up the smears against Paulette, the nearly constant harassment she'd endured since the December 1969 publication of her *Queen* magazine article. And it would also come out that she'd been offered an attractive deal but had turned it down because she insisted on her innocence. And there was the sodium pentothal test, which supported her steadfast denial.

Morvillo appeared impressed that Paulette had scuttled the previous deal by refusing to admit guilt. And how would it look, Zelermyer said, going after her when there were so many more important crimes to solve? Morvillo had, after all, already offered to make the thing go away. Zelermyer pressed him – what's the point of a trial at this point?

After the meeting, Zelermyer called Paulette to give her the news.

There would be no trial on October 31.

Instead, Morvillo postponed the matter and planned to file a declaration of *nolle prosequi* – setting the prosecution aside – if there were no more bomb threats and Paulette kept out of trouble for the next year and also underwent psychiatric counseling (an ironic instruction, given Scientology's hatred for the practice).

In other words, if she kept her nose clean, Morvillo planned to drop the matter entirely.

She wasn't completely out of trouble – there was still the possibility that her indictment could become news, and she worried every day that Scientology would do something to make that happen. She worried that the church might send additional bomb threats, and the next time the government might not back down. But for now, Paulette began to breathe a little easier.

It appeared that she wouldn't have to kill herself after all.

The trial had been averted, but Paulette was still suing Scientology, and it was suing her in multiple lawsuits. She worried about her publisher, Tower Publications. She spent hours talking to Harry Shorten's attorney, Herb Rosedale, trying to make him understand what they were up against.

But Rosedale didn't want Shorten to fight. He told Paulette that she would have to come up with the money to pay for Tower's legal costs, rather than the other way around. When she said she couldn't do that, he then advised that Shorten do what Scientology wanted. (Several years later, Rosedale changed his mind and during the 1980s and 1990s became known as a crusading attorney for families who had been harmed by religious organizations, and he published widely in academic journals.)

On November 27, on Rosedale's advice, Harry Shorten got himself and Tower out of the lawsuit the church had brought against *The Scandal of Scientology*. Shorten paid $500, and addressed a letter to Rev. James C. Mulligan, president of the

Church of Scientology of California.

Dear Rev. Mulligan,
We regret any difficulties caused to the Church of Scientology as a
result of any half-truths or misstatements of fact in the book The
Scandal of Scientology which we have published. Please rest assured
that any such errors were not intentional on our part.
Very truly yours
TOWER PUBLICATIONS, INC.
Harry Shorten

Paulette was bitterly disappointed. She was now on her own defending her book. Within a few months, however, she had an unlikely new source of income that would help her during years of legal battles with Scientology.

In 1973, Maury Breecher was making only $12,000 a year as a public relations man for a hospital. But then his salary more than doubled – to $25,000 – when he landed a new job as an assignment editor at the *National Enquirer* in Boca Raton, Florida.

If the *Enquirer* didn't enjoy the best reputation as a supermarket tabloid, it paid much better than most newspapers, and freelancers knew it. Reporters were constantly trying to break into the *Enquirer*'s pages, and Breecher was one of its gatekeepers. His approval could guarantee a steady stream of income for any writer who regularly got pieces into the paper.

Early in 1974, Maury was asked to speak to a gathering of

the American Society of Journalists and Authors in New York, and Paulette Cooper and her best friend, Barbara Lewis, were in the crowd.

He bombed. Not only was his speech uninspiring, the members of the ASJA generally considered themselves above the celebrity gossip in the pages of the *Enquirer*. Barbara hated what Maury had to say so much, she went up to him afterwards and gave him a piece of her mind.

"You were awful," she said to him.

Paulette felt bad for him, apologized for Barbara, and mentioned to Maury that she'd written pieces for *Cosmopolitan* and other women's magazines. She knew how much hard work went into those stories, and she assumed it was the same at the *Enquirer*, whatever people thought of it.

Maury liked what she had to say, and asked Paulette to submit some of her work. When he liked what he saw, he then asked her to send in some ideas for stories.

Usually, if a new writer sent in half a dozen ideas, Maury might find one that had some potential. But he was pleasantly surprised when more than half of the stories Paulette sent in seemed perfect for the paper.

For many months Paulette had not been able to leave New York – a condition of her indictment – but Paulette's parents had a winter home in Palm Beach near the *Enquirer*'s headquarters in Lantana, so she was happy to accept when the *Enquirer* offered to fly her to Florida for a three-week training session. Paulette not only enjoyed the work, she was surprised how much being in

Florida and getting away from her New York troubles seemed to reinvigorate her.

After she returned to New York, Breecher bought stories from Paulette regularly, paying her rates that were top dollar at that time, about $300 for a day's work. And despite its reputation, the *Enquirer* did care about accuracy – all writers had to tape interviews and submit the tapes with their drafts for fact-checkers to confirm quotes.

Paulette's were always perfect. Maury soon began to rely on her as one of his best freelancers. And gradually, he and his fellow editors began to learn about Paulette's experiences with the Church of Scientology.

In the halls of American Media Inc., owner of the *Enquirer*, there was no love lost for Scientology. Many of the reporters were British, from a country where there seemed to be a greater awareness of Scientology, and one of the reporters had even been sued over a story he'd written about Hubbard. Before long, the editors of the newspaper were fully aware that the work they were providing Paulette was the only thing enabling her to carry on her fight against the numerous church lawsuits.

When Paulette's own supply of story ideas ran low, or when she was so distracted by legal work – depositions, interrogatories, and questions from her lawyers – that she didn't have time to search for leads, Maury and his fellow editors canvassed the office for items she could work on just to keep her income steady. They knew full well that much of the money they were paying her was going to attorneys and depositions and the other numerous costs associated with her court fights.

In part to keep the church from knowing where her money was coming from, Paulette rarely took bylines on her stories at the *Enquirer*. Most of the time, only she and the editors knew that she'd written a particular story. And although an internal Guardian's Office document shows that by 1976 Scientology knew Paulette was working for the newspaper, none of the harassment she was going through in other parts of her life interrupted her work for the *Enquirer*. Before long, she was relying completely on the *Enquirer* to keep her afloat.

In her first year with the newspaper, 1974, her total income from all sources was $15,434. Of that, $13,413 was from the *Enquirer*.

Her stories included one about Richard Nixon and his college roommates breaking into a dean's office at Duke University in 1936 to get an advance look at their grades. (*NIXON'S BREAK IN... 36 YEARS BEFORE WATERGATE*)

Another story featured a boy of 13 whose brain tumor had left him blind and wheelchair-bound. (*DYING BOY NEEDS TO KNOW YOU CARE*). The boy received tens of thousands of letters because of Paulette's article, and his mother wrote the paper to say it had made her son happy before he finally succumbed.

Paulette bared all to get the scoop on Paradise Lakes in Land O'Lakes, Florida (*THE NAKED TRUTH ABOUT LIFE IN A NUDIST CAMP*), and she also handled many of the "Women's Lib" stories for the newspaper. She developed a relationship with a psychologist who could make the case for, or against, the women's movement, depending on what Paulette needed. Privately, Paulette referred to her as her "trained seal." (*HOW WOMEN'S LIB CAN HELP YOUR MARRIAGE*...but also *WOMEN'S LIB BUSTING UP MARRIAGES*)

She dabbled in a few health stories (*20 MILLION AMERICANS SUFFER FROM PINWORMS*), and everything in between, including:

MAN WHO TRACES MISSING HEIRS FINDS SOME PEOPLE WON'T TAKE THE MONEY
HOW TO ENJOY BEING A WOMAN -- WITH YOUR HUSBAND'S HELP
WACKY THINGS THAT DON'T GET INTO GUINNESS BOOK OF WORLD RECORDS
90% POLLED CAN'T THINK OF ONE ACCOMPLISHMENT BY CONGRESS IN THE LAST 10 YEARS
TWICE AS MANY PEOPLE KNOW THEIR ASTROLOGICAL SIGN AS THEIR BLOOD TYPE

Maury Breecher considered Paulette Cooper one of his best reporters, but he and the other editors at the *Enquirer* also knowingly kept her income healthy in order to help her from going under while she fought Scientology.

The newspaper never publicly received credit for it.

10

Don Alverzo

Len Zinberg was told to dress like a bum. It wasn't really much of a stretch – like always, he had almost no money to his name. But he did as he was told and made himself look homeless.

Then he was given a manila envelope that contained about 30 pages of material inside. It wasn't his job to look at them, but he did anyway. They appeared to be pages from a diary written by a teenage girl. They contained complaints about "mom" and "dad" that seemed pretty typical for a girl that age. Also, there were some thoughts about sex and other embarrassing things. Len didn't ask how the Guardian's Office had obtained the pages. His job was simply to deliver them to Ted Cooper.

It was March 1974, and Ted's jewelry office was in a building in midtown Manhattan. Len went up the elevator to the 15th floor, and then approached the receptionist. He put the envelope down on her desk, and told her it was for "Mr. Crooper," purposely mispronouncing it, just as he'd been told by the Guardian's Office.

He then immediately turned around, avoided the elevators, and found the stairs. He rapidly stepped down all 15 floors on his way out of the building.

While the Guardian's Office was still targeting Paulette, she was still targeting Scientology. She had already written a popular book on the subject, and she was writing about other subjects for the *Enquirer*, but whenever she could, she encouraged other journalists and publications to write about L. Ron Hubbard and his controversies.

She continued to hear from people whose children had joined Scientology, or members who had decided to leave and wanted to talk to someone. Paulette became someone who connected them with newspaper reporters or magazine writers, urging them to make such stories public.

Early in 1974, Paulette helped a young reporter in St. Louis who wanted to learn more about Scientology and needed help finding people who could talk about it. Elaine Viets was only 24, but she was already tired of her job as a fashion reporter for the *St. Louis Post-Dispatch*. She felt stuck in a "pink ghetto," never getting to write serious news stories because of her age and her gender. Then, one day she heard from a handyman in her building who knew she worked for the newspaper.

"If newspapers were so great, they'd help my girlfriend," he said. He told her that his girlfriend had joined Scientology, and she'd gotten pregnant by an ethics officer who then wanted her to have an abortion. At the time, abortion was still illegal in Missouri, so Scientology had flown her to New York to have the procedure done. When the young woman later wanted to leave the church, she was told that if she did, they would tell her very Catholic mother about the abortion. For years, they had held it over her, keeping her from leaving.

Viets wanted to tell the young woman's story. She convinced her editors to let her turn it into a major project about all aspects of Scientology with the help of the paper's religion writer. She then looked up Paulette, and with her help found people like Nan McLean and her son, John, who had spent time on the yacht *Apollo* with L. Ron Hubbard.

Elaine's series was the first glimpse for the public of what life aboard the *Apollo* was like. "McLean describes Hubbard as about 65 years old, short and fat, weighing about 250 pounds. He has no teeth and is often sick. He is given to wild mood swings. 'Hubbard has the best of everything possible aboard a ship,' McLean said. 'He has cars, three motorcycles, a stereo system, the best food and clothing, a cook, a valet and a private suite of rooms.' His wife Mary Sue and some of his children, Diana and her husband, [Jonathan] Horwich, Quentin, 19, Suzette, 17, and Arthur, 13, live on the *Apollo*."

McLean said that since he had left the church, his home near Toronto had been picketed by protestors who one day held a "funeral" for the lost souls of the family, and carried a coffin through local streets.

Tony Ortega

In the final installment of the *Post-Dispatch* series, Viets discussed Scientology's reputation for spying on people and harassing them. Paulette was mentioned. Elaine reported that the church denied it took part in any covert activities.

The series was a huge success and was nominated for a Pulitzer. After it came out, Elaine Viets continued to do hard news and didn't have to go back to the fashion pages.

Two months later, the Church of Scientology sued the *Post-Dispatch* for Elaine's series. And despite its public denial that it spied on enemies or took part in covert operations, it sent spies to infiltrate the office of the attorneys representing the *Post-Dispatch*.

One of them was a man named Merrell Vannier, 26, a Scientologist at the St. Louis church who had become a volunteer for the Guardian's Office a short time before. Vannier had been asked to help a more senior agent named Don Alverzo from Los Angeles.

"Don Alverzo" was not the man's real identity. The name was from a 1940s-era radio announcer's test that was popularized by Jerry Lewis: "One hen; two ducks; three squawking geese; four Limerick oysters; five corpulent porpoises; six pairs of Don Alverzo's tweezers; seven thousand Macedonians in full battle array; eight brass monkeys from the ancient, sacred scripts of Egypt; nine apathetic, sympathetic, diabetic old men on roller skates with a marked propensity towards procrastination and sloth; ten lyrical, spherical, diabolical denizens of the deep who haul stall around the corner of the quo of the quay of the quivery,

188

all at the same time."

Merrell didn't know Alverzo's real name. No one at B-I seemed to. But Merrell's impression was that in the GO's spy division, no one was more experienced or skilled than Alverzo. He only knew that Alverzo said he had flown helicopter missions in Vietnam, and he had apparently made his mark for the GO earlier, in an operation in New York. But Merrell didn't know the details.

Alverzo's first idea was to have Merrell (who, besides spying for Scientology, was also taking a break after three semesters in law school) apply for a clerking job at the building where the newspaper's attorneys worked. After an interview, however, Merrell thought his cover had been blown. Then Alverzo noticed that the building had advertised for a night janitor. So Merrell used a different name, applied for it, and got the job.

Merrell would go into the building at 10 pm and leave at 6 in the morning. He cleaned offices all night, and brought back information about the layout of the offices and who worked where. He told Alverzo that he could go anywhere he wanted, but there was one office in the building he couldn't get into—and it was where the lawyers for the newspaper worked.

"Find out where the key is," Alverzo told him.

Merrell asked around, and learned that there was a door key in a small shack on top of the building. He spent some time getting to know the maintenance man who worked there, and asked him why he wasn't asked to clean that one locked office.

"They have their own cleaners, and they unlock it only for

them," he was told.

Merrell reported that information to Alverzo.

"You have to get me that key so I can copy it. Just figure out when he takes his break," Alverzo told him.

Merrell worked on the maintenance man, sharing smokes with him until he trusted Merrell to go into the shack and grab a cigarette even if he wasn't around. Then, Merrell waited for the right time to grab the key when his new friend was on a break. After he obtained it, Merrell ran down to meet Alverzo in the alley behind the building, and Alverzo dashed to get the key copied. Merrell got it back in place only 20 minutes after he'd taken it.

With a copy of the key, Merrell now began entering the locked office at night and mapped it out, bringing to Alverzo its layout and location of files. Then, after they'd studied it, they set a date to begin taking out documents.

Over three nights, Merrell unlocked the door, Alverzo and another agent entered the offices, locked the door behind them, and then copied documents while Merrell stood outside keeping watch. Merrell's heart would race, but he noticed that Alverzo was usually smiling. He seemed unflappable.

After the operation, Alverzo told him that the documents turned out to be very important, providing the church new information about battles it had been engaged in even back to the 1950s.

"You made your bones, kid. You're in," he told Merrell.

In New York, Paulette Cooper began to hold up her end of the bargain she had made with prosecutors, who put off her trial on the bomb threat letters. She started making regular weekly trips to Hastings-on-Hudson, a Westchester County town north of New York City, where Herbert Benglesdorf had an office.

Benglesdorf was on the faculty of the New York Medical College at Metropolitan Hospital, and since 1962 he'd been certified by the American Board of Psychiatry and Neurology. At Paulette's request, Benglesdorf took no notes of their sessions, and he soon came to appreciate why she wanted it that way. Although her motivation to see him might have been about her legal situation, she took the sessions seriously. And Benglesdorf took her problems seriously. Of which there were many.

She worried that the harassment or another scheme to get her arrested might start up again, and she was depressed about how her career had been affected. She had been eating a little better, but she still had little interest in the things other people seemed to care about. Benglesdorf thought her account of what had happened – the harassment, the indictment, the surveillance, the phone tapping – was credible, if some of her fears seemed exaggerated.

She was, in other words, a perfectly normal woman under extraordinary stress produced by matters out of her control.

She told him about her history with men. About Bob Straus, and about how he had drifted away while she was under indictment. In July 1974, when Paulette turned 32, she couldn't help thinking about what might have happened if she'd stayed together with Bob. Maybe it wasn't too late, she wondered.

She called him and left a message. His letter in response surprised and devastated her. For the first time, she learned that Bob had also been targeted with anonymous smear letters which threatened his career as a prosecutor. They had been mailed to his bosses, and contained information he assumed only Paulette knew. "I can come to no conclusion other than that you wrote that letter and the bomb threats," he wrote to her. "I never want to hear of you or from you again," he added.

Reading that, she wept. She had always believed he was one of the few people who had never doubted her innocence. And now he was accusing her of sending the bomb threats. She was stunned.

Benglesdorf talked her through it. Over time, as her mandatory year seeing Benglesdorf progressed, she came to rely on him more and more. She told him about her work at the *Enquirer*. She told him about her adventures with other men. Less and less, she talked about what had brought her to him.

At first, she had resented being forced to get therapy. But as with her experiences earlier, with Stanley Cath in Massachusetts, Paulette enjoyed therapy, and she came to rely on Benglesdorf's counsel. Particularly, it turned out, when a new drama in her life began to emerge. One that had nothing to do with a church or books or spies or the FBI.

It was about a new man that Paulette had fallen in love with.

Four months after the St. Louis break-in, on October 30, 1974,

Don Alverzo flew to Washington D.C. to meet for the first time with a man named Michael Meisner. Meisner was the top Scientology spy in the nation's capital. His title was Assistant Guardian for Information in the District of Columbia (AG I DC). Also present at the meeting at the Guardian's Office at 2125 S Street, NW, were GO operatives Mitchell Hermann and Bruce Ullman.

Alverzo had flown out from Los Angeles carrying with him several pieces of equipment. One of them was a multiple electronic outlet, the kind of thing you plugged into the wall socket so you could then plug in more items. Alverzo explained that the object actually concealed a bugging device. It could pick up the conversation in a room and broadcast it over a weak radio signal to a receiver nearby.

He explained that they didn't have much time. In two days, on November 1, the Guardian's Office had learned that a meeting would be held in a conference room on the fourth floor of the main IRS building—at 1111 Constitution Avenue, NW—and Scientology would be discussed.

Their job, he explained, was to plug the device into a wall socket in the conference room before that meeting started. And they had only a day to figure out how to do it.

Meisner had been preparing for this day for several years. Originally from Chicago, he had first learned about Scientology in 1970 from a friend while he was a junior at the University of Illinois at Urbana. A few months later, he left school to work full time for the church. By August 1972, Meisner was running the mission in Urbana, and the following year, he was recruited to the

Guardian's Office by Duke Snider, a GO official who had apparently been named after the Brooklyn Dodgers outfielder.

Meisner and his wife Patricia were sent to Washington D.C. in June 1973 so each of them could begin their GO training. Meisner was also sent for several months to Los Angeles for special training in B-I's intelligence activities. By January 1974, he had returned to the nation's capital and had achieved the position of Assistant Guardian for Information. And he was in that position as the Snow White Program was finally about to go into high gear.

Since L. Ron Hubbard had formulated the plan for Snow White in April 1973 while he was hiding out in an apartment in Queens, the project to root out government documents about Scientology in the United States was still gathering steam.

On November 21, 1973, seven months after Hubbard had green-lighted Snow White, Jane Kember wrote a letter to Henning Heldt telling him that she had learned that Interpol in Washington had files on Hubbard, and she wanted them intercepted. Kember was the Rhodesian woman who ran the WorldWide Guardian's Office for the Hubbards from England. Henning Heldt was the top Guardian's Office official in the U.S., and he worked out of Los Angeles. "It is important that we get cracking and obtain these files and I leave you to work out how," Kember wrote to Heldt, trying to spur him to action. But the theft still hadn't occurred when, in July 1974, Meisner was prodded by his boss, Duke Snider, to do something about it.

By late 1974, Scientology had been making Freedom of

Information Act requests to obtain documents legally, but the illegal side of the Snow White Program was lagging behind. That changed when Don Alverzo showed up in DC with his bugging devices on October 30.

On the evening of November 1, after he'd spent the day busy with other matters, Meisner was told what had happened that day at the IRS building. The bugging device was taken into the building by Mitchell Hermann. He located the conference room on the fourth floor, and plugged the device into a wall socket. He noticed that the windows of the room faced the driveway of the Smithsonian's Museum of History and Technology across the street.

He went back outside and joined Don Alverzo and the GO's DC secretary, Carla Moxon, as they pulled a car into the museum's driveway and tuned in the car's FM radio to the device's frequency, taping what they were able to hear.

After the IRS attorneys held their meeting about Scientology, Hermann made his way back into the building and up to the conference room, retrieved the bugging device, and also picked up copies of the meeting's agenda which the attorneys had left behind. He took those to Alverzo, who then flew back to Los Angeles with the tape recording, the documents, and the bugging devices.

Reports about the successful bugging were sent to all of the Guardian's Office top officials, including Duke Snider, Henning Heldt, Jane Kember, and Mary Sue Hubbard. Snider, in a note to his boss, a British GO official named Morris Budlong, warned that the Snow White Program had now moved into dangerous new territory. "We must be careful with this transcript as even in the distant future in the hands of the enemy the repercussions would be great. There are new laws on this federally and a strong post-Watergate judicial climate."

But plans were already underway to infiltrate the IRS on a more permanent basis. On November 14, just two weeks after the bugging of the conference room, the Guardian's Office managed to get around a hiring freeze at the IRS and placed an agent, a young man named Gerald Bennett Wolfe, into a job as a typist in the tax division.

A few weeks later, early in December, Meisner and Mitchell Hermann went to the IRS building and stayed around until after 7 pm, when most workers had gone home. Then they went up to the seventh floor to the Exempt Organization Division—which monitored Scientology as the agency fought giving the group tax-exempt status—and lifted files about the church to take back to the GO for copying. The documents in the files added up to a pile ten inches thick. The next day, after the copying, Hermann brought the files back.

Meisner called his boss, Snider, and told him about the theft, explaining that it had been exceedingly easy to pull off. Snider in turn boasted to his boss in England, Mo Budlong, about the operation.

"Duke, such news brings joy to my heart. ARC. Absolutely fantastic. ARC. I can't wait to see the data," Budlong replied in a telex, using the Scientology acronym, "ARC"—for "affinity, reality, and communication"—which generally represented harmonious agreement.

Meisner was finally making happen what L. Ron Hubbard had formulated for the Snow White Program more than a year before, and his bosses were thrilled with his progress. But Meisner himself hadn't met his own spy, Wolfe, who had been placed in the IRS offices.

Hermann brought them together in an Arlington, Virginia parking lot in mid-December, and they went to Hermann's home in Washington for a half-hour meeting. Wolfe wanted a code name, and Meisner began calling him "Kelly." Meisner and Hermann explained to Wolfe how easy it had been for them to take files just a few days before. The told him they wanted Wolfe to begin taking files, targeting an IRS attorney by the name of Barbara Bird, who had been one of the people in the November 1 bugged conference meeting.

On December 30, Wolfe went to Bird's office to case it. He noticed that it had two doors, one of which was locked and blocked by a table. He managed to unlock that blocked door without Bird's knowledge, and then at night or on weekends, after Bird had gone home and locked the main door, Wolfe went through the unlocked, blocked door past the table, and then he could take his time going through her files and copying documents relevant to Scientology.

He passed them to Meisner, who then meticulously recorded and notated them before passing them on to his superiors, who included Mary Sue Hubbard.

Washington DC wasn't the only place where the Guardian's Office was experimenting with burglary. Robert Louis Dardano became a member of the Boston Church of Scientology in 1972, but almost immediately he was in trouble.

His mother objected to the money he was spending on Scientology. She made noise about it, and it got back to the church. Dardano was told he was a "potential trouble source" because of his mother, and he was removed from his job as an "expediter" – basically, he was a gofer with a car – and he was told he wouldn't get his job back until he "handled" his mother.

He got her to calm down, explaining that he wanted to be a member of Scientology and there wasn't anything she could do about it. But two years later, she went to the Better Business Bureau, saying she wanted to take legal action against the church.

As a result, Dardano was cut loose again by the Boston church because of his mother's continued opposition. Eventually, he moved into a Tewksbury, Massachusetts house with another young church member named Bill Foster and five other Scientologists who had been in and out of church jobs.

They were misfits, idealistic Scientologists who wanted to fit in but repeatedly found themselves labeled "potential trouble sources" or had "blown" – left their jobs – for various reasons. With a few other friends who didn't live in the house, the group began to call themselves "Eric's 11" – referring to Bill Foster's code name.

Between September 1974 and March 1975, "Eric's 11" was

a source of volunteers for the Guardian's Office in the Boston area. Initially, Dardano was assigned "overt" work, mostly at local libraries. As part of a crew of five or six, he would go into a library and do research on groups that were attacking Scientology, taking notes that would be delivered to a man named Gerald "Deac" Finn with the Guardian's Office B-I division, who would forward information to Los Angeles.

By the end of 1974, Dardano was running the library crew, and then he was promoted to do "covert" operations. At the time, it had gotten back to Scientology that a reporter at the *Boston Globe*, John Wood, was working on a major story about the local church. The members of Eric's 11 were dispatched to a number of undercover positions, each hoping to get information about what was being said about Scientology, including finding information on the *Globe* story.

Dardano was asked to apply for a job as a security guard at the newspaper, and he got it. Other members were placed in positions at the Federal Reserve Bank, the Consumer's Council, the Lindemann Mental Health Center, the Better Business Bureau, the Consumer Protection Division of the Attorney General's office, the Law Enforcement Assistance Administration, and other places. And a member named David Grace got a job with the cleaning company that serviced the law offices of Bingham, Dana & Gould – attorneys for the *Globe*.

Grace was instructed to gain access to the offices after hours, and look through the files of attorney James McHugh. The B-I believed McHugh was working with Wood on the *Globe*'s story, and the Scientology spy division also believed Wood and McHugh were getting help from a woman named Paulette Cooper.

Grace did what he was told, and one night brought home from the office a thick file from the law office. Grace brought the file back to the Guardian's Office quarters at the Boston church, where Dardano and others sifted through the file, looking for things the GO might need. They were excited when they found in the file a rough draft of Wood's article which McHugh had been reviewing for libel.

At about the same time – February or March, 1975 – another group was sent to a psychiatrist's office in nearby Belmont, Massachusetts. Dardano drove, and he and Bill Foster dropped off Gary Brown and Peter Marquez. Dardano and Foster waited in the car as Brown and Marquez broke into the office of Dr. Stanley Cath, Paulette's college psychiatrist.

After some time, they came out of the building with a thick file, and Dardano and Foster drove them back to the Tewksbury house. They sat in the kitchen, passing around Paulette Cooper's most intimate medical records and therapy notes. It was the high point of Dardano's career as a Guardian's Office volunteer. Later, Bill Foster read to the team a commendation the GO had given all of them.

But soon enough, there was trouble. The methods of Eric's 11 – with so many GO volunteers living together, and sitting around a kitchen table handing each other documents – was completely against GO protocol, which called for individual operatives to know nothing about what anyone else was doing. In March 1975, after the break-in of Stanley Cath's office and the burglarizing off the *Globe*'s attorneys, the house was broken up, and Dardano and Foster and the others were ordered to go their separate ways.

During the first months of 1975, Gerald Wolfe was bringing out so many documents from the IRS in Washington DC—a stack that would eventually reach ten feet high—the Information Bureau gave up trying to label and excerpt them.

The sheer amount of material Wolfe was bringing out wasn't the only problem. Scientology actually wanted to use those documents and make some of them public. But how to do that without making it obvious that they had been stolen?

In May, Meisner was told by another GO employee, Gregory Willardson, about a scheme he had dreamed up to deal with that problem. Willardson had named it "Project Horn," and it was Meisner's job to implement it.

Meisner explained it to Wolfe, and instructed his spy to begin taking not just Scientology files, but others as well. Wolfe continued to target the office of Barbara Bird, but also another attorney, Lewis Hubbard (no relation to the Scientology founder).

Wolfe gathered documents about other organizations that the IRS had been investigating—Sun Myung Moon's Unification Church (the Moonies) and Bob Jones University, whose tax exempt status was under review because of its segregationist policies. Wolfe was also instructed to smuggle out blank copies of IRS letterhead paper, so that fake letters could be created as if written by a fictional, disgruntled IRS employee. The GO wanted to create an IRS whistle-blower who was sending documents about Scientology or the Moonies to those organizations, providing cover for how the documents would be made public.

A "staff member in the IRS," Willardson wrote in his description of Project Horn, "mails out IRS files to the persons/groups mentioned in their files...[it] will provide a cover for [Scientology's] PR and legal [divisions] to expose the documents."

In other words, Scientology had its Snow White Program spies steal documents and letterhead so it could create a fake story to explain why it had possession of other documents it had already stolen.

The job of making photocopies of Paulette's records from Dr. Cath's file took several weeks, for some reason, and then the GO volunteers had to break back into Cath's office to replace the original documents. But perhaps because they were in a hurry, they misfiled Paulette's folder.

Later in 1975, as the Guardian's Office moved on to the next phase of its operation against her, Paulette began receiving copies of her medical and psychiatric records in envelopes with no return address. The harassment was starting up again — after she'd managed to survive the indictment and put her immediate legal troubles behind her. And this time, it devastated her.

The year before, pages from her teenaged diary had been delivered (by Len Zinberg, but she didn't know that) to her father's office. The pages had been chosen for embarrassing comments she had written about her parents when she was 17. She still had no idea how Scientology had managed to get copies of pages from her diary, which she kept in a closet at her apartment.

But now, it was her medical records that were coming in mailed envelopes. She knew they could only be coming from one place. And it suddenly brought back to her how she had felt when she went to Dr. Cath as a college freshman. She was having a personal crisis after, that summer, traveling to Belgium and reuniting with her sister Suzy for the first time since they were separated after the war. Her survival of the concentration camp in Belgium – and the deaths of her biological parents, whom she saw in a photograph for the first time – were almost too much for her. She loved her adoptive parents, but she fought with them like any teenager would, and had written in her diary that she hated them. She also dealt with feelings of survivor's guilt, and feelings of never being good enough for Ted and Stella Cooper and it all combined to send her into an existential crisis in her first semester at Brandeis.

Now, those feelings welled up again as she realized that Scientology agents must have broken into Cath's office. She called him, explaining what was going on. He went to check her file.

"It's missing," he said, not realizing that the burglars had misfiled it.

Scientology, she knew, had some of her most intimate secrets, and the thought of what they might do with them made her nauseous.

In April 1975, the Guardian's Office had Michael Meisner turn his attention to a new target. The church had been locked in litigation regarding the tax exempt status of its church in Hawaii, and it wanted the documents that had been obtained by the government's attorneys in that case, who worked in the Tax Division of the US Department of Justice.

On Meisner's instructions, on May 3, 10, and 17, Wolfe used his IRS identification to enter the Justice Department's Star Building, at 1101 11th Street, NW, and made his way to the offices of two attorneys involved in the Hawaii litigation. He copied documents from 12 files he found there, and each day delivered those copies to Meisner.

Once again, the Scientology spies had found it easy to get into government offices, take the information they wanted, and get out again without being discovered. But now, with so many tens of thousands of documents in their possession, even the Guardian's Office began to wonder about the penalties they might face if their activities were discovered. Memos about the legal definitions of "burglary," "breaking and entering," and "unlawful entry" flew back and forth between Guardian's Office executives.

On May 27, Mary Sue Hubbard grew tired of the handwringing over what they were doing. She sent a note to Jane Kember, the highest-ranking person in the Guardian's Office World Wide after Mary Sue herself: "Our overall strategy with the IRS shall be as follows: 1. To use any method at our disposal to win the battle and gain our non-profit status. 2. To buy all the time we can in terms of years...so we work to win, but *also* to delay as time works on our side, not theirs."

On June 18, the GO's top man in the US, Henning Heldt, sent a response to Mary Sue and Jane Kember, assuring them that he was following those instructions, and that he expected the data-gathering project to finish up soon. The aim, he wrote, was "to use any method at our disposal to win the battle and gain our non-profit status...Bureau I's actions are moving along steadily and full completion is expected in two to three months."

By the time Heldt sent that message, the operatives in Washington had already identified yet another IRS office they wanted to target for more document thefts. They had received information that files about L. Ron Hubbard and Scientology were being held by the IRS Office of International Operations (OIO), and Meisner was tasked with figuring out how to get "Silver" into it. (By now, Wolfe himself was being called "Silver" after the code name had originally been applied to the IRS.)

Meisner was given a deadline: Get Silver into OIO by August 30. Meanwhile, Scientology had more information than ever about where documents about Hubbard and the church were located in government files. In July, Scientology had filed a Freedom of Information Act request with the IRS. That request went to an IRS attorney named Charles Zuravin. By law, it was Zuravin's task to track down all of the documents that might refer to Scientology in IRS hands, and then work from that list to determine which documents the church was actually entitled to under the Act. (Such a list was known as a "Vaughn index.")

Meisner had Wolfe enter Zuravin's office between July and November, periodically stealing copies of the Vaughn index that

Zuravin was compiling. The Guardian's Office then had a record of the number and location of the documents the IRS believed it had on file about Scientology, whether it intended to turn them over or not. It provided the Guardian's Office with a road map of records to steal.

It was almost too easy: Zuravin had even noted which documents were going to be released to the church, and which ones were being held back. So Meisner had Wolfe target the latter, and Wolfe methodically went down the list, using Zuravin's index to tell him right where to look for documents the IRS didn't think Scientology was entitled to.

Into November 1975, Wolfe was still working down the list, stealing IRS documents by the foot. But then, a few days before the end of the month, the IRS suddenly moved its Scientology-related documents to a more secure location. Wolfe couldn't get into it. After months of easy theft, the Guardian's Office was suddenly stymied.

After another month with no progress, it became obvious that something had to be done to get access to the remaining documents on Zuravin's list.

It was time, once again, to bring in Don Alverzo.

11

Locked doors and fake IDs

O n September 16, 1975, the U.S. Attorney's Office for the
Southern District of New York filed a *nolle prosequi* to end
the prosecution of Paulette Cooper. She had, a year earlier, ful-
filled the requirement that she get psychiatric counseling since
her trial had been put off at the end of October 1973. "Under
the circumstances, the government does not believe that further
prosecution of Paulette Marcia Cooper is necessary or in the
public interest," the government's document read.

Her case was now officially over. But she worried that there
was still a cloud over her. It was still possible that a newspaper
might learn that she'd been indicted. She still couldn't really
relax. But she continued to see Dr. Herbert Benglesdorf, well
after she had been required to do so to fulfill her end of the bargain with the U.S. Attorney's Office.

She wanted his advice about Roland, a Jewish Marcello Mas-
troianni look-alike with a French accent who had been born in

Eastern Europe, lived for a while in Israel, then for many years in Montreal before moving to New York. He had a PhD and worked as the chief financial officer of a major corporation.

Roland had spotted Paulette when she moved into the Churchill late in 1972 – he had received the smear letter about her planted by Scientologists, but he didn't connect it with the attractive young woman he noticed around the building. Later he admitted that he would hang around the mail room hoping for a glimpse of her, but she was too preoccupied to notice.

She told Benglesdorf that she had met Roland at a party in the building early in 1975. The party was at the apartment of her friend Sandy, who worked in advertising as an account executive and had known Paulette since her BBDO days.

That night at Sandy's someone was playing the album from the musical revue *Jacques Brel is Alive and Well and Living in Paris* over and over. The songs, in French and written by a Belgian, were significant and intoxicating for her, she told Benglesdorf, and she fell in love with the music and with Roland, who spoke the language.

She was charmed, and fell hard. That summer, she turned 33, and for the first time since she was with Bob Straus, she began to think seriously about marriage. Roland was sophisticated and funny, and he helped her to forget that she had been through so much harassment, she told Benglesdorf. She said that the three of them – Roland, Barbara Lewis, and herself – were each damaged in their own way, and they joked about it. Barbara had never really recovered from her attack. Paulette was still damaged from

The Unbreakable Miss Lovely

her indictment and the ongoing harassment.

And Roland, it was becoming increasingly clear, drank too much.

Paulette began to suspect it when she would hear his refrigerator door open and close after she rang his doorbell. When he wasn't looking, she'd open it and see the only thing in it was a glass of wine. She and Barbara also noticed that frequently, he came into the Churchill carrying a brown paper sack that appeared to have two bottles inside. But what most worried her is that he did his best to hide it from her.

Benglesdorf surprised her by telling her to face facts: Roland was an alcoholic, and Barbara had her own troubles, and each of them were magnifying Paulette's own problems. He suggested that she break off with both of them.

Split with her best friends? Paulette didn't see that happening. The three of them, and sometimes with Sandy, would chip in for joint dinners at Paulette's practically every night. Barbara would bring a steak, Paulette would put together a blue cheese salad, and Roland brought the wine. Barbara kidded Roland about his accent ("I luff you," she imitated him saying to Paulette). Paulette teased Barbara about her habit of making ends meet by making things disappear. ("Great sirloin. Where'd you steal it?") Barbara teased Paulette about not joining her friends in the women's lib movement. "Paulette's years behind in women's lib," she'd say, but Paulette already considered herself sufficiently emancipated.

Then, in the fall, Paulette had a new suitor. An attorney in

England named Eric Leigh-Howard who had been handling one of her lawsuits admitted that he'd fallen for her and wanted her to marry him. He was more than twice her age, so she didn't take it very seriously, but he was persistent, and he asked her to come to London to see what kind of life he could give her. He was quite successful, had a large flat in the exclusive Knightsbridge area facing Hyde Park, and he sent her a first-class ticket to tempt her.

By then, things with Roland were deteriorating. Eric had met him while he was in New York and told Paulette he was a loser, and she began to have second thoughts, mainly because of his drinking. But the more she pulled away, the more he tried to hold on to her.

Adding to her stress, her tiny Yorkshire, Tiki, developed epilepsy, and medicine wasn't helping the little dog fend off the attacks. While she worried that Tiki wouldn't live much longer, she decided to accept Eric's invitation once Roland offered to care for the dog. (She told him she was going to London for legal reasons.)

It was December when she flew to London and spent a week by a fireplace in a large and gorgeous flat reading Agatha Christie novels, eating chocolates, and ringing a bell for a Filipino man and maid servant who brought her things like dishes of Scotch salmon.

But in just a week, she could see that life with Eric wasn't what she wanted. He offered her very little freedom, always wanting to know what she was up to. She was used to more independence. And she was especially upset the night she met Cyril Vosper, someone she had corresponded with for years.

Vosper had written a book about Scientology, *The Mind Benders*, that came out the same year as hers. Like Robert Kaufman, he was a former member who described his experiences in the organization. He also had suffered harassment, and at one point he had been reported falsely to customs as a drug dealer when he was visiting Spain. His luggage had been torn apart and he was questioned intensely. Once he revealed he had written a book about Scientology, the customs agents said they understood and allowed him to go.

Although she had told Eric she'd be gone only an hour, she and Cyril spent three hours talking about their experiences with Scientology. Eric was beside himself when she returned, saying he had been ready to call the police to look for her.

Meanwhile, she called Roland daily, mainly to find out how Tiki was doing. He told her the dog was fine. But then, on her last day in London, he admitted that Tiki had died a few days earlier. Paulette dropped the phone and became hysterical. Eric frowned, "you're crying about a *dog*?" That ended any chances the lawyer had with her. She packed her bags and went home.

When she got back to her apartment, she found out that Roland had not taken Tiki to the vet when the dog became seriously ill. He claimed that he was afraid she would blame him for Tiki's condition, but she wondered if he was just too paralyzed with alcohol to do anything about it.

Meanwhile, she learned that Barbara had told Roland what she had really been doing in London. When Paulette confronted her best friend, Barbara said, "I did it because I love you."

"What would you have done if you hated me?" Paulette asked.

Incensed by what she considered Barbara's betrayal, she realized that Benglesdorf may have been right when he said that Barbara and Roland weren't her best friends but her best enemies.

She broke it off with both of them. And as 1975 ended, she was alone again.

The remaining documents listed on IRS attorney Charles Zuravin's index that the Guardian's Office wanted to get its hands on were being kept in two locked offices in a high-security area, within a "red seal." One office was Zuravin's, the other was the office of Lewis Hubbard. The GO wanted the documents in Hubbard's office badly—they were from an audit of the Church of Scientology of California, the mother church. Michael Meisner was told that Don Alverzo was being sent out from Los Angeles to get into the two locked offices.

On January 17, 1976, Alverzo arrived and met with Meisner, showing him the lock-picking tools he'd brought with him. While Alverzo picked one office door, he wanted Meisner to work on the other one.

The next day, Sunday, January 18, Gerald Wolfe signed in Meisner and Alverzo with his IRS identification card. He took them to the third floor, where the two locked doors to the offices of Zuravin and Hubbard were just a few feet apart.

Wolfe kept a watch out as Alverzo and Meisner went to

work. But more than an hour later, neither one of them was having any luck with the tools that Alverzo had brought with him. Frustrated, Meisner punched Zuravin's door, and it suddenly opened. The three men hurried into Zuravin's office to grab files, run them to another floor to do copying, and then return them to their original place.

Then Alverzo went back to work on the other locked door, the one to Lewis Hubbard's office. He was still having no luck with his tools. So he tried an old trick—he took out a piece of cardboard, and slipped it between the door and the jamb, hoping it might slide back the latch. And it worked. The three rushed in again, rapidly went through Hubbard's files looking for things the church didn't already have, copied them, and left.

They departed the building at 2 am, and later that day, the 19th, Alverzo was on a flight back to Los Angeles with a foot-high stack of documents. Meisner followed him less than two weeks later. He spent most of the month of February in Los Angeles as the GO's top executives spent some time reviewing the progress of the Snow White Program.

So far, almost everything Meisner had been asked to steal from the IRS in DC had been taken. But it still wasn't enough: They gave him six more names of IRS officials whose files they wanted, and sent him back.

On March 4, after getting instructions from Meisner, Gerald Wolfe went to a suite of offices at the main IRS building at 1111 Constitution Ave, NW, used by IRS employee Joseph Tedesco, and surreptitiously removed a doorknob. Later in the evening,

Tony Ortega

after other workers had gone home, he went back to the door missing its knob and pushed his way into Tedesco's offices.

Wolfe took the files he copied to a pool hall in Alexandra, Virginia where he handed them over to Meisner. Meisner's report on the theft was forwarded to the top GO officers, including Mary Sue Hubbard. Six days later, Wolfe made another foray for more files, this time from the office of another target on the list. Wolfe seemed to be doing very well. But in mid-March Meisner was asked by his superiors to get an IRS identification card of his own so he could join Wolfe on the burglaries.

On March 15, Wolfe signed Meisner in and the two of them went to the IRS identification room, forcing their way in with a metal shimmy, and finding their way around with a flashlight. Following the directions they found in a booklet, they fashioned fake ID cards for themselves. The name they typed on Wolfe's was "Thomas Blake," and on Meisner's was "John M. Foster." Over the next three months, they made fake ID cards for another five GO operatives.

The Guardian's Office invasion of the IRS was going so smoothly, an even more audacious scheme was proposed: To infiltrate the offices of a Deputy U.S. Attorney General at the Department of Justice, where the GO suspected that changes to the Freedom of Information Act itself were being planned.

Again, things went surprisingly well. Using their IRS cards (Wolfe used his own valid card, Meisner used his fake "John M. Foster" ID), the two entered the Justice building at 9th and Pennsylvania Ave, NW, and broke into the office of Deputy Attorney

General Harold R. Tyler, Jr., using a metal shim to lift a lock latch.

Tyler was a Princeton grad, a WWII Army veteran, and had served as an assistant US Attorney and a federal judge before he had, for the second time in his career, become a deputy U.S. attorney general, in 1975. Meisner and Wolfe rifled through his office, and found the proposed changes to the Freedom of Information Act. They copied the documents and sent them on to Los Angeles, including to Mary Sue Hubbard.

A few days later, one of Meisner's bosses, a woman named Cindy Raymond, explained to him why they needed him to go back and break into Tyler's office again. At the time, Scientology had made a records request with the Drug Enforcement Agency, but the DEA had turned it down. So the church was appealing the case, and wanted information about the DEA that might help it win its appeal. Raymond learned that the Justice Department had been conducting a widespread investigation into corruption in the DEA, and a copy of that investigation—the "DeFeo Report"—was likely to be in Tyler's office.

There was bound to be a lot of damaging information about the DEA in those papers. Raymond instructed Meisner to get copies of it so it could be leaked to the press to undermine the DEA's credibility and might help Scientology in its legal appeal.

On April 9, Meisner and Wolfe went back to the Department of Justice, and broke into Tyler's office again. In their previous trip, Wolfe remembered seeing papers he thought might be the DeFeo Report, and he quickly found them again, contained in three files which they copied and replaced. Meisner forwarded copies of the stolen documents to Raymond and to Mary Sue Hubbard.

Two weeks later, on instructions of the top officer of the GO's Information Bureau—Bruce Raymond, Cindy's husband—Meisner called up a reporter at the *Village Voice*, pretending to be a disgruntled Justice employee. He mailed the reporter half of the DeFeo Report, promising to give the rest at a later time.

Also in April, Meisner was directed to break into the offices of the IRS Office of International Operations (OIO)—which he had been told to infiltrate the year before. This time, there was more urgency because the GO had learned that L. Ron Hubbard and Mary Sue were being audited, and documents pertaining to it were held by an OIO employee named Thomas Crate.

At about 7 pm on April 14, using their ID cards, Wolfe and Meisner signed into the IRS building at 1325 T. Street, NW, where the OIO was housed. They went to Crate's office on the tenth floor, but the door was locked. As they tried the door and then talked about what to do, a cleaning lady noticed them, thought they looked suspicious, and called a security guard.

After thefts of thousands of government documents over nearly a two-year period, it was the first time they'd come close at all to being caught. When the guard confronted them, they simply showed him their IDs. The guard had the cleaning lady unlock the office door.

Inside, they found the audit of the Hubbards in several large files in the desk of Crate and his supervisor. But they didn't see a copying machine. So Meisner and Wolfe carried the files back to the main IRS building, copied the documents, went back to the OIO building, signed in again, and replaced the files. It was about 11 pm when they were finally done.

(In those OIO files, Scientology found evidence that Paulette Cooper had been feeding information about the Guardian's Office to the IRS in 1974. A document showed that she had encouraged an OIO investigator to talk to Nan McLean, who supplied the investigator with a stack of documents.)

A month later, they did it all over again so they could get even more up-to-date records in the Hubbards' audit. Once more, the cleaning lady let them into Crate's office.

In April 1976, Meisner also began making incursions into the Justice Department building to steal files from the Interpol Liaison Office. Finally, more than a year after she first made the request, Jane Kember's instructions to get Interpol's files on L. Ron Hubbard were underway. Meisner ended up taking so many documents Scientology had records of Interpol's history going back to the early 1950s.

But that same month, a simple question asked in a courtroom by a judge stopped the Guardian's Office in its tracks and changed the focus of the Snow White Program.

Things were also changing for the people who worked directly with L. Ron Hubbard as he decided finally to come back to land. Tonja Burden was only 13 years old when her parents joined Scientology and put her into the Sea Organization, encouraging

Tony Ortega

her to sign a billion-year contract on March 3, 1973. She moved from Las Vegas, Nevada to Los Angeles, where she was put into the Cadet Organization, and lived in squalid conditions with 400 other Scientology kids in two three-story buildings.

After she was interrogated to make sure she wasn't connected to someone who wanted to do harm to Scientology, she was flown to the yacht *Apollo* in September—shortly after L. Ron Hubbard himself had returned to the ship after his 10-month stay in Queens, New York.

She was flown to Lisbon, but the *Apollo* had already sailed. So she caught up with it in Madeira. Surprised by how dilapidated the ship was, she struggled through a difficult conditioning process to turn her into a hardened sailor.

After passing that test, she was assigned to serve directly under Hubbard as one of his "messengers." Like the other young girls in the job, she was taught to carry Hubbard's instructions to others on the ship, running as quickly as she could, and deliver his words with the same tone that Hubbard had used.

Messengers also took care of his most immediate needs, including preparing his showers, washing his clothes, lighting his cigarettes, and getting him dressed. And Hubbard was very particular: he hated any scent of soap in his clothes, and wanted his shirts rinsed 13 times to get any smell out of them. If he did smell something, he would explode at the young girls serving him.

Tonja's duties included running messages from Hubbard to telex operators on the ship that kept the *Apollo* in contact with the rest of the Scientology world.

218

In a cabin below Hubbard's, there was a man whose title was "Snow White" who was busy with a large operation. He had a message board that was covered with papers. Some were pinned with small flags that read "In Progress" or "Done." Whatever was being directed in that cabin, it was obvious to Tonja that it was just another project being done to Hubbard's specifications.

More surprising for Tonja was to see that on a bookshelf in the ship's lounge, there was a copy of a paperback with the name *The Scandal of Scientology*. And later, she heard Hubbard say something about its author, Paulette Cooper.

The incident happened just outside his cabin, and he sounded angry and frustrated. As a messenger, Tonja was trained to respond to such a situation right away. She went to Hubbard to see if there was anything she could do. She got there in time to see him throw something down on a desk as he exploded, "That *bitch*, Paulette Cooper!"

By this time, in 1975, Hubbard was preparing to end his years at sea running Scientology from the *Apollo*. He had first tried to make land in the US in 1974, but he was tipped off that federal agents had been waiting for the ship in Charleston, South Carolina. So the armada had spent another year at sea, wandering the Caribbean, and now, Hubbard was determined to set anchor.

In October, the ship was docked in the Bahamas, and the crew scattered—some to New York, some to Washington D.C., and Hubbard, with Tonja and others in tow, flew to Orlando and then drove to Daytona, Florida as preparations were underway for their real target: taking over much of the gulf coast town of Clearwater.

Tonja and the other messengers were moved to another motel near Clearwater in the town of Dunedin, Florida, and the telexes were set up. She was still carrying messages back and forth from Hubbard to the rest of the Scientology world. And now, early in 1976, Hubbard was beginning to ask increasingly for one file in particular.

It was called Operation Freakout.

12

Operation Freakout

J ane Kember was losing patience with Paulette Cooper. The woman who headed up the worldwide Guardian's Office for Mary Sue Hubbard was used to getting her way. In one note to her underlings, she told them to make sure that any attacks on Scientology, no matter where they occurred, were "reported and handled properly, or both CSG [the 'Commodore's Staff Guardian,' Mary Sue Hubbard] and I will have your heads for breakfast." And she signed it, "Love, Jane."

In the spring of 1976, Kember was getting increasingly impatient that Paulette had not yet been silenced and was continuing to help Scientology's perceived enemies, especially the press. The church had won a small judgment against Paulette in Toronto when she failed to respond to a lawsuit she hadn't even realized had been filed against her. Kember wanted the Guardian's Office to use it as leverage against the author.

"Have her lawyer contacted and also arrange for PC [Pau-

lette Cooper] to get the data that we can slap the writs on her,"
Kember wrote to her deputy, Henning Heldt, the GO's top man
in the US on March 31, 1976. "If you want legal docs, from here
on we will provide. Then if she declines to come we slap the writs
on her before she reaches CW [Clearwater, Florida] as we don't
want to be seen publically being brutal to such a pathetic victim
from a concentration camp."

Kember worried that Paulette would begin to lead criticism
of Scientology after its 1975 program to take over Clearwater had
been exposed. She wanted Heldt to find a way to leverage the
Toronto judgment to handcuff Paulette before she did damage
in Florida.

And Jane Kember wasn't the only one who was fed up with
Paulette and the threat she posed, especially now that Scientology's founder had landed back in the United States for good. The
day after Kember wrote her note to Heldt, on April 1, the Guardian's Office began to spell out the aims and logistics for a complex
and audacious plot aimed to destroy Paulette.

Everything they had tried against her had failed to stop her.
Having her arrested. Spreading spurious slander about her sexual history. Filing multiple lawsuits against her written works.
Posing as close friends to get intimate information about her
plans. Breaking into her college psychiatrist's office to obtain
her records. Tapping her phone. Obscene phone calls and pornography mailed to her. Even trying to compromise her father's
business. Nothing had worked. Paulette was still corresponding
with people about Scientology, still helping other journalists,

still trading information with Nan McLean. Still talking to law enforcement or anyone else who might take on the organization.

L. Ron Hubbard was trying to re-establish himself and his management of Scientology in the United States. And it was in the U.S that he had been unable to neutralize Scientology's single biggest enemy. It made his blood boil. Hubbard wanted, once and for all, to destroy this petite brunette living in New York by hitting her with a multi-pronged assault that had been dubbed Operation Freakout.

The operation was spelled out in six pages, written by Guardian's Office national operations chief Bruce Raymond (whose real name was Randy Windment) to the North East Sector chief, Dick Weigand, with the local Assistant Guardian of Information in New York making sure things got done. The plan began with its overall goal: "MAJOT [sic] TARGET: To get P.C. incarcerated in a mental institution or jail, or at least to hit her so hard that she drops her attacks."

In order to accomplish that result, the highest levels of the Guardian's Office spy bureau, B-1, would coordinate with other national Scientology officials to pull off several consecutive capers intended to make it look like Paulette was losing her mind and had become a danger to herself and the public.

Raymond wrote that the FBI might buy into the subterfuge because it still had lingering doubts about her from the 1972 letters: "The FBI already think she really did do the bomb threats on the C[hurch] of S[cientology]."

To set up the operation, several things had to be put into

place first. Job one was to find a double for Paulette. Several other "field staff members" (FSMs) would also be recruited. Like Len Zinberg or Sylvia Seplowitz in previous years, these were typically local workers at the org who were recruited for a specific task. The Guardian's Office was careful never to tell an FSM anything beyond what was needed for his or her particular role – the "need to know" basis of all intelligence operations.

In this case, one FSM was needed for a crucial phone call, another couple were needed to befriend Paulette to find out something about the clothes she wore or even to obtain an article of her clothing. The document recommended that a "cheap coat" resembling something Paulette would wear should be acquired.

One of them would attempt to get close to Paulette through Transcendental Meditation. Paulette had gone to only a single meeting of the group, paying $75 so she could obtain her mantra. Although her participation was transitory, the Guardian's Office seemed to think she was still actively involved, and could be approached through it.

In order to get their double looking as much like the real thing as possible, the planning document asked if Paulette still had streaked hair and if she was still "skinney." It would be a volunteer's job to find out.

Another would search Paulette's neighborhood for a laundry that she didn't actually patronize—perhaps by staking it out over time and making sure Paulette didn't go there. Also, the woman posing as Paulette had to be ready to change into her disguise on a moment's notice, so she had to carry around her Paulette clothes and her Paulette wig.

Operation Freakout was divided into several different "channels," and each was planned to occur at a set time after the previous one had been achieved. Things would kick off with a telephone call to Paulette on a day during the work week to determine if she was home alone. If she was, then the operation would begin. An FSM who sounded like Paulette would then call two New York consulates for Arabic countries.

"The call should be fast, to the point, and impinge," the planning document said, using a Scientology word for "have impact."

The caller would then follow this script: "I just came back from Israel (pronounce the way it is pronounced in Israel). I've seen what you fucking bastards do. At least you're not going to kill my sister. I can get away with anything. I'm going to bomb you bastards."

Then the FSM was supposed to swear or mumble something in "Jewish." (Meaning Hebrew, presumably.)

The reference to Paulette's sister Suzy was deliberate. Suzy had been living in Israel since marrying an Israeli man in Belgium, and Paulette had been to Israel recently on a travel writing assignment.

On its own, this first caper was not designed to produce much of an effect. But Operation Freakout was carefully laying down a pattern for law enforcement agents to piece together and convince them that Paulette was coming undone.

The next day, the second phase of the operation would begin. At a location away from the Scientology org, an operative codenamed "Max" (whose real name was Charles Batdorf) would construct an anonymous note of the stereotypical sort, with capital letters cut out of magazines and pasted on a sheet of paper.

But not just any magazines. The instructions were quite specific: the letters should be cut out of a copy of *Writer's Digest* and an issue of the latest promotional newsletter from Transcendental Meditation. For the sheet itself, Max was supposed to look for a mostly blank page from *Writer's Digest*, and cross out in pen any printing on it.

When the letters were pasted into place on the page, they should make the following message:

"ALL OF YOU ARE DESTROYING ISRAEL. YOU'RE JUST LIKE THEM. MY SISTER LIVED, YOU BASTARDS. I WAS THERE – I SAW THE WONDERFUL PEOPLE. NOBODY CAN TOUCH ME. I'M GOING TO KILL YOU BASTARDS. I AM GOING TO BOMB YOU. KISSINGER IS A TRAITOR. I'LL BOMB HIM, TOO. IT MAKES ME VERY SICK. I MUST MEDITATE. YOU ARE SPYING ON ME EVEN IN ISRAEL. YOUR DAY WILL COME SOON. I'LL EXPOSE YOU AND BOMB YOU."

After deciding which Arab country was most virulently anti-Israel, Max would get the address of its New York consulate from the library, and then use another set of capital letters to address an envelope, being careful not to leave any fingerprints. The note would then be posted from a mailbox closest to Paulette's Churchill building apartment. If in the process of making the note Max had any suspicion that he had left a fingerprint, he was to throw everything away and start over again. And strict secrecy was crucial: No one but Max could know what he was doing, not even the org's PR officer or "communicator legal."

A week would then go by before the third part of the operation would begin. This part required the most coordination by multiple agents. One of them, who had befriended Paulette, would call her and set up a meeting at a time when the targeted laundry was open. The "friend" would try to get Paulette to a restaurant or bar with the purpose of getting her drunk. Another operative, staking out the Churchill, would immediately report what Paulette was wearing as she left the building to attend the meeting. Then, Paulette's double would rapidly change into similar clothes.

"If Paulette has on blue jeans, change to blue jeans. If she has on her usual coat, put that on...Several different outfits should have been obtained by [Paulette's double] so that when the caper goes down, she can immediately change into the color or type of outfit that Paulette has on."

From the time Paulette left her building and was spotted by the stakeout agent, the double was told to change her outfit in only three minutes. With Paulette on her way to have drinks with her "friend," the double, wearing sunglasses, would go into the laundry that had been chosen, and say that she was Paulette Cooper of 300 E. 40th Street, apartment 3H, waiting for the person behind the counter to write down the information on an invoice.

"Do I have any clothes here?"

When the laundry worker said no, the double would then demand that he check his records. When he said no again, she would then scream: "You're crazy! My name is Paulette Cooper! Check again!"

After the clerk reacted again, the double then "goes PTS 3," which was Scientology jargon for a psychotic episode.

"You're one of them! I'll kill you! You're a dirty Arab. You fucking bastards! I'll bomb you. I'll bomb the Arabs. I'll bomb the president! I'll kill that traitor Kissinger! You're all against me."

The double would then leave an item of clothing that had been obtained from Paulette's apartment, putting it on the counter or dropping it on the floor as she quickly left the laundry to a waiting car outside. In the car, she would immediately take off her wig and change her clothes.

By then, the staff member who had been staking out the laundry—a person not only in some sort of disguise, but also someone who didn't work at the Scientology org at the Hotel Martinique—should be walking up to the shop counter. He would ask an innocuous question ("Do you do suede cleaning?") and then say, as casually as possible, "Boy, was she crazy! I think you should call the police, with all these nuts threatening to kill the president."

Then he would leave, walk about five blocks, and make a call to the FBI from a prearranged location. Disguising his voice, he would quickly describe his reason for calling: "I don't want to get involved, and I don't want to give my name, but some nut girl in a laundry just went crazy and threatened to bomb the place and kill the president. With all these nuts running around I thought you should know. The guy in the laundry heard her too."

Before he could be questioned, he would hang up and leave the area as quickly as possible. He would not be told that the call was being recorded by the Guardian's Office.

The GO volunteers were routinely kept in the dark about what the others were doing. The agents who had been told to befriend Paulette and possibly obtain an article of clothing, for example, would not be told anything about the laundry scene. But they would be asked for any statements Paulette might make in the days after the caper, "for use in other actions."

Ten days after the laundry scheme, if nothing had happened to Paulette, it was time for the next step. A female staffer would call "the Arab Consulate"—presumably the New York consulate of the same Arabic country that had been called earlier—and, covering the telephone receiver with a thin piece of paper to disguise her voice, would ask for the "press attaché" and then say the following (while, unknown to her, the call was being recorded by the Guardian's Office): "I just want to tell you there is some-one—a writer—by the name of Paulette Cooper, who recently came back from Israel. She works for Israel Intelligence. She's also insane. She was in a concentration camp in Nazi Germany. She's been seeing a psychiatrist for years. Her sister is also with Israel Intelligence and lives in Israel. She talks when she is high on drugs or drunk. Lately she's been talking about bombing your embassy. I hate the damn Jew."

The staffer would then hang up and get away from her location quickly.

Finally, there was an additional "channel" rounding out Operation Freakout that was aimed to, once again, surreptitiously obtain Paulette's fingerprint on a piece of paper.

One of the staffers who had befriended her was instructed to take her out to get her drunk. At that point, a male staff member acting drunk would approach them, bearing a joke typed out on a piece of paper and backed with a blank sheet. The operative with Paulette would be careful not to touch the papers, but would laugh at the joke, hoping for Paulette to pick up the papers to read the joke for herself.

Then the "drunk" jokester would pick up the papers, being careful not to touch the blank sheet which now had Paulette's fingerprint on it. In the bathroom, he would carefully fold the sheets so the blank paper was inside, preserving the fingerprint. Then he'd put the sheets into his wallet.

"Drunk is always acting the fool. Drunk leaves," the planning document said.

He would then take the sheets to the Assistant Guardian of Information, who would then put the sheet with Paulette's fingerprint into a typewriter and hammer out the following message...

"You are a traitor to your people YOU BASTERD. I've been there and seen what you have done. You're ONE OF them. I'M GOINg To KILL you I'm going to BOMb YOU. I have a connection. NObody Can touch Me. You arre a German Pig. You Should be in THe Concentration CAMPs. I Feel so Ill Because OF YOu And YOu GodDam PIGs. YoU Die SOOn. It IS a Phalic SYMbol. I ThinK TrAnsFeranCe. EPidus The BOMB Is SET TO gO. MY Sister ISREAL. THey Are Responsible. They Persecute Me I WILL Kill THem AND YOU. YOU are All Against ME. The Arabs"

The letter would be posted from the mail box closest to Paulette's apartment at the Churchill to Henry Kissinger in Washington.

(Why Kissinger? Perhaps because in 1974 the Secretary of State had sent a negative message about Scientology to American embassies in the Caribbean. At the time, Hubbard and his small armada of ships were there, waiting for an opportunity to return to the US.)

Hubbard wanted Operation Freakout to be launched as quickly as possible. In his own handwriting, he scrawled across the top of the planning document "'A' Operation" and the word "Rush" or "Push" and "Hand Route." He also wrote some words across the top of another page: "Op. Freakout 2" and "No Prints!!!!"

(Hubbard's notation suggests that he had considered the earlier scheme against Paulette, to get her indicted for the bomb threat letters, as an earlier form of "Operation Freakout." But there are no other documents that confirm that.)

The top page of the planning document was dated April 5, 1976, and a handwritten notation said it was delivered to the

North East Sector chief – Dick Weigand – the next day, April 6.

According to the plan, the first step—calling the consulates of two Arabic countries with the first fake Paulette call—would take place only two days after the operation was assigned.

Hubbard was in a hurry. He wanted Paulette ruined, and fast. But it didn't happen that way.

A few blocks from the Churchill, at 225 E. 44th Street, between Second and Third Avenues, Costello's bar beckoned to the ink-stained wretches who made a living in New York's news business. Reporters from the *Daily News* and the *Post* would gather there after work. Australian journalist Steve Dunleavy was a regular.

When Paulette Cooper felt like seeing other writers after a day of work – freelancing for the *National Enquirer* could be a solitary pursuit – she'd go to the watering hole to kid around with the guys who covered the city.

It was during one of these nights at Costello's that she noticed a man walking around, showing people a joke he'd typed out on a sheet of paper that was resting on a clipboard. Some of them laughed, some didn't. But he was very insistent about it, wanting everyone to see it. Then he brought it over to Paulette. He held out the clipboard to her, trying to get her to take it from him.

She grabbed it and looked it over, and thought the joke wasn't funny. She went back to her drink. And it wasn't until she was walking home later that it dawned on her what had happened.

She became frightened, worrying that another Scientology operation was starting up. And she kicked herself, angry that she'd fallen for something so blatant. Sure, it was Scientology trying to get her fingerprint again, she thought, using an operative with a clipboard, just like with Margie Shepherd four years earlier.

For days, she wondered what was going to come of it. Would her fingerprint end up on something else that could get her arrested or indicted? And this time, would the government assume she was guilty and throw the book at her?

Around this time, she also noticed that someone was pretending to be her. Friends would call, asking why she had been so rude on the telephone when in fact, she hadn't called the friend recently. Another time, when she went to a meeting of the American Society of Journalists and Authors, someone asked about her trip to Washington. When Paulette said she hadn't been in the capital in a couple of years, she was told that she had called a few days earlier, saying she was in DC recently. Paulette realized that someone was either testing out their impression of her voice, or they were trying to make her friends think she was crazy.

But except for those signs that she was being targeted again, the other parts of Operation Freakout didn't get played out.

L. Ron Hubbard may have been in a hurry, but the Guardian's Office was methodical. It was cautious. It could take months to put the elements in place for an operation. It had been pilfering offices, stealing documents, fabricating letters, and so many other things, and had never been caught. And it wanted to keep it that way.

The Snow White Program that Hubbard finalized in April

1973 took more than a year to get going in earnest. And Operation Freakout also apparently took some time to get into action. Except for the attempt to get Paulette's fingerprint with the joke at Costello's bar and developing someone to make calls in her name, it was taking time to get the staff members into position to pull off the laundry caper and the bomb threats about Henry Kissinger. Months went by. And then, Paulette made it impossible to pull off the operation as it was written.

She moved away.

On April 14, 1976, during a hearing about a Freedom of Information Act lawsuit, U.S. District Judge George L. Hart, Jr. asked a question of Assistant US Attorney Nathan Dodell in the presence of Scientology's attorney, Walter G. Birkel, Jr.

"Have you all considered taking [L. Ron] Hubbard's deposition?" the judge asked.

"It is an interesting thought, Judge Hart," Dodell replied.

"Why don't you take his deposition?" the judge pressed.

Dodell said he'd consult with his colleagues at the Justice Department about the possibility.

Birkel related the incident to his clients at the church. And once the exchange was relayed to the Guardian's Office, near-panic set in.

Part of the reason for the existence of the GO was to protect the Hubbards from being hauled into court for depositions, and here a *judge* was suggesting that it happen. Within days, the GO ordered investigations into both Judge Hart and assistant US attorney Dodell.

On May 7, 1976, Michael Meisner and Gerald Wolfe went looking for Dodell's office at the US Attorney's Office in the federal courthouse on 3rd Street. They went to the third floor, which housed a legal library operated by the District of Columbia Bar Association. Close to the back door of the library and near a key-operated elevator were the offices of the Civil Division of the US Attorney's Office, including Dodell's office, which was locked. After trying to break in with a metal shim, they gave up and left.

Days later, Wolfe returned on his own around lunch time. When Dodell and his secretary left the office to eat, Wolfe rifled through her desk until he found a set of keys. He called Meisner, and they met to make copies. Then Wolfe went back and dropped the original keys in the corridor, thinking that the secretary would assume they had fallen out of her purse.

On the evening of May 21, Meisner and Wolfe went to the courthouse and showed a security guard their IRS cards, saying that they were going to work in the DC Bar Association's library. The guard gave them a key to the elevator, and after they took out some books to make it look like they were doing research at a back table of the library, they went out the library's back door to Dodell's office.

Using their duplicate keys, they went into the office and began copying a stack six inches high of Scientology and Interpol documents in Dodell's files. (Even before Judge Hart's comment, the GO had intended to target Dodell when it learned that his office probably contained copies of Interpol records about Sci-

Tony Ortega

entology. The GO had come into that information by placing a woman as a secretary in the Justice Department.) Meisner then prepared multiple memos for the Guardian's Office about the things they had found in the documents.

A week later, on the evening of May 28, Meisner and Wolfe returned to the courthouse for another invasion of Dodell's office, this time taking a stack of documents a foot high and duplicating them on a copying machine in the US Attorney's Office down the hall.

When they were returning the originals, they were stopped by a man named Charles Johnson who worked as a night librarian for the DC Bar Association. He asked the two men if they had signed in to do their research. They admitted that they hadn't. So Johnson had them sign in, and told them they couldn't return unless they had specific permission from the day librarian.

Meisner and Wolfe returned the original documents to Dodell's office and left. But Johnson had lingering doubts about the pair.

He looked through the library's log and saw that they had signed in as "J. Foster" and "Hoake." But a week earlier, two men with the same handwriting had signed in as "J. Foster" and "J. Wolfe."

Johnson notified the US Attorney's Office, telling them that he had seen two suspicious men using the copying machine in their office. The US Attorney's Office in turn called the FBI, who told Johnson to notify them if he saw the two men in the building again.

236

The Guardian's Office, meanwhile, was determined to get even more information out of Dodell's office, and it wanted Meisner to target Dodell's most personal information. On June 8, the GO approved "Project: Target Dodell," which would "render Dodell harmless."

Meisner didn't want any more trouble with the night librarian, so he requested, and got, a letter from the chief DC Bar Association librarian giving him permission to use the library.

On June 11, he and Wolfe went back to the courthouse on an evening visit. Meisner showed Johnson the letter giving him permission to use the facility. Meisner and Wolfe then went to the rear of the library so they could get into Dodell's office, but they were stuck: Dodell's office was being cleaned, so they had no choice but to sit and wait.

Meanwhile, Johnson called the FBI, as he'd been told.

13

The woman from the FBI

Two FBI special agents soon arrived. One of them was Christine Hansen, one of the first female agents in the FBI's history. She and her partner confronted Meisner and Wolfe, who produced their IDs. Wolfe, rather than use his valid IRS card, produced a fake one that had the name "Thomas Blake" – the name of an actual IRS employee. Meisner showed his "John M. Foster" ID, and told Hansen that he had actually left the IRS and admitted to her that his ID was no longer valid. So Hansen said she was confiscating it.

Meisner said that he and his friend "Blake" were doing legal research at the library, and had used the US Attorney's Office copying machine because it was close by. While Hansen questioned them, her partner went to call an assistant US Attorney. Meisner gave a fake home address and asked if they were under arrest. No, Hansen answered. So Meisner told Wolfe they were leaving, and they made their way out of the building, ignoring

Hansen's partner as he tried to call them back.

Meisner and Wolfe walked for several blocks to make sure they weren't being followed, then they hailed a cab and went to Billy Martin's Tavern in Georgetown, where Meisner called Mitchell Hermann in Los Angeles and used coded language to let him know something major had happened. Hermann replied in code, telling him to hang up and then call again to a pay phone near Hermann's office, where Hermann could speak more freely. Then Meisner told him what had happened.

Hermann told him to sit tight while other Guardian's Office employees retrieved Meisner and Wolfe's cars at the IRS building and the US courthouse and picked the two men up at the tavern. Meisner was taken to a hotel for the night. The next morning, he flew to Los Angeles.

On the sixth and seventh floors of the Fifield Manor— a 1920s building in the style of a French Chateau on Franklin Avenue in Hollywood that had once been home to retired actors which Scientology had bought in 1969—the Guardian's Office top man in the United States, Henning Heldt, and another top official, Dick Weigand, considered Meisner's report about what had happened the evening before at the US courthouse.

Their chief concern, they explained to him, was to prevent the FBI from making the connection between Meisner and Wolfe and the Church of Scientology. If Wolfe was arrested, they told Meisner, he needed to plead guilty to whatever he was charged with, giving a cover story for why he had given a fake ID and was using the US Attorney's Office copy machine. Meisner would then need to turn himself in to the FBI and give the same cover story and also plead guilty.

The next day, however, the Guardian's Office executives changed their minds. There were just too many ways that the FBI could eventually trace Meisner and Wolfe back to Scientology. Heldt argued that it might be better to make Meisner and Wolfe disappear by sending them out of the country.

But Weigand said that would only make the FBI more suspicious, and would increase the likelihood that they would keep investigating until they discovered the Scientology connection. Weigand said the best plan was still to have Wolfe give a cover story and plead guilty if he were arrested, and then have Meisner surrender and give the same cover.

Heldt agreed, and the next day they all planned to meet again and prepare the cover story with Wolfe, who was flying out to Los Angeles to join them. The next morning, June 14, the Guardian's Office began to transform Meisner's appearance. His hair was dyed red and cut short, and he shaved off his mustache. He was given money to obtain contact lenses later that day to replace his eyeglasses.

In the cover story they came up with, Meisner and Wolfe were drinking buddies who, on a lark, made fake IRS identification cards when Wolfe was showing him around where he worked. Wolfe then asked Meisner to help him do legal research, and they had used the DC Bar Association's library at the courthouse because it was conveniently located between the two of them. They hadn't realized that the copying machine they had used was in the US Attorney's office.

That night, still on the 14th, Wolfe flew back to DC and met the next day with Mitchell Hermann, who helped him go over the cover story again. Meanwhile, back in Los Angeles, Meisner continued his transformation. He was now "Jeff Murphy," and he moved in with Weigand and prepared a report about all the burglaries and other illegal activities he had overseen as the Assistant Guardian for Information in DC, a post he now had to give up. He was given a new title: National Secretary for the US, a position bestowed on him by Jane Kember.

Back in DC, Special Agent Christine Hansen hadn't given up on the case. The "John M. Foster" ID she'd taken from Meisner turned out to be a fake, and the "Thomas Blake" who worked for the IRS did not turn out to be the man at the courthouse with Foster – the second man's ID was a fake badge as well. And it bothered her. *Why* were two men using fake IDs to get into a legal library in the US Courthouse, and why were they seen using a copy machine in the US Attorney's office? She found that the IRS was also concerned, and agency officials told her they were willing to cooperate to figure out how and why fake identification cards had been created. Hansen procured a warrant for the arrest of the two men if she could find them again.

On June 30, 1976, Hansen was at the main IRS building, where she'd been talking to technicians about how ID cards were made, when she saw a familiar face in a hallway. It was one of the two men she'd questioned at the DC Bar library. She stopped him and demanded his ID. He clearly recognized her and looked shocked to see her. She, meanwhile, was stunned at her sheer luck.

And so, in a hallway of the IRS building, Christine Hansen arrested Gerald Bennett Wolfe, and the largest infiltration of the US federal government in its history began, slowly, to unravel.

Wolfe was charged with using a forged government pass and was released on his own recognizance on the same day, after providing handwriting samples. The highest levels of Scientology now watched nervously to see what would happen next. In a letter to Weigand, Mary Sue Hubbard complained that they had made everything too easy for the FBI: "All they had to do was trace the common entry points of the log back to both Mike and the FSM [Wolfe] until they arrived at the point where the FSM used his correct ID card" at his IRS job. (Mary Sue didn't know that Hansen's arrest of Wolfe was a result of sheer luck, after she spotted him at the IRS building while she happened to be there.)

Other letters and messages were passed between the top executives as they wondered if Wolfe's cover story—about making fake IDs as a lark—would hold up. At the end of July, however, Wolfe was ordered to testify to a Grand Jury, and on August 5, a magistrate judge then issued a warrant for the arrest of Michael Meisner.

As the GO prepared to send Meisner even further undercover, Mary Sue Hubbard wondered how the FBI had made the connection between "John M. Foster" and Meisner, who had not given his actual identity the night he was questioned by FBI agents, and had also given a fake address—but one that was only a few doors down from where he really lived.

What they didn't know was that Christine Hansen, the FBI special agent, was determined to figure out what was really going on.

She went to the address "Foster" had given, and showed his ID badge to people in the neighborhood until someone recognized him – and told her the man's name was really Michael Meisner. She also learned much earlier than the church realized that Scientology was involved.

Still puzzled about Wolfe and Meisner being seen in the US Attorney's offices, she went to each of the lawyers and their staffs, asking if they were missing any documents, and who might be interested in rifling through their desks. When she got to Nathan Dodell, he told her he knew exactly who would want what was in his office: The Church of Scientology.

The what? she asked.

She quickly began learning about the organization and why it might be burglarizing US government offices.

In Los Angeles, the Guardian's Office was panicked about Wolfe's arrest and Meisner's warrant. Weigand told Meisner that he needed to cut off all ties with the Guardian's Office and keep himself hidden. Meisner moved out of Weigand's house and into a Glendale motel under the name "Jeff Burns," then days later he moved to a Los Angeles motel as "Jeff Marks." After three more motel changes, he settled into a hotel in Burbank on September 15.

A few days later, Weigand and Mary Sue Hubbard discussed their options. Weigand figured there were only two: Meisner would turn himself in and keep his mouth shut about the church, and would face about five years in prison. Or, Meisner would keep in hiding for five years, when the statute of limitations would run out for the kinds of charges he might face

Meanwhile, the Guardian's Office wanted to know more about Meisner's warrant. So it had a Scientologist police lieutenant in San Diego check the National Crime Information Center (NCIC) computer for details on the warrant, which turned out to be for forgery of a government ID. That NCIC check alerted the FBI, and Christine Hansen had the San Diego FBI office question the police lieutenant about making the NCIC inquiry. The lieutenant made up a story about arresting Meisner in San Diego on a jaywalking charge and then doing a routine check on him. GO executives considered it a good false lead to waste FBI resources.

But Hansen wasn't distracted. In late September, she told the DC Scientology church that she wanted handwriting samples for Meisner as the FBI continued to look for him. Mary Sue Hubbard concluded that the FBI was going to search for Meisner's handwriting on sign-in logs at DC buildings, so she asked for the GO to get a full list of all the places Meisner had broken into.

It was a long list.

In the fall of 1976, while Scientology's top officials in Los Angeles were scrambling over what to do with Michael Meisner and Gerald Wolfe, just miles away the church's attorneys were preparing to go to battle with Paulette Cooper. She, however, was doing her own scrambling, trying to find a lawyer who would represent her.

Virgil Roberts had left a large law firm and had gone into business with a few partners. A black man living in Los Angeles, he was interested in civil rights litigation. And a woman he knew on a lawyers' committee on civil rights contacted him in the fall with a case she thought he might be interested in—an author from New York was being sued over the contents of a book she'd written.

He was intrigued, but he was also wary. The client, Paulette Cooper, had only about $10,000 to spend, and in just a month the case was scheduled to go to trial for an estimated six to eight weeks. In addition to the low pay and having very little time to prepare, the case was daunting because Cooper was being sued not only by the Church of Scientology of California but also in Detroit (for something Paulette had said on a radio program there), in the United Kingdom, in Toronto, and in Australia.

The Los Angeles case was the first scheduled to go to trial and would likely have a significant effect on the others. If Cooper lost badly here, there was a good chance she could get overwhelmed by subsequent losses around the world.

Roberts liked the odds. He took the case. Paulette moved to LA to prepare for the trial and had boxes of material that she'd used to write *The Scandal of Scientology* shipped to Virgil's office.

In a libel trial, an author's best defense is the truth, and her pursuit of it. Virgil rapidly began making himself familiar with the research Paulette had relied on, so he could show that she'd worked hard to provide an accurate picture and had not had a "reckless disregard for the truth," which in part defines libel.

As they strategized about the best way to prove to the court that her book had told the truth, they thought seriously of issuing a subpoena for Charles Manson. One of the things about Paulette's book that had bothered Scientology the most was that she had included Manson in her chapter about celebrities and the church. For several years, while he was at McNeil Island Penitentiary in Washington, Manson had become very interested in Scientology and did more than a hundred hours of auditing during the years 1963 to 1967. "I got pretty heavy into Dianetics and Scientology," Manson later said, and Bruce Davis and Squeaky Fromme had also been involved. As Paulette indicated in the book, it was the *New York Times* that had first discovered Manson's Scientology connection, but her book mentioned it on the back cover and featured it in a way that irritated Scientology officials. Wouldn't it be something, she and Virgil discussed, to have Manson testify about his Scientology years in her trial?

Researching Scientology wasn't the only odd part of the case for Virgil. There was also the judge, Thomas C. Yager. Eleven years earlier, in 1965, Yager had married a wealthy heiress 14 years his senior—he was 47, she was 61. They had honeymooned on Catalina Island, and sailing back to Newport Harbor four days after they had tied the knot, his bride vanished, presumably falling overboard somewhere in the Pacific Ocean. Yager claimed that he'd gone below decks briefly, and when he came back up, she was gone. He didn't call the Coast Guard, he said, because his radio wasn't working.

Yager wasn't charged with wrongdoing, but he did have a more difficult time getting reelected at the next local election. Now, in 1976, he was only a couple of years short of retirement.

At one point, Yager called Roberts and Paulette into his chambers. While they were talking about several different matters, he mentioned that he couldn't accept a copy of *The Scandal of Scientology* they had given him, just as he couldn't accept a copy of *Dianetics*, which the church had sent. But, he said, he would accept donations to a new church he'd started, "The Community Betterment Service." Paulette tried not to show how stunned she was.

Despite his oddnesses, Yager didn't hand Scientology any favors. For the two weeks leading up to the trial date, Scientology attorney Joel Bennett entered dozens of motions asking that passages in Paulette's book be considered "libel per se." In other words, the church wanted Yager to agree that there were statements in *Scandal* that were defamatory on their face, and would obviously cause the church harm. If the judge agreed, the church would not have to prove to a jury that the statements were untrue, and could then argue how much damage they had caused.

For example, Bennett pointed to Paulette's reference to a quotation by L. Ron Hubbard, that before he published his book *Dianetics* in 1950, he had said to friends that the only way to get rich was to start a religion. (Hubbard had actually said it multiple times to numerous people, including to a teenaged Harlan Ellison.) Bennett argued that the statement essentially called Hubbard a liar, implied that he was out to commit fraud on the IRS, and therefore made him out to be a criminal.

But Virgil pointed out to the judge that Paulette had merely quoted Hubbard verbatim, and if those were the implications of his words, it wasn't Paulette's fault.

The judge sided with Paulette on that point, and on every single one of Bennett's dozens of other motions, clearing them all away so that trial could begin. The church was going to have to prove that the book had libeled the church and none of the statements were going to be considered defamatory on their face. To prove libel, they would have to show that the passages in the book were not only untrue, but that Paulette had maliciously disregarded the actual facts.

Judge Yager, in other words, had made the church's job much harder. And Virgil was feeling good about Paulette's position. Although he'd had only a few weeks to prepare and had worked around the clock to get ready, he really believed she had a good chance to win.

Meanwhile, the church was doing what it could to improve its own chances. Each day, when Virgil went from the courtroom to his office in Century City, he would see them—dozens of Scientologists, standing on the sidewalk outside his 28th floor suite at 1900 Avenue of the Stars. When he asked about it, he was told they were concentrating on him and his office, hoping to affect his mind with their thoughts. They were also filling the courtroom each day, hoping similarly to affect Judge Yager's mind.

Through their brain waves, the Scientologists were determined to win the lawsuit.

But the day before trial was to begin, Virgil was surprised when Bennett, the church's attorney, showed up at his office.

By now, Virgil knew quite a bit about his opponent. He knew that "Bennett" wasn't his original name, for example. Joel was Jewish, but had given himself a WASPy last name when he wanted to marry a blueblood heiress of his own.

And it wasn't only his name he'd changed to win her over. He had overextended himself at his firm to give his wife what she needed to live the life she was accustomed to. And initially, he told Virgil, working for Scientology had been very lucrative. But now, the church wanted results and the payments were coming less frequently.

Bennett told him that he couldn't afford to lose this case. And he admitted that his chances at the trial weren't looking good. He needed to have a settlement, and he needed it now, he said as he broke down right there, in Virgil's office.

"I'm in way over my head," he blubbered.

Virgil had other reasons to consider a settlement. There was Paulette herself. He knew he'd have to put her on the stand, and he wasn't looking forward to it. Paulette had told him about the harassment she'd been through, and she couldn't talk for more than a minute about Scientology without becoming heated.

He knew that if she did that on the stand, it wouldn't go well with a jury. She sounded too angry, and not like a journalist who had merely written a book about a subject she had no connection to.

And then there was Ted Cooper. Paulette's father had called Virgil, making sure he knew about the bomb threats and the indictment and the phone tapping.

"Mr. Roberts, can you just make this go away?" Ted had asked him.

Virgil was disappointed. He knew he had a good chance to beat Scientology at trial. But he knew Paulette was also hungering for a settlement. She hated being away from New York. She didn't enjoy driving on California freeways, which made it hard to get around. She missed her friends. And court proceedings not only produced a lot of anxiety for her, they were also tedious in their detail. She dreaded the thought of several more months living like this. And what Judge Yager had said in his chambers made her think he was too strange to handle the case correctly.

So Virgil set about trying to get Paulette the best deal he could. There were the other lawsuits around the world, for example. He told Bennett he'd get a settlement only if they were all withdrawn as well.

On the church's side, Bennett wanted the copyright to *Scandal*. By 1976, five years after its original printing, the book was no longer in print, so Paulette agreed. The settlement required Paulette to turn over every copy she still had in her possession, save for one copy for herself. She also would not republish the book or comment on it publicly, and the church agreed to pay Virgil's attorney's fees. (A church spokesman told the press earlier that Cooper's side had asked for $25,000.) The church attached a list of 52 statements from the book that Cooper was required to sign, saying that she had no personal information about them (they contained things she had included based on newspaper reports, such as the *New York Times* story about the involvement of Charlie Manson in Scientology). The church promised not to use the list "for any other purpose than to clarify or correct statements concerning Scientology." (Scientology soon broke this promise, however, and published the list in a book of its own, and claimed Paulette had admitted to errors, when she hadn't.)

When the deal was signed on December 5, 1976, Judge Yager congratulated Virgil on wrapping things up so neatly. For now, the battles between Paulette Cooper and the Church of Scientology were over, from Los Angeles to the UK to Australia. But if the lawsuits were over with, her book was no longer her own – a price she wasn't unhappy to pay.

Paulette had never had an attorney work so quickly and effectively. She was relieved and grateful.

At Mary Sue Hubbard's request, Michael Meisner made a list of all the places he'd broken into on behalf of the Church of Scientology. Meisner wrote that he'd illegally entered the Department of Justice, the IRS, the Office of International Operations, the Post Office, the Labor Department's National Office, the Federal Trade Commission, the Department of the Treasury, the U.S. Customs Building, the Drug Enforcement Administration, the American Medical Association's law firm, and the law firm representing the *St. Petersburg Times*.

On October 8, Special Agent Christine Hansen served a subpoena for Meisner's handwriting samples on a young Guardian's Office employee named Kendrick Moxon, who turned over nine pages of handwritten material. Meisner was told that Moxon had been instructed to turn over fake samples of his writing.

Meisner himself moved into an apartment in Los Angeles—keeping him in a motel was costing the GO too much money. And a new cover story was dreamed up for him. He had been breaking into offices because he was a journalist working on a story about lax security in government agencies. And Mary Sue Hubbard added another layer to the story: Meisner should say he was having problems in his marriage because his wife was more successful than he was. In order to prove himself, he had tried to show how much he could do on his own.

In November, Meisner moved again, into another Los Angeles apartment, and he wrote a letter to Mary Sue Hubbard, telling her that a new problem was developing. Even if he turned himself in and stuck to their latest cover story, there was still a big question to answer: Where had he been since June? The longer his hiding went on, the harder it was going to be to convince the FBI that there wasn't a larger conspiracy to uncover. He suggested a new cover story, that he'd been visiting a friend in Canada.

Through December, as the grand jury in DC continued to investigate Wolfe, the GO kept working on an ever-more elaborate cover story for Wolfe and Meisner to use to throw off the FBI. But the cover story by now had become so complex it was taking months for the GO to get it all written down. Into March, 1977, Mitchell Hermann was still coming up with details for it.

Meanwhile, Mary Sue Hubbard fully understood the risk that Scientology was facing. On March 25, 1977 she sent out a memo to B-I staff, describing a new "red box" system that would keep sensitive documents ready to be whisked away in case of a government raid. "All the red box material from your areas must be centrally located, together and in a moveable container (ideally a briefcase), locked, and marked." Signing under a code name, "Judy," she gave her staff three days to get the "red box" containers ready.

As for what would go into them: "Proof that a Scnist is involved in criminal activities." Specifically, anything that would impact L. Ron Hubbard or Mary Sue, and in particular the documents the Guardian's Office had stolen from so many government offices should go into the briefcases.

Meisner, meanwhile, was complaining that things were taking too long, and the GO seemed to agree, as it replaced Hermann and others who were supposed to be handling the Wolfe affair. By the end of March, Meisner asked to be sent to DC to take the matter into his own hands. He also began to question the wisdom of having him plead guilty once he did return and was arrested. Meisner said he wanted to go to trial, and he thought he could convince a jury that Special Agent Hansen's identification of him as the person she confronted at the courthouse library was faulty.

On April 20, Jane Kember angrily dressed down her employees for letting the matter take so long, and she repeated the game plan: Wolfe would plead guilty and take a light sentence as a first offender. Meisner would surrender and also plead guilty, giving a cover story for where he had been for seven months.

A week later, Meisner said he was going to leave by the end of the month for either Canada or DC and get things moving. But on April 29, he was told that the GO was keeping him in Los Angeles, and was placing two guards at his apartment.

At 2:15 am on April 30, Dick Weigand, two other GO operatives, and three guards showed up at Meisner's apartment. They searched it for any evidence of his connection to the Church of Scientology. Meisner was given a handwritten note from Mary Sue Hubbard, telling him that if he followed orders, the GO would eventually remove the guards.

The next day, on May 1, three GO operatives and two guards arrived and told Meisner that he was being moved to a more secure apartment. He refused to go, so he was bound and gagged and put on the floor in the back of a car. After he was moved, Meisner realized it was useless to resist, so he gave the guards no more trouble, and the situation relaxed.

In DC, Gerald Wolfe's behavior was mystifying government prosecutors. Through April, he had indicated interest in a deal: He would plead to a misdemeanor in return for cooperating with the grand jury still investigating what the break-ins were really all about. But then, after getting a new attorney, Wolfe changed his mind about cooperating with the grand jury. On May 13, he pleaded guilty to a felony, the wrongful use of a government seal. Prosecutors were stunned, and angry.

Meisner, meanwhile, was told he would not be allowed to

surrender until the IRS had granted tax-exempt status to the Church of Scientology of California. But Meisner had had enough of waiting. On May 29, while out walking with his guard, he broke away, jumping into a taxi and asking to be driven to a Greyhound Bus Station. He took a bus to Las Vegas and checked into a cheap motel. The next day, he called the GO in Los Angeles. Agents were sent out to talk him into returning to LA.

When he did, he met with Henning Heldt at Canter's Deli on La Brea. Heldt told Meisner that both L. Ron Hubbard and Mary Sue were concerned about him and were doing everything they could. Heldt told him he needed to think of his guards as friends. Meisner was moved to an apartment in Glendale, and for another month was under constant guard.

In DC on June 10, Gerald Wolfe was in court for his sentencing. Prosecutors told the judge it still concerned them what they didn't know about Wolfe and his partner, and why a person with no criminal record would plead guilty to a felony with a potential five-year prison sentence. It seemed to make no sense. Wolfe's attorney, however, once again put it down to a drunken prank. And he said that the government didn't have any evidence that Wolfe had taken any sensitive government documents. (At least, the *government* had no evidence of it. Not yet.)

Wolfe was sentenced to probation and 100 hours of community service, to be served in Minnesota, where he was from. But before he could leave, he was subpoenaed by the federal Grand Jury, which was still trying to figure out why Wolfe and another man had used fake IDs, and whether they had stolen documents.

And again, why?

Under oath, Wolfe stuck to the cover story—that he was doing legal research at the DC Bar Association library with his friend, "John Foster." Wolfe then told the GO what he'd testified to, so Meisner could make sure his own testimony matched it when he eventually surrendered. But Meisner was complaining again that the Guardian's Office wasn't really concerned about his welfare. This time, he got a handwritten note from Mary Sue Hubbard, warning him that if he ran again, he'd be on his own. He promised good behavior, and then was so cooperative, the guards relaxed around him again, even leaving him alone overnight.

Then, at 6 am on June 20, Meisner made another escape. He packed up a few clothes, caught two successive buses, and went into a bowling alley to make a phone call. Meisner called an Assistant US Attorney in DC and explained the situation. Two hours later, three FBI agents arrived at the bowling alley to pick him up. They immediately took him to Los Angeles Airport, where he was put on a plane to DC.

Christine Hansen, however, wasn't there to celebrate. There were so few women in the FBI, she had been pulled away from the DC office (where there were two female agents) to another division which needed one. She had no choice in the matter. And the Meisner-Wolfe investigation was taken out of her hands and given to another agent, who soon was telling her that he planned to drop it. She complained, and it stayed open. But she wasn't involved when Meisner himself finally showed up to become a witness. Meisner was given a court-appointed attorney, and he agreed to plead guilty to a felony conspiracy charge in return for cooperating fully with the Grand Jury. He was also put under protective custody of the U.S. Marshal's office.

Meanwhile, back in LA, the Guardian's Office discovered immediately that Meisner was gone, and that he'd left behind a note saying he would be unreachable for a week. While there was some panic about Meisner's escape, Mary Sue Hubbard counseled calm. She figured that Meisner was worried about the time he'd have to serve in prison after he surrendered, and she predicted that he was researching the legal situation in a library somewhere to reassure himself, probably in the San Francisco area.

On June 29, 1977, nine days after Meisner disappeared, a GO operative received a letter from Meisner postmarked from San Francisco, saying that he just needed some time to himself. Reassured that Mary Sue had been right, the GO continued to work on Meisner's cover story, figuring that he'd be back soon.

But that's not what happened.

14

The raid

In July 1977, Paulette Cooper's travel writing career took her to Senegal and Gambia. She had been asked to write about the history of the slave trade, and had made the obligatory trip to Gorée Island, off of Dakar, where the majority of slaves bound for America were said to have begun their hellish cross-Atlantic trip. After she wrote her story, her editors at the *New York Times* asked Paulette to consult a historian to back up her material, and she was surprised when the historian told her that the story was apocryphal. A few slaves had been processed there, but it was hardly the hub that stories made it out to be. The *Times* never printed her story, and other newspapers kept printing the legend.

On the flight home, Paulette picked up some newspapers to pass away the hours. And she was somewhere over the Atlantic when she started leafing through a copy of the *International Herald Tribune*. She noticed a short item that had been picked from the *Washington Post* wire. It said that on July 8, the FBI had conducted a massive raid in DC and Los Angeles, the largest raid in the bureau's history, involving more than a hundred agents.

The target: The Church of Scientology.

The story was very short and contained no real detail. But Paulette read it over and over again. And tears streamed down her cheeks.

At 6 am on July 8, teams of FBI agents swarmed two locations in Los Angeles. A smaller team ran into Fifield Manor, the French chateau on Franklin Avenue, heading for the sixth floor offices of Henning Heldt. About 80 agents, meanwhile, poured into the large complex on Fountain Avenue that had previously been the Cedars of Lebanon Hospital. At the same time, another set of agents rushed into the Scientology church in Washington DC.

The night before, the agents had been briefed on the 33-page affidavit that went with the warrants they would be serving. Based on what Michael Meisner had been telling the FBI in the two weeks since he had become a government witness, the agents had compiled a detailed list of 162 specific documents and files that had been stolen from government offices.

The agents were instructed to find those documents to prove that the thefts had happened. They were told to be disciplined about their searches – Meisner had told them where the documents would probably be found, and they were not to go off searching elsewhere, inviting legal trouble from an organization which already, by 1977, had a litigious reputation.

By 10 in the morning, the agents were finding so much evidence of the Snow White Program and the infiltration of government offices, a call went out for reinforcements. Eventually, 156 agents were poring over records in Scientology's headquarters in three locations and 30 separate rooms, and 48,149 files with 100,124 pages of documents were seized in total. A large truck was needed to carry it all away.

The raid lasted 21 hours, and the last of the agents didn't leave the premises until after 3 in the morning.

A week later, on July 15, L. Ron Hubbard abandoned a ranch east of Los Angeles where he'd been living since October and went to a secret location in Sparks, Nevada. In 1975, Hubbard had come back ashore after running Scientology at sea. While church agents began a surreptitious takeover of Clearwater, Florida under a front named United Churches of Florida, he had to flee when a local reporter heard he was in town from a local tailor Hubbard had purchased a suit from.

With his cover in Florida blown, Hubbard grabbed his nurse, Kima Douglas, and her husband Mike, and the three began driving for New York. Hubbard was on his way to hide out in Queens again, just as he had two years earlier. But nearing the city, they thought better of it and headed for Washington DC, where they moved into a brownstone and set up the telexes.

Through late 1975 and 1976, as Michael Meisner and Gerald Wolfe and Don Alverzo were burglarizing federal offices, L. Ron Hubbard was living just blocks away, and was kept informed about the project.

He was also briefed about a GO operation in March 1976 that took place in one of his favorite places in town, Rock Creek Park. It was there that Michael Meisner and Sharon Thomas – the GO operative who had managed to become a secretary at the Department of Justice – staged a hit-and-run accident in order to discredit Clearwater mayor Gabe Cazares. The mayor, who had resisted Scientology's takeover of his town, was in DC for a conference, and on March 14 Thomas had been introduced to him by a Scientologist pretending to be a local reporter. Thomas offered to show him the town in her car, and as she drove through Rock Creek Park, she seemed to lose control of her car and appeared to strike a pedestrian – it was Meisner, who played his part and flung himself as if he'd been hit and pretended to be injured. Thomas then sped off. The next day, GO operatives discussed how they might use the incident later to end the mayor's political career.

On June 11, Meisner and Wolfe were stopped and questioned by Christine Hansen at the federal courthouse, and after he was told about it, Hubbard predicted that it would result in big trouble. He told Kima Douglas that it was time to abandon another residence, and they took a flight to Los Angeles, where once again he was in temporary digs until something more permanent could be found. In October, Hubbard moved to the ranch in La Quinta, and he appeared to relax. Then, on November 17, news arrived that his oldest son by Mary Sue, Quentin Hubbard, had committed suicide in Las Vegas.

"That stupid fucking kid! Look what he's done to me!" Hubbard was heard to say. Quentin's homosexuality had been a nuisance to Hubbard. Now, Hubbard took his son's suicide as a personal slight.

As 1977 began, Hubbard turned his focus to a process he was developing to combat drug abuse. He called it the Purification Rundown, and he came up with it after researching LSD addiction by talking to two drug users. Hubbard claimed that he'd made a great discovery, a combination of sauna use and niacin intake that he thought might win him a Nobel Prize.

But his ruminations about Nobel success were cut short with the news of the FBI raid in July. A week after it happened, he left in the middle of the night from the La Quinta ranch, being driven in a car whose headlights were kept off until it reached the main highway. The car didn't stop until reaching Sparks, a low-rent town in Nevada where Hubbard holed up while he waited to see if the FBI was coming after him. And while he waited, he noticed that the world seemed to have gone mad for the kind of science fiction – space opera – that he spent so many years cranking out in the 1930s and 1940s.

In May, a movie called *Star Wars* had opened, and by July it was a phenomenon. Director George Lucas had created a major motion picture that paid homage to his favorite childhood serial, Flash Gordon, and it was setting box office records. Hubbard could be forgiven for thinking he could cash in. While he hid out from the FBI in an apartment in Sparks, he began turning Scientology's most secret upper-level teachings – space opera about a genocidal galactic overlord named Xenu – into a screenplay, calling it *Revolt in the Stars*.

While Hubbard scribbled away at a script about space battles, the church itself was locked in a very real war.

Almost immediately, the July 8, 1977 FBI raid on Scientology became a battle royal of litigation. And in DC, at least, the church found some success: On July 27, Judge William B. Bryant agreed with Scientology that the FBI's warrant had been invalid, and ordered the government to return the documents it seized at the DC org. The government appealed, and Bryant's decision was overturned. But Bryant then found that even if the warrant was valid, the FBI had improperly used it to go on a fishing expedition during its search for records. That decision was also overturned.

The church also attacked the searches in Los Angeles, and while those matters were being litigated, the FBI and the Department of Justice were under instructions to do nothing with the seized documents.

So while the government had to remain silent about why it had raided the church, Scientology went on a public relations campaign to portray itself as a victim of outrageous federal overreaching. Church spokesmen told reporters who were curious about the raid that Scientology had actually been investigating *government* wrongdoing, which is why the government had then retaliated with a show of force.

The church put together binders of documents and news reports going back 20 years in order to portray itself as a victim of government meddling. The binders were sent out to friendly columnists, who then portrayed the FBI as heavies picking on Scientology.

In August, syndicated conservative columnist James J. Kilpatrick obliged, writing that "Over a period of 23 years, commencing in 1954, the federal government has thrown its whole massive weight into a malicious persecution of this religious sect."

Liberal columnist Mary McGrory also received a copy of the binder put together by the church. "The church has always excited the unfriendly interest of the government, nobody is entirely sure why," she wrote.

But if the FBI agents and prosecutors at the Justice Department couldn't talk publicly about what was in the documents, they were rapidly going through them, and began building a case. And that included reaching out secretly to someone they were surprised to find named in Scientology's records.

On October 12, Paulette was working at her desk in her apartment when her telephone rang. A man on the line identified himself as Russ Cicero, and said he was a special agent with the Federal Bureau of Investigation.

Sure he was, she thought.

Assuming it was a Scientology trick, Paulette told him to give her a number at the FBI where she could call to make sure he was telling the truth.

He gave her a number.

She called it, and it turned out to be the FBI. She asked for

Cicero, and was patched through. So why was the FBI calling her? she asked.

Cicero said that what he had to tell her was confidential, but the Bureau wanted to know if she was interested in helping out with an investigation. He could only tell her a few general things about the results of the raid on Scientology, and the tens of thousands of documents that the FBI had seized. For the last three months, agents had been painstakingly going through them, and were stunned by what they found. Not just documents that spelled out the Snow White Program, but many other things. Including, he said, documents about Paulette.

Had she ever heard, he asked, about something called Operation Freakout?

Paulette wept after she put the phone receiver back down, not only because Cicero told her the FBI had documents which showed that the church planned to frame her in 1976 in something called Operation Freakout, but he also described other documents which made it clear that she had been framed with the bomb threat letters in 1972.

Finally, after eight years of harassment, an indictment, the lawsuits, the expense, the harm to her career – finally, she was going to be publicly exonerated. When, she didn't know. But now that the FBI was on her side, things were going to be very different.

But that's also what made her break down after the call. She thought about what she had lost. She thought of Bob Straus.

They had talked of marriage. He had wanted lots of kids. But her depression during those days had pushed him away, and the smear letters had made him doubt her innocence. Now, she knew there was proof of it. But it had been more than three years since they last saw each other. She didn't even know if he was still single. If he was, she still thought there was a possibility for them. She steeled herself, and called Bob's office. She reached Bob's secretary, and put on a cheery tone.

"I'm an old friend of Bob's, and I was putting together my Christmas card list. But I'm embarrassed, I can't remember the name of Bob's wife. Can you help me out?"

Paulette thanked the woman after she reeled off not only the name of Bob's wife, but also their two children.

Paulette hung up. Somehow she had already known that it was far too late to resurrect what she had with Bob. Maybe she just wanted him to know that she had been right, and that he shouldn't have doubted her. He had believed she was innocent, she knew. But the smear letters, the harassment, had turned out to be too much. She could understand why he felt that way. The Church of Scientology's campaign against her had, in this case, been successful and had done immense harm to her life.

But now, things were turning, and her disappointment about Bob Straus gave way to the elation she felt after her call from Russ Cicero. He asked Paulette, did she want to help the FBI prosecute the Church of Scientology?

Oh, did she.

The only people she told about the phone call from the FBI

were her parents, who were both relieved and concerned – they still worried about her 1973 indictment becoming known and what it might do to her career, even if the FBI now believed she was innocent. They told her they always believed her, and they begged her not to get involved again. Forget the whole thing, they said, worrying that if she helped the FBI, the harassment would intensify again.

But she told them there was no way she couldn't help the FBI in the investigation. Finally, law enforcement was on her side, and she told them she wanted Scientology to pay for the years it had stolen from her. She wanted badly to see the documents about her that the agents had seized. But she was told she wasn't going to see them, not while they were still being litigated in court.

Even as agents began coming over to her apartment at the Churchill to talk to her about Scientology, they were careful not to show her the Operation Freakout documents or anything else referring to her. It was disappointing, and she had no idea how long she'd have to wait before she could see what they had found.

But they did show her photographs. And what they showed her stunned her.

One showed Paula Tyler. She was the young woman from California Paulette had helped get an apartment in her building. The young woman who had been introduced to Paulette by Margie Shepherd after Margie had showed up at her door canvassing for Cesar Chavez. The woman who, after moving into the Churchill, had come over constantly to talk with Paulette about her troubles. The woman who had introduced her to Jerry Levin.

The woman who suddenly had to go to Europe after Paulette had spotted a photograph of someone who looked like her in a Scientology magazine.

That Paula Tyler.

The FBI showed Paulette photographs they had taken of Scientologists in their investigations, and she spotted Paula. She told them about her. And about Margie Shepherd. And about Jerry Levin. All of them, she now began to realize, were working for Scientology.

She thought of her teenage diary, tucked way back in her coat closet. It was Jerry, she suspected, who had taken it out and copied pages of it for the church so they could be dropped off at her father's office three years ago. It was Jerry who always wanted her to come up to the roof. To look at the view from the ledge, where she always felt nervous.

It was Paula and Jerry she had confided in, telling them her fears as she was at her absolute lowest, while awaiting trial in 1973. And everything she had told them, she knew, had gone right to Scientology.

She wanted to throw up.

Despite the FBI's caution with her documents, and Paulette's own care speaking only to her parents about what she was going through, the story about her frame-up that was spelled out in the documents seized by the FBI finally became public on April 28 and 29, 1978 in two stories by journalist Ron Shaffer in the *Washington Post*.

Paulette was taken by surprise. Although Shaffer had talked to two of her attorneys – Paul Rheingold and Virgil Roberts – Paulette herself was in Europe on a travel writing assignment in the days leading up to the story and hadn't heard it was coming out. But someone in the Bureau had talked to Shaffer, and had spelled out pretty clearly what was in the Snow White Program and Operation Freakout documents.

Finally, five years after it had happened, the indictment of Paulette Cooper was public information.

In 1973, it was her greatest fear that newspapers would find out she had been arrested and indicted, and she had decided she would kill herself if a trial actually happened. But now, it was finally out in the open, and she was thrilled. Finally, she could talk about what she'd been through.

"The 'attack and destroy' campaign carried out by the Church of Scientology's 'Guardian's Office' to silence critics has involved illegal surveillance, burglaries, forgeries and many forms of harassment, according to sources close to an intensive federal investigation of the Scientologists' activities," Shaffer wrote in the first of his two stories, and briefly described Paulette's situation without actually naming her: "Scientologists obtained the personal stationery of a woman, typed a bomb threat on it, mailed it to a Scientology office and reported the threat to police. The woman, who had written a book critical of Scientology, was arrested, charged with making a bomb threat, and then charged with perjury when she denied doing it. She suffered a nervous breakdown before the case eventually was dismissed."

The story also detailed the hit-and-run scheme that was designed to ruin the political career of Gabe Cazares.

The next day, Shaffer's second story was all about Paulette.

"According to informed sources, FBI agents have found in church records evidence that the Scientologists framed Cooper by stealing her stationery and sending the bomb threat to themselves.

"The Scientologists deny they were involved in any such scheme. 'It's totally ridiculous and typical of outrageous false statements that some people feel they need to pass on regarding the church,' George Layton, a Church of Scientology spokesman, said."

Also that day, a story by another *Post* reporter, Timothy Robinson, revealed that the day before, after Shaffer's first piece had come out, Scientology's attorney, Phillip Hirshkop, had asked a judge to force Shaffer and the newspaper to turn over any FBI documents or notes on those documents that Shaffer had used. A judge refused. Clearly, Scientology was extremely unhappy that Shaffer had revealed what was in the FBI's possession.

Less than a month later, on May 25, 1978, the Church of Scientology of California filed suit against Paulette Cooper, accusing her of helping the *Post* produce Ron Shaffer's stories, which it said was a violation of the settlement agreement she had made with them at the end of 1976.

"Cooper will not utter, publish or republish to any public gatherings or in the press…information or material concerning the Book, Cooper's prior writings and statements concerning

Scientology, and past litigation between Cooper and Scientology, including but not limited to the terms and provisions of this settlement agreement," the 1976 settlement read.

Scientology had no evidence that Paulette had discussed her book or the *Queen* magazine article or her prior litigation with the *Post*, and the agreement didn't cover Scientology's own behavior – surveilling Paulette, harassing her, or framing her, or planning to do more. But the church decided that the *Post* story was enough to convince a jury that Paulette had violated the agreement she signed to end all litigation in 1976.

Paulette was ready for a fight. She'd been on the defensive for years, but now, even if she didn't have the Snow White and Operation Freakout documents in her possession yet, she knew they existed, and she knew the FBI was becoming as interested in seeing Scientology punished as she had been for many years.

Paulette filed a counterclaim against the California church, asking for $10 million in damages. In June, the Church of Scientology of New York filed its own breach of contract lawsuit against her. And in August, she counterclaimed against the New York church, asking $20 million in damages.

The litigation war was back on.

On August 15, 1978, nine members of the Guardian's Office, including Mary Sue Hubbard, were indicted in federal court. (Two others – Jane Kember and Mo Budlong – lived in England, and extradition proceedings began against them.)

Their cases were then assigned to Judge George Hart, Jr.,

the same judge who, in 1976, had raised the question of L. Ron Hubbard being deposed in a Freedom of Information Act lawsuit – a suggestion that had set off a Guardian's Office investigation of Hart and the plundering of assistant US Attorney Nathan Dodell's office, which itself eventually resulted in the arrest of Gerald Wolfe and Michael Meisner.

After a few months, when it looked like Hart wasn't going to be receptive to their objections and legal maneuvers, Scientology's attorneys, in January 1979, took an extraordinary step. They asked Hart to recuse himself because, they admitted, the GO had targeted him with overt and covert operations that might have been illegal. As a target of that kind of behavior, they argued, Hart couldn't be impartial.

He agreed, and recused himself.

The cases were next assigned to Judge Louis Oberdorfer. But in 1969 he had handled a tax case involving the church. So he recused himself on Feb 5, 1979.

The cases then were assigned to Judge Charles Richey. Richey was a Richard Nixon appointee, but a liberal. Scientology's attorneys initially said they were pleased that he had taken the case. To accommodate the defendants, Judge Richey traveled to Los Angeles in the summer of 1979 to hear three weeks of testimony and arguments about the FBI's raid of the church. And because he had received several death threats, Richey traveled to LA with two federal marshals.

After hearing evidence, Richey denied Scientology's motion to suppress the documents the FBI had seized. With a trial looming, and the prospect of even more bad publicity, the defendants, including Mary Sue Hubbard, waived trial and agreed to sign a "stipulation of evidence," a lengthy document written by the Justice Department that explained in detail the activities of Meisner and Wolf and the other GO operatives. For their part, the government dropped 23 of the 24 criminal counts. Most of the defendants were then facing a single count of conspiracy to obstruct justice.

Now, it was up to Judge Richey to make a decision. After reviewing the evidence, on October 26, he convicted all nine on the "overwhelming evidence of guilt." He scheduled sentencing for the nine defendants on December 9.

But before that happened, Scientology did two things. It filed a motion to have Richey recused from the case, and it hired a Washington DC private investigator with a legendary reputation.

While the Guardian's Office prosecutions were happening, Paulette Cooper was running into more legal trouble, and from a different source.

Ted Patrick billed himself as the father of "deprogramming." He was a high school dropout from Tennessee who had moved to San Diego, and in the late 1960s he turned his interest in cults into a specialty in helping parents retrieve their children from abusive groups. Completely self-taught, Patrick used an aggressive style of confrontation and had even used force to isolate a target for his methods of persuasion.

On September 2, 1979, he detained a young Scientologist

named Paula Dain in Laguna Beach, California. Dain's parents had been referred to Patrick by Paulette Cooper, and shortly after Dain was detained, Nan McLean went to the scene to see if she could help Patrick, who paid her expenses to come.

After she got there, however, Nan realized that Dain was not there of her own volition, and was being held in a hotel room as a prisoner. She called Dain's parents and said she was leaving, wanting to have nothing to do with it.

Dain's parents persuaded her to return, saying they would pay her expenses. But when she returned, she was still convinced that Dain was being held against her will, and persuaded Patrick to let her go – 38 days after he had first isolated her.

Dain then filed a $30 million lawsuit against Ted Patrick, Paulette Cooper, and Nan McLean, but Paulette and Nan were later dropped for lack of evidence.

Still unhappy at the tactics Patrick had used, Nan agreed to testify against him on behalf of Paula Dain, and it became the first serious rift in her relationship with Paulette. Testifying against Patrick was the same as helping out the Church of Scientology, Paulette felt, and she couldn't believe Nan would do it. She did what she could to talk Nan out of testifying on Dain's behalf. (Dain later filed a $30 million lawsuit against Paulette for trying to keep Nan from testifying.) Years later, Patrick was ordered to pay only $7,000 to Dain because a jury found he did not have "evil intent" when he detained her.

If the case didn't amount to much in the long run, it had a devastating effect on one of Paulette's closest relationships. For years, she and Nan McLean had talked on the phone almost daily. Paulette had gone to McLean's home – north of Toronto – many times, including for a wedding of one of Nan's children. She was such a part of the family, she participated in a prank that was popular at the time – streaking with the rest of the wedding party and jumping in the lake. But now, their relationship was seriously strained, and wouldn't really recover for many years.

15

Fifteen Sixteen Uniform

On October 20, 1979, somewhere 8,500 feet over the state of New York, the engine on a Cessna 206, tail number 1516U, suddenly stopped. A little more than an hour earlier, the small plane had taken off from Lawrence, Massachusetts after its pilot, a Boston attorney named Michael Flynn, had made a thorough pre-flight check which included examining the two wing-mounted fuel tanks and a fuel sump under the engine to make sure there were no signs of water.

Their lives suddenly in danger, the people in the airplane each reacted in different ways. Behind him, Flynn's 12-year-old son sat still and didn't say a word. An attorney next to Flynn's son panicked and barfed. The Marine lieutenant and Vietnam veteran sitting next to Flynn in the front passenger seat grabbed a chart on Flynn's directions and began looking for a place to land.

Flynn tried to remain calm as he calculated how far the plane could glide before hitting the ground. It was dropping at about

500 feet a minute, and he figured it could get about seven miles at that rate. The lieutenant located an airfield in the general direction they were flying: It was 15 miles away.

As they glided to Earth, Flynn kept checking his gauges, but everything appeared normal. He switched up the fuel tanks and goaded the fuel pumps, trying to figure out what had happened. But mostly, he needed to find a field to land in.

"Fifteen Sixteen Uniform! Fifteen Sixteen Uniform!" he yelled into his radio, identifying his plane and declaring an air emergency.

With the ground rapidly coming up, he found a farmer's field to land in that was flat and wide. There would be no trouble with trees or power lines. He guided the plane at the field, still calculating the rate of descent.

But then he noticed that the furrows in field were perpendicular to his approach. Flynn knew that after the wheels hit the ground, there was a good chance the furrows would cause the plane to flip.

He yelled at everyone to brace for impact and get their heads down between their knees.

Then, just hundreds of feet above the ground, the engine suddenly roared back to life.

Flynn gunned the engine and pulled up, powering back to 10,000 feet.

And then the engine died again.

As he prepared all over again for an emergency landing, the engine came on and off, sputtering to life and dying, and the plane yo-yoed up and down.

Now, he could see the airfield that the lieutenant had picked out from the chart, and he aimed for it. With the engine sputtering and the plane yo-yoing, Flynn managed to put down and roll to a stop.

His son had never said a word through the entire ordeal.

As Flynn and his passengers recuperated from their fright, a mechanic at the airfield began to take apart the plane to find out what had happened. He came over to Flynn and asked him where he'd flown from.

Lawrence, Massachusetts, about an hour and fifteen minutes of flying.

That's impossible, the mechanic said.

Why? Flynn asked.

Because there's enough water in your fuel tanks that this plane should never have got off the ground. There's no way you took off from that far away.

But they had.

The mechanic drained the tanks and fuel injectors, put the parts back together, and told Flynn he could fly on. But Flynn had declared an air emergency, so he should file a report, the mechanic told him.

And Flynn eventually did. But first, he had a football game to catch. His three passengers got back into the plane, he started up the engine, and Flynn continued on to their destination – South Bend, Indiana, to see Notre Dame take on USC.

Flynn could never prove how so much water had appeared in

his fuel tanks after he'd inspected them and flown for more than an hour. He was told that CIA operatives had been known to sabotage airplanes by putting water balloons into their fuel tanks so they would burst during the flight. But Flynn could never prove that someone had done that to his plane.

Earlier that year, Michael Flynn had agreed to represent a woman, LaVenda Van Schaick, who had left the Church of Scientology. She told Flynn about Scientology's Guardian's Office, about its use of secret codes and undercover agents. Flynn was intrigued, and he read what he could about Scientology, and learned about a writer named Paulette Cooper. After absorbing what he could, Flynn wrote a letter to the church on behalf of LaVenda, asking it to return her personal files, and for a refund of the money she had spent.

The church declined, and tried to intimidate Flynn.

So he sent a second letter, saying that LaVenda's request was rescinded, and if the church wanted to work out a settlement short of litigation, it would need to be in the million-dollar range.

After sending that letter, Flynn then began getting calls from people he hadn't heard from in years. Lawyers he'd worked with (or against) in previous lawsuits. Law school classmates. College classmates. Even high school classmates that he hadn't talked to in decades.

The FBI, they all told him, was calling and asking about Flynn. What was happening, Mike?

Flynn knew that it wasn't the FBI tracking down virtually everyone he'd ever known or worked with. He understood that he'd become the subject of a Guardian's Office "noisy" investigation. He sent the church another letter, telling them that he was going to recruit more plaintiffs so he could file a class-action lawsuit for hundreds of millions of dollars.

It was after he had sent that letter that, in the air over the state of New York, his Cessna's engine had quit.

On Saturday, December 15, 1979, Clearwater city councilman Richard Tenney organized an anti-Scientology rally that drew 10,000 local residents to Jack Russell Stadium, the spring training home of the Philadelphia Phillies. Two weeks earlier, Tenney had held a gathering of about 3,000 people at Clearwater City Hall. In the wake of the FBI documents becoming public, with revelations that besides the spying and burglarizing in the nation's capital Scientologists had also infiltrated the local government and the local newspapers, people in Clearwater who had stood by to watch Scientology take over the downtown had had enough.

The local citizenry had been inflamed in part by a November 27 editorial by the *Clearwater Sun*. "The cult has been here four years. For a time, the possibility might have existed that a form of detente could be worked out between the Scientologists and the people of Clearwater. But the recent release of thousands of Scientology documents in Washington, D.C. has put such a possibility forever behind us," said the newspaper. "Scientology is not a religion, as it claims to be, but rather a for-profit group that uses religion as a guise to escape taxes and separate credulous men and women of large sums of money in exchange for superficial training in mental and emotional disciplines…Scientologists of both high and low rank have in behalf of the cult, engaged in lying, theft, burglary, breaking and entering, conspiracy, and illegal harassment of private citizens."

(About a month earlier, the *Sun* had written about the FBI documents and referred to the Scientology plans as "Operation Snow White." The name stuck, and the press ever after called it by that name. But in Scientology documents, it was always known as the Snow White Program.)

Two of the people who attended the December 15 rally at Jack Russell Stadium were Paulette Cooper (who spoke to the crowd and received three standing ovations), and Michael Flynn. It was the first time the two of them met.

Paulette was dazzled by Flynn, who not only talked about Scientology like no other attorney she'd met, but was also handsome, with penetrating blue eyes. Paulette soon found that Flynn's female associates and clients talked about his looks as much as they did his cases.

For years, Paulette had been frustrated by attorneys who had counseled her to be cautious, and told her that it might be better not to be so outspoken. Flynn said the opposite. He knew her story well, having read most of the articles that had come out since the *Washington Post* first made her story public in April. He said he was horrified by what had been done to her, and she believed him. But more than sympathizing with her, Flynn said he was determined to do something about it. He wanted to put

Scientology out of business.

It was precisely what she wanted to hear. The FBI documents were so damaging, she didn't see how they could fail. With Flynn gathering together numerous clients who had been harmed by Scientology, they could go directly at the church in a way that had never been done before.

Between Flynn's heady suggestions, and the validation of 10,000 admiring Clearwater citizens at the December 15 rally, Paulette was feeling more confident than ever that she had it in her power to help destroy Scientology, and that its days were actually numbered.

That attitude was reflected in the newsletter she had begun mailing around the country.

Every quarter, she collected news about Scientology, typed up summaries of press reports, and mailed them out to hundreds of people, including members of the government and even the White House. She called it "Scientology Clearing-House: A Quarterly Summary of Scientology news (non-objectively) edited by Paulette Cooper."

Around the same time she had met Flynn that December, her optimism about Scientology's numbered days was reflected in articles she typed up that predicted its imminent demise.

"SCIENTOLOGY REALLY SEEMS TO BE HURTING," she wrote in one of her newsletters. "I'm sure most of you will be pleased to hear that missions seem to be closing and orgs seem to be losing people en masse.... Large orgs like Phoenix and Washington D.C. have very few people in them. Many major orgs (New York, Michigan, Pennsylvania) have moved from the affluent suburbs into bad sections of N.Y., Detroit & Philadelphia. Scientologists always told their people that public opinion of them was good but that just the press and the government disliked them. Now they are telling their people 'we've got 7 months to turn public opinion around'!"

Paulette was sure that momentum was shifting against Scientology in a major way, and she was determined to help accelerate it. The FBI and the Department of Justice not only were trying to put the leaders of the Guardian's Office into prison, but they told Paulette they wanted to punish the people who had framed her over the bomb threat letters. While a New York grand jury contemplated charging people criminally over her harassment, Paulette had filed her own litigation against the church, and she began to think it would be more effective if she put it into the hands of Michael Flynn.

She also continued to encourage other journalists to write about the documents seized by the FBI, and about her framing. She was pushing on multiple fronts, hoping that enough effort could deal a killing blow to the organization that had spent so many years trying to destroy her.

She was getting so determined, so single-minded, she lost sight, briefly, that Scientology would never lie down and surrender to her. And at the very moment she should have been most careful, she didn't anticipate its next operation against her.

Scientology's attempt to get Judge Richey to recuse himself after he convicted the first nine Snow White defendants in October was submitted late in the case and was technically flawed. Richey denied the motion, and then sentenced the nine to terms from six months to five years. (They paid $10,000 each the day they were sentenced so they could stay out of jail while they appealed their sentences.)

Richey also decided that once he had sentenced the defendants, he could now, finally, make public the documents that had been seized by the FBI more than two years before. Scientology appealed that decision, but the appeal was denied on January 21, 1980.

Paulette Cooper and Nan McLean were each in Washington DC and in line the very first day the Snow White Program documents were made available. *Toronto Globe and Mail* reporter John Marshall captured the scene. In a cramped, windowless room at the Justice Building, there was a long table covered with boxes of documents, a sizable portion (but not all) of the evidence seized in the 1977 raid.

As they began going through the 23,000 documents made available by Judge Richey's order, Marshall described Paulette as "a finely honed, long-haired accumulation of nervous energy."

"If you see anything about Operation Freakout, please let me know," she told him.

Besides Paulette and Nan McLean, there were nine other journalists and a couple of young Scientologists from the church's magazine, *Freedom*. Outside, in a foyer, a U.S. marshal checked to make sure no original documents left the room. A copying machine was in constant use.

Marshall knew Paulette's story, and he knew that the FBI now considered her bomb-threat indictment all a frame-up by the church. And then he found a document that confirmed it.

It was a June 1974 letter from Dick Weigand to Henning Heldt, describing a Guardian's Office staff member's work for the church: "Conspired to entrap Mrs. Lovely into being arrested for a felony which she did not commit. She was arraigned for the crime."

"Mrs. Lovely" was clearly Paulette, as other documents showed.

And then, Paulette found the notes that had been written by Jerry Levin.

"Oh, this is it," Paulette said, and began to read them. But Marshall said it was too much for her. She copied the documents to read later.

"I need to read these with friends beside me," she told him.

Later that night, at dinner with Marshall and Nan, she read Jerry's notes about her. "We have Mrs. Lovely in a very perplexing position," Jerry wrote to his GO bosses a few days after Paulette was indicted in May 1973.

Paulette knew that she'd shared with him intimate details about her life, and here was proof of it. The time she had told him about her first sexual experiences—fooling around with Robert Smittini on the cruise back from Europe in 1960 when she was 18, and losing her virginity to a professor a couple of years later at Brandeis—she now read about in notes Levin had sent to the

Guardian's Office.

At her lowest point, in the summer of 1973, she had told Jerry that she had contemplated suicide, and that was in there, too. At the time, Jerry had seemed very sympathetic about her emotional state. But now, she saw what he had written about her suicidal utterances to his spy bosses.

"Wouldn't this be a great thing for Scientology?"

Finally seeing the Operation Freakout and Jerry Levin documents about her from the 1977 raid only made Paulette more determined than ever to make Scientology pay for what it had done to her. And then, after she had met Michael Flynn and was dazzled by his plans to bring down the church, Paulette met another man, Richard Bast, who said exactly the things she wanted to hear.

She had been told about Bast by a private investigator, Tom Spinelli, a man she had met through his work for the American Medical Association. Spinelli told her that Bast was a well-known private eye in Washington DC and had been asking about her. Bast had worked with columnist Jack Anderson and with politicians who needed help getting out of sticky situations.

Paulette wasn't aware of his reputation. But on the advice of Spinelli, someone she already trusted, she contacted Bast and they started talking about Scientology.

On February 13, 1980, Dick Bast took Paulette to dinner at The Palace, one of the most expensive restaurants in the city. The monument to decadence was at the eastern end of 59th Street, having opened five years earlier by Frank Valenza, the same daring restaurateur who had operated Proof of the Pudding, the place where Paulette had lived over more than ten years earlier on 64th Street and where the smell of garlic had motivated Paulette to work harder so she could afford to dine at such places one day.

Dinner for the two of them would run about $200, Paulette knew, which was a fortune for a meal in 1980. But Bast wanted Paulette to know just how serious his mission was, and how serious was the money of the man backing him. As if to emphasize it, he carried a briefcase which he rested on the floor.

Bast wouldn't tell Paulette who his benefactor was; he would only tell her that he'd been hired by a wealthy Swiss man whose daughter had joined Scientology and then had committed suicide. The wealthy man wanted revenge, Bast said, and he was willing to pay dearly for it.

Based on the work she had done in the past, they wanted Paulette on their team, and they were willing to pay her $2,000 a month plus expenses. She would do legwork for them, digging up documents, doing interviews, and helping Bast with plans to bring Scientology down.

The offer stunned Paulette. It was enough money that she could quit freelancing and dedicate herself full time to digging up dirt on Scientology. She would be paid decent money to do what she wanted to do anyway. It was an offer nearly as tasty as the courses of food brought out by the Palace's servers.

Bast pushed Paulette for an answer, bringing out a contract for her to sign. The sooner she signed it, the sooner she'd start getting paid to work against Scientology. She looked it over, and noticed a clause that gave her a jolt: "The Independent Contractor herein expressly gives to the Employer her prior consent to intercept any of her wire/oral communications."

She asked Bast about it, saying that it seemed unusual for a simple employment contract.

"It's meaningless. Just standard language for a private investigator contract," Bast said.

She shrugged it off and signed. Here, finally, was what she had been looking for – someone with the money and will to expose Scientology fully, and she wanted to be a part of it. If she had any qualms about the language in the contract, they quickly melted with the butter and cream swimming in the Palace's concoctions.

Signing with Bast and his nameless Swiss benefactor felt like the best possible timing. Paulette was still fuming after what she'd read in the FBI documents a few weeks earlier, which not only vindicated her but revealed how gleefully the Scientology operatives had celebrated her misery and the misery of others.

She was happier than she'd ever been in her life. She had the evidence that she'd been targeted for ruin, she had law enforcement finally on her side, and now she was even being paid a good wage to exact her revenge on Scientology.

Things could not have been going better. She couldn't wait to get to work for Bast.

Two weeks after Paulette signed her contract with Richard Bast at the Palace in New York City, in the California town of Hemet, a man named John Brousseau opened up the back doors of a Ford van. Inside was a foam mattress and some bedding and pillows that Brousseau had laid down in the floor of the vehicle for the journey.

Then he helped L. Ron Hubbard climb in. The 68-year-old man, his famously bright-red hair now greying and hanging in long unkempt locks, sat down on a corner of the mattress and rested his elbows on his knees. Then he held out a hand for Brousseau to shake.

"All right, John. Thanks for everything. I'll see you," Hubbard said. Brousseau closed the doors.

For several years, Brousseau had been Hubbard's personal driver, part of a small staff that took care of the man's needs as he lived in semi-seclusion in Southern California. He helped shuttle Hubbard from an apartment complex in Hemet to the 500-acre compound that was still being built out in a place called Gilman Hot Springs. He also went on walks with Hubbard, and coveted the private time he had with a man who had so many entertaining stories of his days as an aviator, or of what he saw in the war. Like other "Sea Org" workers, Brousseau considered L. Ron Hubbard a great man. But as his driver, he got to know him in a private way that few others did, and Brousseau treasured it. But now, he waved goodbye. A young couple named Pat and Annie Broeker got into the van, and Pat started it up and drove off.

It was the last time Brousseau – and nearly everyone else in the Church of Scientology – ever saw Hubbard.

He finally had gone completely into seclusion.

Richard Bast lived in Virginia, outside Washington D.C., and over a three-month period Paulette made several trips to meet him. When she came to town, he rented her a room in the Washington Hilton. They would either talk at the hotel or at his office, which was in his house in a pricey enclave where his neighbors included U.S. senators. Even at home Bast was usually wearing an expensive suit, but his assistant, a man named Fred Cain, tended to be more casually dressed. Bast's wife would also tiptoe in and out of the room.

Paulette told Bast about the dozens of articles and programs about Scientology she was helping journalists put together with the use of the documents seized in the FBI raid. Some were harshly critical about the church, others less so. But Bast wanted to know about every story being prepared, and Paulette did her best to check on all of them.

There was an NBC *Prime Time* investigation of a Scientology school. A Boston NBC program that would feature her attorney, Mike Flynn. A *TIME* magazine story that had been put on hold. A PBS documentary that would be sympathetic to Scientology's claims that it was being harassed by the FBI and the Justice Department. There were also articles in the works by *Christianity Today*, the Religious News Service, *American Lawyer*, the *Clearwater Sun*, Australian News Limited, the *Denver Post*, the *Las Vegas Review-Journal*, the *Boston Herald American*, the *Boston Globe*, the *Detroit Daily News*, and the BBC.

Paulette expressed frustration that the *New York Times* was dragging its feet about doing an article, but she was thinking of approaching *Mother Jones*, a publication that reached college kids targeted by Scientology.

But most of all, the thing that excited Paulette and convinced her that the popular tide was really turning against Scientology were two big projects in the works – both of them with key help from her.

An editor at *Reader's Digest*, Eugene Methvin, was preparing a lengthy and harshly critical piece about the church, and a producer at *60 Minutes*, Allan Maraynes, was working with Mike Wallace on a devastating piece about Scientology spying. Each of them were relying heavily on Paulette's participation, and each of them were bound to reach huge audiences – perhaps as big as any print and television news stories could possibly reach.

Bast insisted that Paulette audiotape all of her telephone calls with other journalists. She offered to paraphrase the conversations, but he said it wasn't the same. He wanted to hear directly what they were saying about the stories as they were developing. When she resisted his assignments, the former Marine barked orders at her, and she didn't want what was a dream job to end.

A researcher working for Methvin, Jane Smith, read an entire rough draft of the *Reader's Digest* story over the phone as Paulette secretly taped it. She played it back for Bast so he knew the entire contents of the story. She also pointed out how she'd saved *Reader's Digest* some serious headaches by catching numerous passages that were not only factually incorrect but potentially libelous. The magazine was fortunate to have Paulette helping out.

Paulette kept detailed notes of everything she was doing as she worked for Bast. On March 1, 1980, for example, her notes showed that she talked to a Boston cult deprogrammer about having dinner the next night. She picked up copies of news clips for another deprogrammer and Mayor Gabe Cazares of Clearwater. She spoke to a third deprogrammer and a man who had recently left Scientology. She photocopied a news article about Scientology's chief litigation attorney, Phillip Hirschkopf, so she could get the copies to Ray Banoun – the assistant US attorney who was prosecuting the Snow White case – as well as to Judge Charles Richey, and several journalists.

Her notes showed that she was actively encouraging reporters to write stories about Scientology, she was putting them together with law enforcement officials who could provide information, and was also trying to influence litigation against the church.

Bast seemed thrilled. But he wanted more than just reports about what other journalists were doing. He and Paulette spent hours talking about more direct action against Scientology. Some of it, though largely hypothetical, was risky and probably illegal. They talked about having a young man Bast had recruited, Dave Williams, infiltrate the DC church. Once he was in place, he would need to know what to do that would cause the most distress for Scientology.

Some of the plans were outlandish – they talked about planting drugs in the org so it would be found during a raid, for example – and there was crude talk, too. Bast swore constantly and used sexually suggestive language, and he encouraged Paulette to curse as well. Paulette mostly wanted to talk about the news stories she was helping to happen, but Bast seemed only partly interested in that; he kept coming back to ideas about sabotage, and even suggested that Paulette might sleep with people to get more information or place people in compromising situations.

Bast told Paulette that she would have to keep their working arrangement a secret, even when she was deposed in her lawsuits with the church. Paulette told him not to worry, she was good at forgetting things.

She had gotten used to hours and hours of questioning during depositions, and Scientology's lawyers spent much of the time digging for information about her friends and sources. She was a hub of information, and she knew that if she named people, they could be harassed and sued. She had gotten used to saying that she didn't remember things in order to protect other people.

Paulette introduced to Bast the idea of bringing in her friend, John Seffern, the attorney who had worked with the Greens and Robert Kaufman, and who had become a close friend to Paulette. Because of his work with the Greens, Seffern had been targeted by the Guardian's Office for harassment, and it managed to get him disbarred in 1976. Paulette told Bast that he could use some work, and Bast offered the attorney $150 a day. Seffern joined them for conversations at Bast's office, and the three of them talked about the operation's various schemes and subterfuges.

Increasingly, Paulette became concerned that Bast was squandering money that she wanted to go to fighting Scientology. He spent lavishly on their meals and hotel costs. She became concerned that the Swiss millionaire bankrolling the operation didn't realize that Bast was wasting money that could be better put to use.

Paulette took some of the money Bast paid her and flew to Switzerland to warn their benefactor. She knew the name of his attorney. So Paulette tracked him down. Like Bast himself, the attorney wouldn't tell her much about the man who was financing the operation, but he promised to get the man any message Paulette wished to give him. It seemed suspicious, but Paulette returned to the United States hoping that she'd done the right thing.

On June 1, 1980, *60 Minutes* aired its 17-minute story about Scientology taking over the town of Clearwater, focusing on the Florida town as an example of the subterfuge that had been discovered in the FBI documents.

Paulette was seen speaking at the Jack Russell Stadium rally the previous December. She then sat down with Mike Wallace, and succinctly described her situation after Scientology had faked the bomb threat letters.

"I was arrested. I was indicted on three counts. I faced up to 15 years in jail if I was convicted. The whole ordeal fighting these charges took eight months. It cost me $19,000 in legal fees. I went into such a depression, I couldn't eat, I couldn't sleep, I couldn't write. I went down to 83 pounds. Finally I took and passed a sodium pentothal, or truth serum, test and the government dropped the charges against me in 1975."

Wallace then showed some of the Operation Freakout documents on screen, and noted that one scheme against Paulette involved the use of graffiti.

"They put my name up on walls in New York City where I live, with my phone number, so people would call me. They put my name on pornographic mailing lists, so that I would get all kinds of disgusting mail. You see, for years I was saying that these types of things were going on and people thought 'Well, what is she talking about? This is a church.' And finally, after 11 years I see that everything I said was true and that Scientology turned out to be worse than anything I ever said or even imagined."

Wallace managed to convince two Scientology officials to sit down with him and answer questions about what was found in the FBI documents. One of them was David Gaiman, the church's top public relations man in England and a high-ranking member of the Guardian's Office.

When Wallace confronted Gaiman with the documents spelling out Scientology's smear attacks against Clearwater mayor Gabe Cazares and against Paulette, he looked disappointed and shocked. "Bizarre...I cannot defend the intention and the statements within this documentation," Gaiman said.

Wallace said Gaiman blamed the actions on "overzealous" members of the church. "Part of us, part of we the Guardian's Office, fell into the arrogance of the ends-justify-the-means, which is wrong and alien to Scientology," Gaiman said.

Gaiman insisted that L. Ron Hubbard had nothing to do with the actions of the wrongdoers. But Wallace then confronted him with Hubbard policy letters which encouraged exactly the kind of behavior the church was accused of. "Gaiman still insisted we were taking Ron Hubbard's words out of context," Wallace said.

What Wallace didn't say, and perhaps didn't know, was that Gaiman himself had authored detailed instructions for how public relations officers in the church should attack journalists. Wallace also didn't point out that Gaiman himself was named by the Justice Department as an unindicted co-conspirator in the Snow White Program investigation. And it also never came up that it was Gaiman who met Paulette Cooper at the Edinburgh airport ten years earlier with what amounted to an intimidation attempt. Even so, the *60 Minutes* segment was a powerful indictment of Scientology on the most-watched news program in the country, and Paulette was prominently featured.

She could not have been vindicated any more thoroughly.

But any euphoria she felt rapidly dissipated. What might have been her most satisfying moment was quickly turning into another nightmare.

16

The tapes

A few days after the *60 Minutes* broadcast, John Seffern called and asked Paulette to meet him at the Front Porch restaurant on 82nd Street and Broadway. He had something important to tell her. He and Paulette had both worked for Dick Bast. She had recommended John, knowing that he was desperate for cash after being disbarred. They had both been to Bast's house, and had discussed the operations that Bast wanted to run against Scientology.

"Sit down," he told her when she arrived.

He began telling her that he had concerns about Bast. She felt the blood draining from her face. What did he mean, he had concerns?

"There is no client," he said.

Paulette didn't understand. Was he saying that Bast himself was financing the fight against Scientology?

"Well, there *is* a client, but it's not who we thought it was," he continued. "It's Scientology."

Paulette thought she was going to pass out.

"He's working for them," Seffern continued. "There's no father wanting to avenge his daughter. No rich benefactor in Switzerland. It's all been Scientology."

John said he'd discovered the truth when Bast asked him to tape his conversations with Paulette and admitted what was really going on. Paulette could hardly process what he was saying. It was the biggest and worst shock she'd received since that day in the New York grand jury chambers when she was told her fingerprint was on one of the bomb threat letters.

Seffern tried to put a positive spin on it. This is great, he said. Now we'll get them. I'll make believe I'm going along with it and feed them disinformation.

But Paulette wasn't listening. She was still in shock. And she knew it was over. The grand jury looking into her harassment. Her lawsuits and all the time and money she'd spent on them. Her credibility in her fight against Scientology. Everything that she'd been working for.

Seffern said that Bast had admitted he was really working for Benjamin Brown, an attorney for the Washington D.C. Church of Scientology. Seffern said Bast had offered him $10,000 to tape his conversations with her. Bast knew that Seffern was hard up for cash, and figured he'd do anything or that amount of money, including betray Paulette. But he'd miscalculated on that score.

Paulette knew immediately that what Seffern was telling her made sense. Bast had insisted that everything be taped. Her phone calls. Her meetings. Even her talks with Bast in his office. She suddenly remembered seeing a red light on his VCR, and when she asked him about it, Bast said he was taping a television show.

The attorney in Switzerland Paulette had tracked down, who was supposedly working for the shadowy millionaire that she now realized didn't exist at all? That attorney worked for Bast, not the other way around.

Her mind raced, thinking about what she'd been taped saying over the last few months. The conversations. The reports. The telephone calls.

She'd walked right into another Scientology trap.

At the same time that Richard Bast had been working Paulette Cooper, he was also looking into Judge Charles Richey. In fact, that may have been why Bast cultivated Paulette the way he did. Not so much for what Paulette knew, but for *whom* she knew. For years, Paulette had developed sources at newspapers, law enforcement agencies, and the FBI in particular. And Bast was looking for any way into the world of Judge Richey.

He nosed around until he made contact with a federal marshal named Jim Perry who had been one of Richey's bodyguards during the Los Angeles trial in the summer of 1979. Bast discovered that he had a mutual friend with Perry, who told Bast that Perry had been grousing about missing out on some disability pay. Bast engineered a meeting with the unhappy marshal, and used his inside information to get the man talking. Eventually, after he'd loosened up, Perry said that he'd seen quite a lot of things in his nine years as a marshal, enough to make a good book. Bast encouraged him, and said he'd pay Perry an advance of $2,000 to produce a manuscript.

Perry got to work, not realizing that he was actually writing notes for a Scientology operation. And his notes included the allegation that during the summer trial, when Richey was with Perry and another marshal staying at the Brentwood Holiday Inn, the judge had paid for prostitutes.

Bast told Perry that his book needed confirmation before they could print such an allegation, and that's the excuse he used for flying Perry out to Los Angeles to track down one of the women who had supposedly been paid by Richey. Bast then paid the woman $300 a day for her time as he interviewed her and had her sign a sworn statement that Richey had paid her for sex. In July 1980, Judge Richey formally pulled out of the trial against the two remaining Snow White defendants, citing health reasons.

For his work for the Church of Scientology, Bast was paid $321,000 plus $84,000 in expenses.

Paulette made a vodka and tonic to dull the pain as she sat down to listen to hours of tapes that Bast had made of her once copies of them were turned over in litigation. She needed to listen to them and take notes, her attorneys said, and it was a chore she wasn't looking forward to. They needed to know the worst.

On tape after tape, Paulette was heard plotting against Scientology. She thought she had the backing of a wealthy, unnamed

European millionaire. She was ready to do to the church what it had been doing to her for years.

In one scheme, she and Bast talked about sending a friend inside the Washington DC church, and once he had infiltrated it, he could plant drugs for a raid that Paulette would then call down with her contacts in law enforcement.

Paulette: *The point I want to make is if we have any kind of police raid this gay friend of mine…. probably get us some, a couple of things you might want to consider leaving them there that might make much bigger headlines. Like cocaine.*

Bast: *Ho, ho, beautiful.*

Paulette: *Because he snorts with his friends.*

Bast: *Ho, ho. We could set them up there. A drug bust would be a much bigger thing. We get the DEA in there, we have friends in the DEA. So why don't you get some … and knock out a little plan for that. I mean if we're gonna do it, we, who knows, maybe the material that Dave got will check out.*

Paulette: *Well, that's what I'm saying, it's gonna be right in that area. Dave's gotta watch his fingerprints on the thing—everything else. I'm saying that in any depositing of any glassine envelope has to be sure there's no prints on it. But I think that can be arranged.*

Bast: *OK, beautiful. In other words your friend can get glassine envelopes and we can just….*

Paulette: *I know this guy has snorted coke with his friends, OK?*

Bast: *How tight are you with him?*

Paulette: *Very.*

Nothing was ever done to plant her friend or the drugs, but simply hearing herself discuss it was painful. She also trashed Nan McLean, her old friend, for Nan's "stupid honesty." When the two of them had copied thousands of pages of Snow White documents, Paulette had fibbed about the amount she'd copied in order to pay less, but Nan refused to cheat. Now, Paulette made fun of her to Bast.

Paulette: *You know, getting back to Nan and her stupid honesty. Do you know what I managed to cheat down my photocopy bill down to? Get this . . .*
Bast: *What's that?*
Paulette: *$89.50.*
Bast: *Really?*
Paulette: *Now, Nan and I photocopied, I did three-quarters of what she did, OK? That's the way it generally went. . .*
Bast: *Yeah.*
Paulette: *She's paying an $800 bill.*

On a tape made February 20, 1980, Paulette could be heard criticizing Nan for the way she couldn't shade the truth during depositions. From her disbarred friend Seffern, she said, Paulette had learned some tricks about how to be less than truthful under oath.

Paulette: *Yeah, this is where Nan and I fight so badly. She refuses to have lapses of memory. The one thing we have compromised on is* *that on some things, during depositions, she says "I don't know. You'll have to ask Paulette. That's all Paulette told me."*

Bast: *Who says that? Nan does?*

Paulette: *Right. We've agreed to a semi-lie. If she won't totally lie then she's to say . . .*

Bast: *Then at least lie halfway.*

Paulette: *. . . then she is to say . . . for example, "Am I in touch with Mike Meisner?"*

Bast: *Yeah.*

Paulette: *"mmm, mmm . . . . No, but Paulette is."*

Bast: *Yeah.*

Paulette: *In other words, so that she can then pass the buck, and then I say "I'm not in touch with him," because as far as I'm concerned . . . I have a very . . . I have a lawyer friend who's extremely dishonest, and he, on the side, has trained me that when you are in touch with someone, put up your finger, then we are in touch. If we write letters, we're not in touch. I mean, in other words, he says you can take every single thing and comfortably lie about it.*

Bast: *Yeah.*

Besides the cute trick about being "in touch," Paulette implied that she was talking to Michael Meisner, the key witness against Scientology in the Snow White prosecutions. It was another surprising claim, since Meisner had gone into a witness protection program, and had vanished. (Paulette later insisted she never communicated with Meisner, and was just trying to impress Bast that she had important connections.)

The material on the tapes seemed devastating. Paulette knew that if she ever tried to testify in court again, the things she'd said to Bast would be brought out to impeach her. Her credibility as a witness was shot.

But the federal grand jury looking into her frame-up was having other troubles. Scientologists who had taken part in the scheme against her and who were brought in to testify simply refused to speak. James Meisler, the public relations man at the New York church, said he wasn't going to talk, not because he was taking the Fifth Amendment protection against self-incrimination, but because he claimed the First Amendment protected what he'd done in the name of his religion.

One Guardian's Office operative, Charles Batdorf – who had been listed as "Max" in the Operation Freakout documents and whose job it was to type up a bizarre letter to be sent to Henry Kissinger in the scheme – went to jail for eight months rather than testify to the grand jury.

FBI agents told Paulette that the documents seized in the 1977 raid spelled out clearly that she'd been targeted, but in order to get indictments and then convictions, they needed more specific details about what the church operatives had actually done.

As it became clear that eleven of the church's top officials were going to prison for what they had done in Snow White, Paulette was told by her FBI sources that she should take some solace in that, since some of the same people were involved in both operations.

The grand jury looking into her harassment, however, returned no indictments after her comments about her memory ruined her credibility, and her own discussions of dirty tricks against Scientology became known.

Meanwhile, Scientology wasted no time using the Bast tapes to its advantage in its litigation with Paulette. Merrell Vannier, the GO volunteer who had helped Don Alverzo break into the offices of attorneys representing the *St. Louis Post-Dispatch* in 1974, had joined the Guardian's Office itself in 1980, and was put to work transcribing the tapes from the Richard Bast operation. He then used what he found in them to trip up Paulette in her lawsuits with the church.

Vannier zeroed in on the tape Paulette had made of herself with *Reader's Digest* researcher Jane Smith. Paulette had also talked with Eugene Methvin, the editor whose byline would appear on the May story, "Scientology: Anatomy of a Frightening Cult."

Paulette had told Bast that she was reluctant to discuss her connections to other journalists when she was being deposed – she knew the church would only harass or sue people who dared to work with her. Knowing that she would minimize her role in the *Reader's Digest* story, Vannier submitted questions about it for Scientology attorney Jonathan Lubell to ask during a deposition, asking Lubell to drop the questions in intermittently so Paulette wouldn't catch on that the church already knew the answers from hearing the Bast tapes. In other words, it was another setup, and only further eroded her credibility as a court witness.

And then, after the set-ups and schemes to destroy her, Scientology reached out to Paulette Cooper in the strangest way possible.

Tony Ortega

A few months after the Bast operation ended, Paulette received a phone call from one of Scientology's legal affairs officers, a man she had gotten to know slightly during numerous days of depositions. She was surprised to hear from him, especially after what the church had just done to her. But she heard him out.

He told her that Scientology planned to sue *60 Minutes* over its June 1 segment. Naturally, she knew what was coming – she was going to be sued as well. Many of her lawsuits were the same. She was pulled in as a defendant based on another person's book or article or radio program. And now, she'd find herself dragged into a suit with CBS.

But she was told there was an alternative. It was clear to Scientology that she had been instrumental to the segment, and had worked closely with its producer, Allan Maraynes. Maraynes was more important to them than she was. Would she be willing to help gather information about the producer in return for being left out of the lawsuit?

Paulette could hardly believe what she was hearing. She was told that someone from Scientology could come over to her apartment to "set up some things" – presumably imaging equipment – and then Paulette should invite Maraynes over and get him talking.

She could tell, from the way it was pitched to her, that the idea was for her to seduce Maraynes, sleep with him, and get him to say things about how *60 Minutes* had intended to make Scientology look bad. If she did that, she wouldn't find herself defend-

306

ing yet another lawsuit.

Not interested, she said, and hung up. Later, she told Maraynes about it and they laughed. She had gotten to know him during the filming of the segment, but he was recently married and had never expressed an interest in Paulette. She assumed Scientology had listened to the Bast tapes and heard the way Bast salaciously suggest that she sleep with people to get information and had gotten some ideas.

It was just the way Scientology operated, she knew.

The Bast operation only made Mike Flynn angrier. He told Paulette that the Bast tapes would only end up helping her in court, not the opposite. "Whatever is on them, the fact that they hired someone to befriend you, given your vulnerabilities, will only backfire on them. Whatever you said would pale in comparison to what they put you through," he told her.

Looking over the things Paulette had said to Bast, Flynn told her that they only showed how damaged she had become after years of harassment. If anything, they would only make a jury *more* sympathetic.

"If a jury heard the whole thing? In fact, *we* may even introduce the tapes as evidence," he told her.

On March 9, 1981, Flynn filed his first lawsuit on Paulette's behalf, against the Boston church, L. Ron Hubbard, and Mary Sue Hubbard, asking for $25 million.

The suit named specific grievances related to the Boston organization—the burglarizing of Paulette's medical records from Dr. Cath's office, for example. But it also referred to her entire history of harassment, as well as schemes carried out by the Boston church that had little or nothing to do with Paulette. (The infiltration of the *Boston Globe*, for example.)

Flynn wrote the complaint to encompass the entire Scientology conspiracy as described in the FBI documents, and focused it on Hubbard and his wife. "L. Ron Hubbard and Mary Sue Hubbard throughout the period set forth in this complaint have been engaged in illegal and criminal activities designed to perpetrate a nationwide scheme of fraud and infliction of personal injury. As a result, they have established a nomadic life-style for the specific purpose of avoiding legal process."

Mary Sue Hubbard was actually appealing her Snow White conviction and was not in hiding. It was her husband who had gone into seclusion the year before. But clearly, the language in the lawsuit made it obvious that Flynn was aiming high. This wasn't just a lawsuit about the Boston church and its involvement in breaking into Cath's office for Paulette's records. It was the first salvo from Flynn and Paulette in a larger battle.

He was still talking about a massive class-action lawsuit, and he knew Paulette would help him attract more clients ready to take on the church. If the government had let her down with its grand jury, Paulette still believed that with Flynn, the tide was turning against Scientology.

But her life wasn't only about fighting the Hubbards. After her disastrous months working with Bast, Paulette returned to her work for the *National Enquirer*. She enjoyed working with the editors of the paper, and she liked the pace: she often had a dozen or more stories working at any one time, which helped feed her need for constant intellectual stimulation.

But there was a side to working for the *Enquirer* that bothered Paulette. The focus on celebrities and inside information about them had her editors asking her to do things that made her uncomfortable.

When Orson Welles fell ill and was hospitalized for a while, Paulette's editor wanted her to sneak into the facility and interview him. When she said she didn't want to bother the man, her editor tried to talk her into it by explaining that people recuperating in hospitals are usually lonely and are happy to be interviewed. She refused.

She also balked when she was asked to visit the Pennsylvania family of Mary Jo Kopechne, who had died in 1969 when the car she was in was driven into a pond by Ted Kennedy. The family later talked to another reporter, but Paulette didn't mind losing the story to another writer.

Not that she didn't hate missing a scoop. At one point, she tried to get John G. Husted Jr. to tell his story. He was relatively unknown at the time, but through her research Paulette had learned that he had been engaged to Jacqueline Bouvier before she broke off the engagement and married John F. Kennedy. In a letter, Husted told Paulette he wasn't interested. Years later, when he did give an interview about Jackie, Paulette was irate.

Another time a big story eluded her, Paulette had asked an old friend for an interview with Betty Ford. The friend was a former classmate from Brandeis who had become the First Lady's press secretary. With that advantage, Paulette was hoping she could get the first story about Betty's battle with breast cancer—but her friend blanched, and called it a "disgusting" subject. Sure enough, Betty later gave an interview about it to someone else.

When Yul Brynner fell ill and was hospitalized, the *Enquirer* wanted Paulette to interview him. They told her to find out which Manhattan hospital the actor was in. She went into the coffee shop of a major hospital, waited until there were no other customers, and then, on a whim, she told the woman behind the counter that Brynner was there. Yes, the woman replied, and told Paulette that he was on the 14th floor and had checked in under the name "Robbie Lee." Paulette went to the 14th floor, but then suffered a pang of conscience. The first show her parents had ever taken her to after her adoption was a production of *The King and I*. So rather than bother Brynner, she called in the tip to the newspaper. The *Enquirer* flew someone else from Florida who bribed nurses for information. (Paulette still got paid because she'd located Brynner.)

In general, celebrity interviews made Paulette squirm. Dick Clark was condescending. Marlon Brando mumbled. Throughout his interview, he stood sideways to her and never met her gaze.

After Paulette introduced herself by phone to Paulette Goddard, the actress thought she was being mocked and refused to believe that Paulette's name was the same as her own as she slammed down the receiver. June Havoc believed in ghosts. Vicki Carr's family had risen up from ditch diggers (that interview Paulette enjoyed greatly). Lillian Carter, Jimmy's mother, was a pain in the ass and gave her 10 minutes after Paulette's long trip to Plains, Georgia. But then, struggling to find something to talk about, she discovered that Lillian loved professional wrestling – the bloodier, the better. It made for a great story.

Al Hodge had been "Captain Video" in the early 1950s in television's infancy, but by the 1970s he was broke and in poor health. Paulette found him working as a security guard at Cartier. None of his old shows were still in existence (recordings of them had been sold for scrap), so he couldn't cash in on the 1950s nostalgia craze starting to take hold. Paulette loaned him money after writing about him, even though she knew he'd probably drink it up. She even brought him around to parties, and she treasured an engraved ashtray that he gave her as a gift—until someone broke it. Hodge died in 1979 at only 66.

When Pat Boone talked about finding God, he would go into a strange trance-like state. After Paulette's story about him ran, she came up with an idea for a book. At the time, the early 1980s, celebrities finding God was a hot topic, and she proposed a book that she and Boone could do together. She wanted to call it "Jesus Christ's Superstars," but he liked "Hotline to Heaven." They disagreed on terms, and the project never got off the ground.

Another born-again celebrity she profiled was Graham Kerr, the "Galloping Gourmet." Her *Enquirer* story was titled "*I GAVE AWAY MY 3 MILLION FORTUNE FOR CHRIST.*" Kerr was one of the few people she interviewed whom she told about her struggles with Scientology. He was sympathetic, and he and his wife Trena clasped her hands and held a prayer circle.

The celebrity Paulette ended up chasing the longest was Jackie Onassis. When Jackie's husband, the Greek shipping tycoon Aristotle Onassis, died in 1975, the *Enquirer* became obsessed with her, vowing to write something about her in every issue. Paulette was sent to interview her butcher (Lobel's), her hairdresser (Mr. Kenneth), the store where her secretary consigned Jackie's clothes (Encore), and Paulette was asked to get information about Jackie from her psychiatrist, Dr. Marianne Kris.

Kris had also treated Marilyn Monroe. Paulette took the assignment, but rather than ask Kris about Jackie, which she knew would be futile, she instead discussed her own life so she could write a story about what it was like to get therapy from such a famous figure.

For years, Paulette tried to get close to Onassis for the *Enquirer*, and followed her to a formal event at the Hotel Pierre. The *Enquirer* paid the astounding amount of $450 for Paulette's ticket. For that kind of money, Paulette knew she had to take her best shot at getting Jackie alone for a talk. When she saw the former First Lady head for the restroom, Paulette followed her in.

She knew it might be her best chance to actually talk. So, there in the woman's room, she made her play, asking if she could interview her. "No, thank you," Jackie said sweetly in her breathy way, and walked out of the room.

It was the closest she came to an actual conversation. So Paulette then just had a good time at the gala, and ended up dancing with Sargent Shriver, who called her "a cute little monkey." Paulette still ended up with a big story when she noticed that Jackie's supposed friendly relationship with the Kennedys was just a put-on. The *Enquirer*'s headline for her piece was, "*JACKIE SNUBS THE KENNEDYS AT A SOCIETY PARTY AND THEY SNUB HER BACK*." And the evening was also memorialized for her in another way: A photo of Jackie, with a dressed-up Paulette in the frame, ended up on the cover of the June 8, 1976 issue of the *New York Post*.

Paulette had better luck getting close to a celebrity when she decided to pull a hoax on the great hoaxer himself, Allen Funt. At the time, Paulette had been doing some articles with Alan Abel, a professional prankster, and they thought it might be fun to trip up Funt. So they presented him with a birthday cake and wouldn't leave even though it wasn't actually his birthday. It wasn't a brilliant gag, but Funt took it good-naturedly.

And then, to Paulette's surprise, he asked her out. He was nearly 30 years her senior, but she thought, initially, that he was fun to be around. But as she and Funt dated, wherever they went, people would find a way to come up to him and say, "Smile, you're on Candid Camera." When they would go to a restaurant, the waiter would bring over a note from another table: "Smile, you're on Candid Camera." Before long, it drove Paulette nuts. But Funt took it with a smile—whoever sent the note always thought it was the most clever thing in the world. Funt knew he couldn't escape it, and never would.

He also couldn't escape Paulette's constant talk about Scientology and became appalled by what he heard. Funt wrote a check for $10,000 to one of Paulette's attorneys to help him fight Scientology – and Paulette worked hard to keep Funt's name out of her depositions for fear that he would be subpoenaed and harassed.

She and Funt dated occasionally for about six months. Her fling with writer Jerzy Kosinski was even more short-lived. She had sent him a copy of her *Medical Detectives* book, and the Polish novelist suggested they get together at a Sixth Avenue French restaurant where he was a regular. They dated a few times, but it soon ended. She went out occasionally with Ira Levin, author of *Rosemary's Baby*, *The Stepford Wives*, and *The Boys from Brazil*. She also dated some of the men she met in law enforcement.

In 1979, Paulette had purchased a new bed, only to learn that Scientologists ran the store that sold it to her. Taking no chances, she called people she knew at the FBI, and an agent came over to sweep the mattress for listening devices. After a few dates he ended up sleeping with her on it. Later, when his indiscretion was discovered, he was fired.

He wasn't the only man who lost his head around Paulette. She repeatedly found herself considering opportunities of the most unusual sort. Perhaps none stranger than a man who, a few years before the mattress incident, had formed an attachment for her because she had saved his son from Scientology.

After the publication of *The Scandal of Scientology*, for years

Paulette was sought out by parents who were panicked because their children had joined Scientology or were considering it. In some cases, Paulette would get personally involved, and this time, she had talked a young man out of joining without much trouble. He was only in the very first stages of fascination for L. Ron Hubbard's ideas, so Paulette was able to turn him away from it with only about an hour of conversation.

The young man's father was grateful. And rich. His name was Mitch and after Paulette helped him out with his son, they became occasional tennis partners at the Grand Central Station courts, and he would take her to lunch at the Metropolitan Club, where he was a member. He enjoyed hearing her stories not only about fighting Scientology, but also about her childhood and how she got to America.

Another time, he took her to an expensive lunch spot and they were seated at a cramped table near the kitchen. And there, with other diners so close they couldn't help but overhear, Mitch asked her to have his child. He would spend at least a million dollars supporting her and the baby over the years if she agreed.

She didn't know what to say before she managed to get out "That's interesting."

"I'll say that's interesting," said one of the men seated nearby in the cramped dining room.

"I was talking about the sauce and not the conversation," she said, and they all laughed.

But Mitch wasn't kidding. His own wife was past childbearing years, he explained, and his grown son – the one Paulette had talked out of joining Scientology – was a disappointment to him. He wanted another child and would support Paulette if she would agree to it.

She turned him down. She found out later from his son that Mitch had changed his last name to hide the fact that he was actually Jewish. Paulette suspected he had chosen her because of her childhood stories and to assuage his guilt over changing his name. But Paulette wanted to be a writer, not a mother. And she wanted to make her own money, not get it from a man.

17

'You must be one hell of a woman'

In August 1981, Paulette Cooper picked up her 18th lawsuit from Scientology. She was in Los Angeles on assignment for the *Enquirer*, and planned to visit the American Psychiatric Association convention at the Bonaventure Hotel to look for stories. While she was in town, she heard from some of her sources – a Redondo Beach couple named Curt and Henrietta Crampton, who had lost their daughter to Scientology.

The Cramptons told Paulette that Scientology was planning a celebrity auction at the Hollywood Palladium. It alarmed them that Scientology had advertised the auction without a reference to the church. Several Hollywood actors, including Carol Burnett, had agreed to donate items.

The proceeds of the auction would benefit the Fifield Manor, the French chateau on Franklin Avenue that had been one of the locations raided by the FBI four years before – by now it had been renamed after becoming the newest location of Scientology's "Hollywood Celebrity Centre."

The Cramptons and Paulette were certain that Burnett and the other celebrities had no idea they were supporting the Church of Scientology. Paulette began making phone calls to the actors and their agents, informing them who was really behind the event.

The Cramptons told Paulette they were going to stand outside the event at the Palladium and hand out literature, and they asked her for a recommendation of what to distribute. She told them about Eugene Methvin's 1980 article in *Reader's Digest* that she'd been interviewed for. They made copies, and the day of the auction the Cramptons stood outside the venue and handed them out.

Paulette didn't attend the event at all. But the church moved fast, slapping a lawsuit on the Cramptons at the Palladium, and served papers on Paulette at the APA convention, finding her between talks that she was attending. Scientology claimed that the trio's sabotaging attempts had ruined the auction. Several celebrities had backed out after phone calls from the Cramptons. And after spending $40,000 to put it on, Scientology had only taken in $13,000 in donations.

The lawsuit would generate days more of depositions for Paulette, who had already been through weeks of questioning over the life of all of her lawsuits.

While Paulette's legal cases grinded on, Mary Sue Hubbard lost her appeal that year. In a footnote to the written decision that would send Mary Sue to prison, the panel of three judges acknowledged that all along, Scientology had complained that it was being put on trial because of its beliefs.

That simply wasn't true, the judges pointed out. "The crimes charged here are not 'ideological offenses.' Those who formulate conspiracies to obstruct justice, steal government property, burglarize, bug, harbor fugitives from justice, and commit and suborn perjury before the grand jury have no constitutional right under the first amendment to conceal the documentary evidence thereof...freedom of religion is not endangered but encouraged when criminal conspiracies are suppressed that attempt to hide behind religion."

Calling itself a church (while telling its members that Scientology was an exact science of the mind, not a belief system) had been very effective against criticism. But now, gradually, word was getting out about Scientology's actual methods.

Paulette Cooper and Mike Flynn had met at a rally in Clearwater in 1979. Now, three years later, they returned to the town for a spectacle. In May 1982, the city of Clearwater held five days of hearings about Scientology and its takeover of the city's downtown. The hearings were televised locally and ran from May 5 to May 10. Flynn had been hired to represent the witnesses and put them on, one by one.

A former executive at the Flag Land Base testified that the complex brought in between $400,000 to $1 million each week from the Scientologists coming to take high-level courses.

Another former member testified that Scientology often made health claims that were bogus. Others talked about the incredibly long hours and low pay of church employees, and that secrets they gave up in interrogations were later used against them as blackmail. Children suffered some of the worst conditions of all, the commission was told.

On Saturday, May 8, Flynn brought in Paulette to testify.

"I don't know how you could survive what you have survived, and I think you must be one hell of a woman," Paulette was told by Charles LeCher, the city's mayor. "I don't know how you even—you can trust anybody anymore. A man that you might meet that he is one of them and trying to get you again."

LeCher was a city commissioner who had been selected to be mayor on April 12, 1978 when Gabe Cazares resigned. LeCher had been re-elected in 1981. He asked Paulette how she managed to support herself while she had been a defendant in so many different lawsuits.

"I work day and night to support the lawyers," she said a bit acidly. "I figured out just recently that it's cost over fifty thousand dollars for legal fees on the suits."

Paulette then began to tell her story. That she was a freelance magazine writer who had written hundreds of stories—only two of which were about Scientology. She said that the church was telling the people of Clearwater that it had turned over a new leaf and it was behaving better than it had when the FBI raided five years earlier. If Scientology had changed, Paulette noted, "I certainly haven't noticed it...The eighteenth lawsuit was just served on me last week." Like the others, it was more about causing a nuisance than anything else.

"I am being sued now repeatedly by individual Scientologists who, in some cases, I don't even know. Suits for supposedly distributing literature at functions I didn't even attend," she said.

Up to this point, she had spent nineteen days doing depositions for Scientology litigation, and had four more scheduled in just a couple of weeks. The harassment that had started in 1969 with the publication of her *Queen* magazine story was still ongoing. Even today, she was still getting harassing phone calls, and so were her parents.

In the past, one way the church tried to smear her was to exaggerate or mischaracterize her legal situation. Letters about her being the subject of investigations by the district attorney or the state attorney general would get sent to the Justice Department or the IRS.

Her mother was still getting visits by operatives. Just a few months earlier, Stella Cooper had been approached by a woman in a beauty parlor as Stella was getting her hair done. The woman said she had a son, and she was curious about Stella's daughter, who sounded perfect for her son to ask out. Stella was shrewd enough to know that the woman was trying to set Paulette up with a Scientologist, and she left the salon. Shaken, she called Paulette and told her about it. Paulette briefly referred to the incident as she continued to detail her harassment for the Clearwater commission.

Despite that incident, and some problems she'd had with

canceled flights in her travel writing career, 1982 was much better than previous years, she said. But she wanted the commission to know what it had been like to speak out about Scientology in the late 1960s and early 1970s, when very few people were doing so.

At one point, it seemed like the only three people who dared talk about Scientology in the press were Paulette, Nan McLean, and then-Clearwater mayor Gabe Cazares.

She then explained how she had gotten interested in Scientology, with a friend who had taken some Scientology courses and then got the idea that he was the reincarnated Jesus Christ. That led her to take a course as she began investigating Scientology and realized that it seemed to keep enemies lists on former members. And it struck her as odd that when she tried to track down an article about Scientology she found a reference for at the New York library's card catalog, the article would usually be missing, cut out neatly from its magazine or newspaper.

After her *Queen* magazine story came out, the death threats began. Over the next four years, she said, she was sued four times, "one of which was for somebody else's book," a reference to the libel suit against Robert Kaufman's book, *Inside Scientology*. (Paulette was sued for encouraging Kaufman to publish it.) But then Paulette had sued the church for harassment in 1972, "and this was actually shocking to them because Hubbard had written that....no one would ever sue Scientology, that they had too much to hide."

Later that year, the smear letters began appearing, five in total, that were sent to the residents in her apartment building, to her boyfriend, and one to her parents. One of them had called her a prostitute. "You can imagine how upsetting it is to open up something like that and read it," she said.

The smear letters were part of the reason she had moved into the Churchill in December 1972, hoping for better security. She explained that her cousin Joy had taken over her old apartment, and then had been attacked by a man with a gun.

Paulette described that the FBI let her know they were investigating a couple of bomb threats at the New York church, and asked to fingerprint her. Then she learned she was the target of the investigation and was indicted.

"The next eight months were a terrible, terrible nightmare in my life that I still feel sometimes that I suffer from to this day."

She explained that her biggest fear was the indictment becoming public and hitting the press. She knew that the public wouldn't understand the difference between an indictment and a conviction.

"I was most concerned about my parents, who had adopted me when I was six years old, and how humiliating it would be for them and their friends to have to explain to go through a trial like this."

She said that her attorneys only made things worse by telling her that they would need her parents to sit in the front row and make a good show for her. But such a thing would kill them, she tried to explain. And then there was Jerry Levin, who moved in with her and seemed like such a friend. At one point, she was even considering using him as a character witness in the trial.

She then explained that months of not eating from the stress and nausea of what she was going through had left her so underweight, they had a hard time finding a doctor to perform a truth serum test on her. But after they did, and she passed it, the U.S. attorney's office had "saved face" by postponing the trial and asking that she be ordered to get psychiatric help.

(She didn't mention that Jay Zelermyer had talked Bob Morvillo out of prosecuting the case. After the trial was postponed, she got into a dispute with Zelermyer and Charles Stillman when they wanted another $5,000 for getting her out of a trial after she and her father had already paid them $19,000, and she felt they had made mistakes that complicated, not helped, her legal situation.)

She said that after threat of a trial disappeared, she tried to get back together with Bob Straus by inviting him to a party. But only then did she learn that a smear letter about her had been sent to his bosses, and he'd decided to cut off all ties with her.

After the charges against her were formally dropped in late 1975, a new form of harassment had started, she said, with people imitating her over the phone to her friends. And then someone had tried once again to obtain her fingerprint, using a written joke in a bar. Now, she realized these were probably early steps in Operation Freakout.

She talked about settling her lawsuits at the end of 1976, and then working with the FBI after it raided Scientology in 1977. She finally got to see the documents seized in the raid at the beginning of 1980, some of which proved that she'd been framed with the bomb threat letters. The documents also proved that she'd been sued for telling the truth, that her father had been targeted for harassment, and that Paulette had been under close surveillance for years.

"It was incredible vindication to look at these documents and see that everything I had said about Scientology since 1968 was true, and that they had turned out to be worse than anything I had said or even imagined."

And that was why it was hard to believe that Scientology was really turning over a new leaf, which is what it had told the city of Clearwater.

"I've only briefly told you some of the things that they've done to me, so that you're not deceived by their true nature," she said. "I believe that Scientology has never changed, will never change, and will keep issuing statements to people saying that they've changed."

Paulette's testimony was a highlight of the hearings. But there were other notables in town who were taking part. Nibs, for example. He had switched sides once again, and was now wearing a new name, Ron DeWolf. But Paulette still suspected that he had taken part in her frame-up a decade earlier.

"Cooper has questioned DeWolf's credibility, suggesting that he is really in Clearwater to make a fast buck. And DeWolf has returned barb for barb," said the *Clearwater Times*.

On June 14, a few weeks after the hearings and while Michael Flynn was still in Clearwater staying at the Holiday Inn Surfside, he got a call from Boston. The man on the phone, Joseph Snyder, reminded Flynn that they had met several months earlier when Flynn gave a talk about Scientology's history of spying to the American Society for Industrial Security.

Snyder, like the other people who heard Flynn's speech, protected companies from corporate espionage, and was interested to hear about Scientology's long record of snooping and burglary. Snyder asked if they could get together when Flynn returned to Boston. Snyder didn't want to say much over the phone, but he indicated that a client had hired him to find L. Ron Hubbard.

When Flynn flew back to Boston, Snyder picked him up at Logan Airport and explained that he was working a strange case for his client, the Bank of New England. About a week earlier, two men had come into a branch of the Middle East Bank in New York City, and had tried to cash a check for $2 million. The check, made out to "Aquil Abdulamiar," was signed by L. Ron Hubbard and was drawn on his account at the Bank of New England. After the two men failed to turn over any identification proving one of them was Abdulamiar, they departed, leaving the check behind. It turned out to be a forgery.

The bogus check was a clever copy of a real check for more than a million dollars that Hubbard had written earlier in the year from his Bank of New England account to a tax shelter in California. Someone had apparently obtained that cancelled check and used it to create the fake one. But who? And what did Hubbard know? Hubbard's bank wanted to find him to ask him about it, but Snyder didn't know where to look.

Flynn didn't know what the check scheme was about, but he did help Snyder with what he knew about Hubbard—that no one seemed to have seen him since early 1980, and that Hubbard's own wife, Mary Sue, hadn't seen him since late 1979.

After talking to Snyder, Flynn wondered, was the bogus check a sign that Hubbard had died, and that someone in Scientology was trying to cash in on his identity before news of his death got to the outside world?

Hubbard's son, Ron DeWolf, agreed with Flynn that there were other strong signs that his father had died. Inspired in part by the check-kiting caper, in November, with Flynn's help, DeWolf filed a petition to the Riverside County Probate Court, asking it to determine if Hubbard was alive and to rule on the status of his estate.

It was the most serious, direct attack by Flynn on Scientology yet. DeWolf told reporters that if his father were alive, he would have to show up in court to prove it. Instead, Hubbard sent the judge in the case a handwritten letter assuring the court that he was still alive and in possession of his faculties. Affidavits and a fingerprint were also submitted, though Hubbard still concealed his actual location. The court was satisfied that he still lived.

DeWolf's legal assault was a failure, but for about a year it generated some of the worst publicity in the church's history. Flynn was becoming the most dangerous enemy Scientology had ever faced. And it was time to do something about him.

The same year as the Clearwater Hearings, Paulette learned that

Barbara Lewis had fallen seriously ill. They hadn't talked much since the end of 1975, when Paulette had angrily cut off ties with Barbara because she'd told Roland about her trip to London to see a man who wanted to marry her. But Paulette still harbored strong feelings for Barbara; they had been best friends during the worst of her days under indictment.

That summer, in 1973, Jerry Levin was spending a lot of time with the both of them, and he would also go alone to Barbara's apartment to complain about the way the Scientologists were treating Paulette. Now they understood that Jerry was just trying to get Barbara talking about Paulette to pump her for even more information. At the time, it seemed like Jerry was being a good friend.

Barbara went through a lot of guilt during those days. She admitted to Paulette that it still bothered her the way the man who had attacked her so brutally years before had been prosecuted and sent to prison. She had been under a lot of pressure to choose his mug shot out of a photo-lineup. The police were certain that the young Puerto Rican janitor had committed the crime – he had run to Puerto Rico, just as a guilty person would. But Barbara had never really gotten a good look at the man who had tied her up and raped her so brutally over several hours. She would never forget the sound of his voice though, and she found herself wishing that she could have heard the young man speak before police took him into custody.

And then, watching Paulette suffer for something she didn't do made Barbara feel even worse. She couldn't help thinking that the young man she'd sent to prison might be going through the same thing. The young man's friends would sometimes call and tell Barbara that she had put away an innocent man. She told Paulette she found herself wishing the man himself would call her, so she could hear his voice.

But then, Paulette and Barbara had stopped talking to each other, and over the years they only gradually became friends again.

In July 1982, Barbara began bleeding. She was barely able to pay her rent, and had no money to see a doctor, so she didn't have it looked at until September. At that point, she was diagnosed with terminal ovarian cancer.

She lived two more years, receiving help from a couple of boyfriends, one of whom was a medical reporter for NBC and used his connections to get her a large room at NYU's hospital with a view of the Hudson River. And that's where Paulette often went to visit her as her health declined.

On Paulette's final visit, Barbara was barely conscious. She had sunk down on her bed, and was unable to see the lovely view of the river from her large wraparound room, the kind usually reserved for celebrities or the very rich. Her thin frame, down to only around 70 pounds, was lost in the bed sheets and blankets. Paulette held Barbara's emaciated hand while she slept.

Barbara died on July 10, 1984. When her obituary appeared, Paulette and Barbara's other friends were in for a slight shock. They had assumed (and Barbara let them think) that Barbara was in her mid-40s. In fact, she had died on her 56th birthday.

Paulette was thankful that she had known Barbara, especially during her lowest point when she was thinking of killing herself. Paulette was a wreck in the summer of 1973, and Barbara was one of the few people who helped get her through it.

Once in a while, Barbara would tell her that when the mess with the church was over, the Scientologists responsible for the spying and harassment would be caught, and Paulette would win a million dollars from them in court. Paulette always answered that even one day of what she was going through wasn't worth a million dollars.

Two weeks after Barbara's death, on July 24, 1984, a press conference in Los Angeles was held by the Church of Scientology in order to make a rather astounding claim. In charge of the conference were the president of the church—a man named Heber Jentzsch—a church attorney named John Peterson, the church's spokesman, Robert Vaughn Young, and a private investigator named Eugene Ingram.

Ingram had been hired the year before to gather evidence about the forged L. Ron Hubbard $2 million check made out to "Aquil Abdulamiar" that two men had tried to cash at a bank in New York in 1982.

In January, Ingram had taken out ads in the *New York Times*, *Washington Post*, and the *Boston Globe* offering a reward of $100,000 for information that would lead to the conviction of the people who had tried to pass the bogus check. And now, the church was ready to reveal the results of its investigation. The culprit, they announced, was Paulette Cooper's attorney, Mike Flynn.

Their evidence for this was a legal declaration signed by a forger serving time in a prison in Naples, Italy. Ingram, the church's private eye, had gone to Naples to get the declaration from the man, Ala Fadili Al Tamimi, who claimed he had created the bogus check and had gone to the bank with his brother, pretending to be Aquil Abdulamiar.

But the scheme, he claimed, had been masterminded by Flynn. Al Tamimi said that Flynn used connections he had at the Bank of New England to get a legitimate check out of the bank for Al Tamimi to create a counterfeit version of it. And now, the church had the lawyer dead to rights. It called for the arrest and conviction of Flynn.

But that didn't happen.

Eventually, Al Tamimi would recant his story. Ingram, meanwhile, turned out to be a disgraced Los Angeles cop who had been fired for, among other things, being accused of running a prostitution ring on the side.

A few days after the press conference, a judge in Los Angeles, Paul Breckenridge, called the allegations against Flynn "garbage" as he dressed down Peterson, the church attorney, for even being involved in such a transparently bogus attempt to smear Flynn. It was desperate behavior, even by the standards of the Church of Scientology.

But by the summer of 1984, Scientology was frantic about Flynn. He had filed 20 lawsuits, and the church had filed 13 against him. Flynn had spent $400,000 of his own money in liti-

Tony Ortega

gation, and it was beginning to pay off in greater press coverage
and successes in court. Scientology was doing whatever it could
to distract public attention from what was happening in court-
rooms in Los Angeles and London.

A month before the press conference, on June 22, 1984,
Judge Breckenridge announced a decision that Mike Flynn and
many others thought might signal the beginning of the end of
Scientology. That court decision was in the favor of a man named
Gerry Armstrong, who was quickly supplanting Paulette Cooper
as Scientology's most feared and hated enemy.

Armstrong had grown up in Chilliwack, British Columbia
and had first learned about Scientology from a friend in 1969,
when he was 22. In 1971, he moved to Los Angeles to join the
Sea Org. Before long, he was sailing with L. Ron Hubbard on the
Apollo, and became a trusted aide to the "Commodore."

After Hubbard moved back to land in Florida and then
ended up in California, Armstrong was part of his "Household
Unit," making sure Hubbard's quarters were up to his standards.
While renovating one home at a 500-acre compound the church
had purchased near Hemet, Armstrong discovered a collection
of boxes that contained a huge trove of Hubbard's original documents.

Everything from Hubbard's baby booties to his teenage
journals to some of his most private, intimate writing about his
sex life were in the stacks of documents. Until Armstrong saved
them, the boxes were going to be discarded in the renovation.

On January 8, 1980, Armstrong wrote to Hubbard, asking

permission to create a biographical archive from the papers. Hubbard agreed, and then the next month he went permanently into hiding.

Later that year, a professional writer named Omar Garrison was hired by the church to author a biography of Hubbard, and Armstrong began working with him closely, cataloging the documents for Garrison's use.

But as he did so, Armstrong was shocked to see how much Hubbard's actual records contradicted the things Hubbard and the church said about his life and exploits. To his followers, Hubbard had been born an adventurer – he'd grown up on a massive Montana ranch owned by his grandfather and by four years old had become the blood brother to a local Indian tribe. He was the youngest Eagle Scout in the history of the Boy Scouts, he had traded ideas with eastern shamans and mystics during extensive travels to Asia in his teens, he was one of the first atomic scientists in the country after his distinguished college career, he'd set records as a daring glider aviator, he'd been a war hero who had survived being machine-gunned as the first casualty in the Pacific theater of World War II. He'd captained "corvettes" that had engaged and sunk Japanese submarines, and after the war he'd healed his serious combat wounds with a new method that became Dianetics. It was a heroic, larger-than-life account of a man who had lived enough for a dozen men.

And Gerry Armstrong knew that all of it was, to one extent or another, a fabrication. Hubbard's own documents showed that he had lived a fascinating, varied life, and with many accomplishments to be proud of. But that's not the story he told or the one promoted by the church. That worried Armstrong. He knew that Scientology made itself vulnerable by putting out claims about Hubbard that could be debunked by official records. In late 1981 and into 1982, he repeatedly went to his superiors, urging them to correct the record and to begin putting out information about Hubbard that actually matched what was in the documents.

Instead of acting on his advice, the organization excommunicated him, "declaring" him a "suppressive person" on February 18, 1982.

In April, when he learned about the declaration, Armstrong knew what he was probably in for. Investigations, harassment, maybe even something worse. He trusted Garrison, and turned over boxes of the Hubbard documents to him. He then copied about 10,000 of the documents for himself, and turned them over for safekeeping to his attorney.

He'd hired Michael Flynn.

On August 2, 1982, Scientology and Mary Sue Hubbard filed suit against Armstrong, accusing him of theft, and asking for the return of the Hubbard archive. Armstrong argued that he'd had to take the records as a form of insurance to guarantee his safety. Without them, he was afraid for his life.

When Mary Sue filed the suit, she was still appealing her conviction in the Snow White Program prosecutions. But a few months later, those appeals ran out. On January 8, 1983, she was ordered to a federal prison in Kentucky to serve a 40-month sentence, but only a year later she was released.

In May 1984, the Armstrong lawsuit went to trial, and Judge Paul Breckenridge presided over four weeks of testimony. After deliberating for two weeks more, on June 22 he made one of the most devastating assessments of Scientology ever put to paper by a judge.

"The organization clearly is schizophrenic and paranoid, and the bizarre combination seems to be a reflection of its founder, L. Ron Hubbard. The evidence portrays a man who has been virtually a pathological liar when it comes to his history, background, and achievements. The writings and documents in evidence additionally reflect his egoism, greed, avarice, lust for power, and vindictiveness and aggressiveness against persons perceived by him to be disloyal or hostile. At the same time it appears that he is charismatic and highly capable of motivating, organizing, controlling, manipulating, and inspiring his adherents. He has been referred to during this trial as a 'genius,' a 'revered person,' a man who was 'viewed by his followers with awe.' Obviously, he is and has been a very complex person, and that complexity is further reflected in his alter ego, the Church of Scientology. Notwithstanding protestations to the contrary, this court is satisfied that LRH runs the Church in all ways through the Sea Organization, his role of Commodore, and the Commodore's Messengers. He has, of course, chosen to go into 'seclusion,' but he maintains contact and control through the top messengers. Seclusion has its light and dark side too. It adds to his mystique, and yet shields him from accountability and subpoena or service of summons," the judge wrote.

As for Mary Sue, Breckenridge called her a "pathetic individual" who wanted the court to believe that Armstrong's possession of her husband's documents constituted a "mental rape" of her. Breckenridge pointed out that as Scientology's "Guardian," she had personally directed members of the Guardian's Office to cull damaging information about church members from their confessional files for "internal security." She really wasn't in a position to complain about collecting private information about other people. And besides, he continued, Hubbard had clearly given Armstrong and Garrison permission to use his documents for the proposed biography.

It was a total victory for Armstrong, and assured that eventually, journalists and authors would have access to the documents that spelled out the uncomfortable realities of L. Ron Hubbard's life.

From London, meanwhile, there was more bad news for the church. A child custody suit there had resulted in another judge denouncing Scientology. The case involved a Scientologist couple who had split up and were fighting over custody of their two young children. The mother and her new husband had left the church, the father had not. The mother and stepfather introduced a huge amount of material about Scientology, in part with the help of a man named Jon Atack who had recently left the church himself. Their goal was to convince Sir John Latey, Justice of the Old Bailey, that Scientology and its policies were so damaging, the father should not be awarded custody. After hearing testimony, Justice Latey agreed with them, and awarded the mother her children.

"Scientology is both immoral and socially obnoxious," Latey wrote in his decision. "In my judgment it is corrupt, sinister and dangerous. It is corrupt because it is based on lies and deceit and has as its real objective money and power for Mr. Hubbard, his wife and those close to him at the top. It is sinister because it indulges in infamous practices both to its adherents who do not toe the line unquestioningly, and to those who criticize or oppose it. It is dangerous because it is out to capture people, especially children and impressionable young people, and indoctrinate and brainwash them so that they become the unquestioning captives and tools of the cult, withdrawn from ordinary thought, living and relationships with others."

Latey made his decision public on July 23, 1984. The next day, Scientology held its press conference in Los Angeles accusing Mike Flynn of masterminding a fraud scheme against L. Ron Hubbard. Flynn said the timing wasn't accidental: The church was doing its best to distract attention from the Breckenridge and Latey decisions, which each found Scientology to be rotten to its core.

When the *New York Times* reported on the church's claims about Flynn in a September 3, 1984 story, Paulette Cooper denounced the accusations against her attorney. "Now they're trying to do the same thing they did to me to Michael Flynn," she told the newspaper.

In fact, Scientology had been trying to ruin Flynn for years, not only with the Al Tamimi declaration, but with multiple bar complaints and investigations and lawsuits. But at the same time, Flynn had not only attracted clients like Paulette Cooper and Gerry Armstrong and Ron DeWolf (L. Ron Hubbard Jr.), but also several others.

With the stunning Armstrong decision, Flynn seemed to have Scientology on the ropes, increasing the chances that Paulette would also benefit as Flynn handled several of her lawsuits from California to Boston. But that's not how things turned out, because Paulette was becoming increasingly tired of being one of Mike Flynn's famous clients.

18

Breaking away

Mark Rathbun had been a Scientologist for almost a year before he was allowed to go "Over the Rainbow" for the first time, in 1978. Before he could be taken to where L. Ron Hubbard was living, the man who was going to drive him there, Steve Pfauth, told Rathbun that he needed to come up with a code name. (Pfauth's was "Sarge.")

At the time, the Marty Robbins song *El Paso* was playing on Pfauth's car radio, and it resonated with Rathbun. He asked Pfauth, who agreed with his choice, and ever since, most people have known Rathbun as "Marty."

Rathbun was taken to Hubbard's La Quinta ranch, but he never met the man himself. The closest he came to meeting Hubbard was hearing the man's booming voice through the walls of his house as Rathbun sat on a lawn chair outside, guarding the place. But within a couple of years, Rathbun had risen quickly through the ranks until he was among the most trusted of the new generation of Scientology executives who were beginning to take over after the prosecutions of the Guardian's Office.

The GO was associated with Mary Sue and her conviction and imprisonment, along with the other top GO operatives, which doomed the spy operation. Hubbard began to turn Scientology's most essential operations over to a group of younger followers he'd been grooming for years – his "messengers."

The first "Commodore's messengers" had been young girls on the *Apollo*, like Tonja Burden. But some of them were teenage boys, and one of them, a short kid from south Philly named David Miscavige, was quickly rising as one of Hubbard's most favored aides. After the Snow White prosecutions, the Sea Org and its Commodore's Messenger Organization (CMO) took over real power from the Guardian's Office and assumed its own legal and spy operations with a division called the Office of Special Affairs.

By 1981, that power swap was just about complete. And that's when Hubbard asked his new young team to accomplish a lofty goal.

Hubbard had been in total seclusion for a year by then. No one saw him, except for Pat and Annie Broeker (two young executives who had come up through the CMO), but Pat Broeker made regular secret drops with David Miscavige at pre-arranged locations in the San Bernardino area to deliver Hubbard's latest communications. Miscavige, in turn, delivered Hubbard's orders to the rest of Scientology. And in 1981, those orders included what came to be called The All-Clear Signal.

Miscavige put Rathbun on it, and Marty spent the next five years working exclusively on the project: To defeat or settle every single lawsuit or criminal investigation facing the Church of Scientology so that Hubbard could come out of hiding once and for all.

Rathbun was only 24, but he found himself overseeing dozens of legal actions for the church over the next several years. And one of his biggest headaches, naturally, was Boston attorney Michael Flynn and all of the clients he represented, who were suing Scientology for hundreds of millions of dollars.

Collectively, and with Flynn pushing the litigation, the group of defendants was a nightmare for the church. Rathbun decided the best strategy would be to pull Flynn's clients away from him, one by one, and get them each to settle on more modest terms. Flynn was being demonized with the press and public to only limited success but the public didn't matter. If Scientology could create doubt in the minds of his clients, it would make them easier to pick off.

By late 1984, Paulette was wearying of the whole thing. Despite Gerry Armstrong's huge victory in Los Angeles that year, she felt stuck with Flynn, who seemed like he was the only attorney in the country who dared to take on Scientology cases. And Armstrong's victory actually worried her: With so many clients in Flynn's stable, she guessed that her slice of whatever ultimate financial victory might happen was getting smaller and smaller.

She also knew that her credibility had taken a big hit after the Bast affair, and wondered if she still had a realistic chance to get the same kind of clear victory won by Armstrong. And if Flynn had won a couple of rounds against the church, Scientology seemed to be fighting more aggressively than ever. Now it was consumed by two new big fights that didn't involve Flynn – the lawsuits of Lawrence Wollersheim in Los Angeles and Julie Christofferson Titchbourne in Portland, Oregon. Each of them were former church members who were claiming that Scientology's counseling processes were harmful, and the church was pulling out all stops to defeat them. (In each of the two cases, courthouses were mobbed by Scientologists making a big show of opposition.)

Despite Flynn's victory for Armstrong, Paulette thought that his chances of winning for her were slipping away with the church fighting so hard against Wollersheim and Christofferson. It was an indication of how tired Paulette had become of fighting Scientology in court by 1984.

After reviewing her records, she found that over the life of all of her lawsuits, she had endured 50 days of depositions, many of them in blocks of five days in a row. They usually featured multiple church attorneys peppering her with questions. In one of them, she had faced five Scientology lawyers at the same time. They were always men, and there were few bounds about what they could ask. "How long does your period last?" they asked at one point. Another time, she was asked to give a stool sample.

"If you want one, you'll get it – on your head," she told the nervy lawyer. They stopped asking for it after that.

Much of the time, she was trying not to give them names of people she had talked to, people she knew would be harassed or sued if she named them. She would say she didn't remember, even when that wasn't entirely true. But that wore her down. She knew there would only be more days of depositions, more avoiding telling the truth, and she didn't like what it was doing to her moral compass.

More than 20 of her friends had also been deposed simply because they knew her. And what they might be asked about her added to her stress. But the worst was that her parents had been pulled into the litigation and had also been questioned. Paulette worried that her father might keel over and die during the brutal interrogating. And she believed that was exactly what Scientology was hoping for.

She worried less about her mother, who was indignant about being questioned. She told Paulette that when she found herself in an elevator with one of the church attorneys, she asked him, "How can you defend people so low that if you lifted up a rock, the lowest thing that would slither out from under it would be your clients, the Scientologists?"

He paused, and then answered, "Because they pay me."

"Whores get paid too," her mother said to the stunned lawyer.

Besides answering questions in live testimony, Paulette was also sent countless pages of interrogatory questions – she figured at one point that she'd had to respond to about 50,000 of them. Some required actual research to answer, and others seemed nonsensical, like the one that asked her to name which nights she had lost sleep because of Scientology, and how much sleep she had lost. It was all so ridiculous, and costly, and exhausting, and time-consuming, and it was keeping her from writing and making a living.

As Marty Rathbun tried to come up with a way to neutralize Paulette, he wasn't aware that she was so close to being ready to stop fighting. He believed that Paulette would be among the toughest to pull away from Flynn. She was the only non-Scientologist among Flynn's clients, and she'd fought Scientology for so long and so viciously, Rathbun and his cohorts thought of her as "the Wicked Witch of the East." There was almost no chance, he thought, that she'd want to play ball.

He didn't realize that by 1984, she felt she'd done enough. She would even think on occasion about how she'd still like to get married and live a calmer life. So, in the end, it didn't take very much at all for Rathbun to lure her away from her attorney.

Paulette heard it from the Cramptons, the couple she had been sued with over the celebrity auction in Los Angeles. They had a connection inside the church who claimed Scientology wanted to settle Paulette's lawsuits, and was willing to pay $10,000. But the church said it hadn't heard from Michael Flynn, and assumed there would be no deal.

Ten thousand? That must be some kind of joke, Paulette thought.

Paulette decided that if Scientology was willing to pay a small amount, it might be willing to pay a much larger amount.

She decided to negotiate on her own, and to hell with Michael Flynn. She would pay him from what she negotiated rather than the other way around.

Flynn's focus on a grand scheme featuring multiple plaintiffs was becoming an obstacle, and she needed to get herself out of it. She told the Cramptons to let it be known that she was willing to meet with Scientology legal affairs officer Lynn Farney. Tell them she wanted to talk, she said.

Marty Rathbun was thrilled when he heard. He then prepared Farney, and walked him through the steps of how he wanted to settle with Paulette. Paulette had no idea, of course, that it was Rathbun's plan all along to pull her away from Flynn and have her negotiate a deal with Farney. She didn't know that Rathbun – who was overseeing all of Scientology's major litigation – was informed of every step of their talks as she sat down with Farney to talk numbers.

They met at Aiello's Pizza Emporium on 32nd Street and 2nd Avenue. ("Aiello" would become a code name for their negotiations.) Paulette ordered Buffalo wings, which was a new treat at the time.

Paulette wasn't sure what to think of Farney. In the 1970s, he'd played bass for Tower of Power when the group was already past its prime. Now he was balding, wore glasses, and seemed anxious – he seemed like the last person who would take a stage in front of a crowd. Rathbun had worked to give Farney a harder edge, to make him seem less mousy and come off more unreasonable and intimidating. But Paulette wasn't intimidated. And soon, she began to think she was getting the better of him.

After they had talked for a while, Farney reached into his shirt pocket and pulled out an envelope. He put it on the table and pushed it over to her. She opened it and saw that there was a certified check inside made out to her for $50,000.

They didn't think they could buy her off that easily, did they?

But then she noticed something. Farney's shirt was made of such cheap lightweight material, she could see through the pocket where several more envelopes were inside. When he pulled out another envelope, with another $50,000 check in it, she could clearly see that there were more envelopes still in his pocket.

What an idiot, she thought.

Eventually, nine envelopes came out of Lynn Farney's pocket and were put down next to Paulette's plate of chicken wings.

And she told him, no deal.

That night, Paulette drank champagne at Michaelina Martel's Park Avenue apartment. The Romanian model was well known in Europe, and had had an uncredited bit part in a 1969 film, *Stiletto*. The long, narrow corridor into her place was lined with magazine covers and other photos of her life in front of a camera.

Michaelina had finally regained her health following a year spent in hospital after she was hit by a taxicab while rushing for a dinner with Burt Bacharach's mother. Now she had found love with her young, handsome boyfriend, Greg, who played guitar while they sang.

Paulette drank and felt lighter and happier than she had in

years. She was going to get out of this thing with Scientology, she now knew. She had just turned down $450,000 and would soon start a real series of settlement negotiations that would recoup the small fortune she had spent in lawyers and court costs over the years.

(Sadly, not long after the party, while coming home from an amusement park in New Jersey, Martel was seriously injured in a car collision that put her back in the hospital for months. Her boyfriend Greg, who was driving, was killed.)

The day after the party, Paulette turned to her old friend and attorney Albert Podell, who agreed to handle settlement negotiations with Farney.

She called Mike Flynn to tell him the news, but he was not happy to hear that the client he had been representing for four years was about to go it alone. His strategy had been to hold together a large group of plaintiffs and go for a huge global settlement. When Paulette told him the story about Farney and his checks, he said the amounts they were talking about wouldn't even cover his bill. Paulette was stunned. He'd let her take nothing after what she'd been through and what she'd spent? She no longer cared about his larger strategy and the millions he was shooting for. She had found a way out.

Paulette and Podell met with Farney over several more days at Aiello's to hammer out the details. Eventually, in February 1985, they reached a deal for an undisclosed amount, and Mike Flynn signed off on it and was paid from the settlement.

But there was another part of the deal Flynn didn't sign. It was a brief affidavit, signed by Paulette. In it, Paulette said she'd been in litigation with the Church of Scientology since 1971, but that all of the lawsuits had now been settled.

In 1978, she had sued Scientology in California but Flynn had convinced her to file another suit in Boston and replace her attorney in the California lawsuit. She did that, she said, because Flynn had come up with a strategy she thought would quickly win her cases.

"He explained that this whole strategy was based upon conducting an attack against Scientology founder L. Ron Hubbard by naming Mr. Hubbard as a defendant in my lawsuits," she wrote.

She claimed that Flynn told her Hubbard had "severed his ties" with the church in 1979, and if they named him as a defendant, the church would settle to protect him. In other words, Flynn knew that Hubbard was no longer running Scientology, she said, but that wouldn't keep them from filing lawsuits accusing Hubbard of being in total control.

"However, I never had any real evidence or reason (other than the word of my lawyers) to believe that Mr. Hubbard was in control of the activities of the Church of Scientology, and my attorneys never presented me with any evidence that such was the case. It is clear to me, on the basis of my conversation with Mr. Flynn on this subject, that the allegations concerning Mr. Hubbard's control over day-to-day Scientology activities had no basis in fact, but were being made solely for strategic reasons in pursuit of a default judgment."

It was a devastating accusation to make. Paulette was blaming Flynn for making allegations he knew were untrue but that the church couldn't afford to refute and would cause the church to settle. Flynn, in other words, was extorting the church through his knowledge of what was really going on—that Hubbard had actually ceded control.

Whether that was actually true was debatable. Hubbard had gone into seclusion in February 1980. With Pat and Annie Broeker as his companions, he kept hidden in an apartment in Culver City, California and then in nearby Manhattan Beach before the three of them settled into a ranch north of Los Angeles near the town of Creston in 1983. (None of this was known to anyone beyond Hubbard, the Broekers, David Miscavige, and a few other people who worked at the Creston ranch.)

And although Hubbard kept out of sight, his instructions for the Scientology empire were carried by Pat Broeker to Miscavige, who met in the middle of the night in parking lots near all-night diners in the San Bernardino area, each meeting spot with a different code name. Miscavige would take Hubbard's instructions to the rest of the Scientology world, and in that manner "the old man" kept his hand on the church's rudder.

But by 1985, his health was beginning to fail, and Broeker and Miscavige were wielding greater control—no one else had access to Hubbard, and didn't dare question their authority when they said what Hubbard wanted Scientology to do.

So when Paulette Cooper signed her affidavit in March 1985, claiming that Hubbard was no longer in control, she may have been at least partly correct. Still, Flynn considered her affidavit a stunning betrayal. He hit back by telling the *Clearwater Sun* that he was preparing to file his own court document that would say Paulette had told a cult deprogrammer she had been paid by Scientology to settle her suits and include the affidavit.

Paulette didn't comment in the press. But privately, she felt her own sense of betrayal by Flynn, and believed that her affidavit would be meaningless. Within weeks of signing it, Scientology approached her again, this time through one of its private investigators, who offered her another large amount, asking her to spy for the church.

She turned it down.

She was done.

Scientology's secretive ranch near Creston, California was 160 acres of bucolic serenity with horse stalls, a house, a trailer, and a Bluebird bus. Locals who went to the place to deliver things or do day work would usually deal with a young woman or a ranch hand who went by the name Joe Carpenter. Occasionally, they might spot an older man named Jack Farnsworth.

Farnsworth was actually L. Ron Hubbard, looking more bedraggled than ever, with long greying locks and sideburns – he knew that he was increasingly resembling Colonel Sanders, and joked about it.

Joe Carpenter was actually Steve "Sarge" Pfauth, who worked the ranch and grew close to Hubbard as he helped care for him. But it was the young woman – Annie Broeker – who spent the most time with the old man, seeing to his needs.

Her husband, Pat Broeker, was seen less and less at the ranch. Pat and Annie had been Hubbard's sole companions during his first few years of seclusion, but after they had settled at the ranch some distance had started to grow between Hubbard and Pat.

By early 1985, Pfauth could see that Broeker was actively avoiding Hubbard, and Broeker would only come to the ranch late at night and leave before Hubbard rose in the morning.

Pfauth didn't know what the falling out was about. He did know that Hubbard still badly wanted the All-Clear Signal to happen – the mission that Marty Rathbun and others were working so hard to make happen so Hubbard could emerge from hiding and rejoin the action at Scientology's main headquarters. They referred to that compound, near Hemet, with the code name "S," and it was only a few hours away by car. But as much as Hubbard wanted to go there, he knew he couldn't leave the Creston ranch as long as he was named in so many lawsuits.

By early 1985, Hubbard had quit smoking, but he had to be hospitalized for a few days for pancreatitis. As soon as possible, they got him back to the ranch, and were fortunate that news of his sickness hadn't become public.

Hubbard lived in the Bluebird bus, and would take walks around the ranch to stretch his legs. One evening, at twilight, he ran into Pfauth, and pointed up at some stars that were just coming into view in the deepening dark.

"There's nothing but a bunch of cowboys out there," he told the ranch hand. "Yeah, they're all cowboys, they kill each other and shoot each other, and they're just a bunch of cowboys out there."

As 1985 wore on, Hubbard's health continued to decline. In October, he told Annie Broeker that he wanted Pfauth to construct something for him, and she summoned Sarge to the bus to hear it from Hubbard himself.

Scientologists used a machine they called an "e-meter" in counseling they called auditing. The device was a cheap contraption (Texas Instruments gave a quote of $40 when they were asked to make them in 1981) that ran a small amount of electricity through a couple of sensors (soup cans, originally) held in a subject's hands. The e-meter measured tiny fluctuations in the galvanism of skin, making a needle move. According to Hubbard's philosophy, the machine was actually measuring the "mass" of a subject's thoughts. Conditioned to believe that the machine was all-knowing, Scientologists become convinced that they could not hide negative thoughts from the e-meter.

At higher levels, after a church member spent years in the organization, he or she learned that the meter could also be used to rid the body of unseen entities which Hubbard named "body thetans" or "BTs." These entities, Hubbard explained in confidential documents only the highest-level members were allowed to see, were the disembodied souls of extraterrestrials that had been placed on earth by a galactic overlord named "Xenu," who had stranded the aliens on earth 75 million years ago.

Now, with his health failing, in October 1985, Hubbard told Pfauth that he wanted him to construct a special e-meter with enough voltage that could, once and for all, rid him of all of his BTs, and also "kill the body."

Pfauth was stunned when he realized what the old man was saying: Hubbard wanted to commit suicide through electrocution. Pfauth wanted nothing to do with it, so for several weeks he dragged his feet. Then, in late November, Annie angrily told him that if he didn't construct the special e-meter, Hubbard would have an electrician in town do it – and imagine what a disaster that could be, she said. So Pfauth took apart his own Mark VI e-meter, and modified it with "some Tesla coils and some up-transformer things," he told Marty Rathbun years later. The machine was still battery-operated, so there wouldn't be enough voltage to harm Hubbard, but it would put on a good show when he used it.

Hubbard did use it late in November or early in December, and the machine fried itself in a spectacular show that probably gave him a good jolt. Hubbard may even have been burned. But it didn't kill him. And that was the end of talk about an e-meter.

By late December, Hubbard was declining quickly. He would wander around the ranch in his nightgown and slippers, following Pfauth and telling him about how "rose perfume" was a conspiracy of the "goddamn psychs." (Hubbard had always hated flowery scents, in his laundry and otherwise. At some point, he began telling people that the scents in laundry detergent were part of some vague plot against the populace by the psychiatric profession.)

In early January, Hubbard began seeing body thetans at places around the ranch, and Annie would ask Sarge to go find them, apparently to mollify Hubbard.

Just before Hubbard died, Pfauth was present as the old man was asked to sign papers about his estate. Hubbard was impatient, and complained of a headache, and Pfauth thought he was in no shape to be signing important documents.

On Friday, January 24, 1986, Hubbard breathed his last. Three days later, Pat Broeker and David Miscavige spoke to a gathering of Scientologists at the Hollywood Palladium, and told them that Hubbard had voluntarily decided to leave his body, which had only become an impediment to the higher-level research that he wished to accomplish. Hubbard's attorney, Earle Cooley, assured the crowd that Hubbard had actually been a very healthy man.

Hubbard was 74 when he died.

When she heard about it, Paulette thought briefly of contacting the press and making a statement. Since she had signed her final legal settlement a year before, by choice she had gone completely silent about Scientology, and was getting used to the idea that she would no longer be the person reporters called for quotes about the church.

Now, for a moment, she hungered to be heard once again. To tell the world what Hubbard had tried to do to ruin her life. That he had been obsessed with her for years. That the organization he left behind was as corrupt as ever, and would remain a danger for other people who dared to speak out.

She thought about it, and was very tempted. But she knew

her parents were relieved that finally she was no longer in the fight, and she also knew that speaking out might start the harassment all over again – and Ted and Stella Cooper would never forgive her if that happened.

Paulette's life was going in another direction, and she decided it was best to let things be.

February 25, 1987 was Albert Podell's 50th birthday, and the attorney who had handled Paulette's settlement two years earlier had come up with an interesting way to celebrate it. On March 6, he rented out the Bouwerie Lane Theater – at Bond Street and The Bowery in Manhattan's East Village – for a performance of *School for Scoundrels*, and invited about 100 friends, half married couples, half singles.

Among the singles he invited were his old friends Paulette Cooper and Paul Noble. They hadn't seen each other since they dated briefly after the last time Podell had invited both of them to a party at his Sullivan Street apartment in the Village, 19 years earlier.

Like the previous time, they easily struck up a conversation – Paulette admitted to Paul that she wasn't enjoying the show, and asked him, "Will you help me get a cab at intermission?" They quickly caught up on their way out of the theater, and Paulette mentioned that she was now living on the east side. Paul said he played tennis near her apartment building.

"Hey, pop by for a takeout dinner after you play tennis sometime," Paulette said as she got into the cab. A few days later, Paul did just that.

The last time they had met, Paul was producing *The Alan Burke Show* for local television. Now he was producing shows for WNYW Channel 5, the Metromedia station that had become the flagship station for Rupert Murdoch's new Fox network created the year before.

For years, Paul had produced local talk shows, and had met and become friendly with many of the era's big celebrities. When he took Paulette on their second date to the opening of a movie at the Carnegie Hall Cinema, Ingmar Bergman's daughter Isabella Rosselini stopped and said "Hello, Paul!"

Paulette couldn't help being impressed. Paul's timing was also impeccable: Paulette craved companionship, but for years she'd worried that any man she dated might turn out to be another Scientology spy – another Jerry Levin or a Richard Bast. She had almost given up the idea of finding someone she could really trust. But she had first met Paul in 1968, before any of the problems with Scientology had begun – he couldn't be a plant, she knew.

Within a year, they were engaged, and ten weeks later, on May 17, 1988, they were married at the Harmony Club in New York. One of their guests was Dr. Ruth Westheimer, who Paul had brought to television to appear on his talk show.

Paul seemed to know everyone, and Paulette felt completely at home in the world he gave her access to. At an Emmy gala, Paul introduced Paulette to another of the famous figures he had gotten to know producing television shows. It was Henry Kissinger.

Paulette couldn't resist. "Did you hear about a plot, in 1976, to send bomb threats to you in a woman's name?"

Kissinger said that yes, he had, actually.

"I was that woman!" Paulette exclaimed, and they laughed. She sent Kissinger, a dog lover, a copy of a book she had written on pets, and he sent her a thank you note as if it were written by his dog, Amanda.

Early in their marriage, Paul and Paulette discussed her past and her fights with Scientology. Paul skimmed her book, but found that it creeped him out. He told her that he didn't want that part of her life to return. He was proud of what she had done, but he wanted her to drop the whole thing. She agreed.

But each of them knew it was a promise she would have a hard time keeping.

19

Resurfacing

While Paulette was beginning a very different life with Paul Noble, L. Ron Hubbard's death in 1986 suddenly opened the floodgates for another generation of writers to take on Scientology. Three major books about Scientology appeared in the four years after Hubbard's death, and each of them owed a huge debt to Gerry Armstrong, who had won the right to keep his trove of Hubbard documents in the 1984 Breckenridge decision.

After Paulette had peeled away from Michael Flynn to sign her own settlement at the beginning of 1985, Armstrong and the other Flynn clients wrapped up their cases with a large deal at the end of 1986, ending 16 suits for about $5 million.

Hubbard finally had a big part of his all-clear, but it was too late to benefit him.

As Flynn faded away, the new authors appeared to become Scientology's latest torment. Jon Atack, the former church member who had helped in the child custody case which produced the other big 1984 court decision against Scientology, connected with Flynn to get copies of the Armstrong documents as he became one of the most thorough researchers ever to study the church. Atack shared his manuscript with British author Russell Miller, who in 1987 published the best book ever written about Hubbard, *Bare-Faced Messiah: The True Story of L. Ron Hubbard*. Atack came out with his book about Hubbard and the church, *A Piece of Blue Sky: Scientology, Dianetics, and L. Ron Hubbard Exposed*, in 1990. And in the U.S. a New Zealand expatriate, Bent Corydon, who had once been a Scientology mission franchiser in Southern California, wrote another book with the help of Ron DeWolf (the new name Nibs had given himself), who backed out before publication in another of his habitual flip-flops. Corydon's book, *L. Ron Hubbard: Madman or Messiah?* came out in 1987.

Like the cluster of books that had come out years earlier by George Malko (1970), Paulette Cooper (1971), Cyril Vosper (1971), and Robert Kaufman (1972), each of the new books was attacked with fierce litigation and harassment by Scientology. And each, just like the 1970s books, were soon hard to find in bookstores or libraries.

In the press about the books and their legal problems, mention was often made of Paulette and her earlier struggles. She was not forgotten, if some of the details of what she had been through began to get muddled. But even though the struggles of the new books brought her new mentions in the press, Paulette kept quiet. She was done with Scientology, and she had other concerns.

Tony Ortega

In August 1990, she brought her sister Suzy to New York from Israel for safety during the Gulf War. Suzy moved into Paulette's old apartment at the Churchill. Suzy had lived a hard life. Unlike Paulette, she had not been brought up by a family of means. And although she had excelled in school, she gave up any thoughts of college in order to support the aunt and uncle who had brought her up.

After she moved from Belgium to Israel, her husband was in and out of hospitals with ailments from his experience in Israel's wars. Suzy became a widow, and was bringing up two children by selling jewelry 12 hours a day.

Paul Noble took an early buyout from Fox and retired in 1991. But a couple of years later, one of his former interns was made the head of programming at the Lifetime network. Paul went to work there in 1993, and helped develop its movie programming, which became so successful Lifetime became the number one basic cable channel for two years running.

Paulette continued to write, but she was focused on less controversial topics. She put out books on travel, missing persons, and psychics. And she became a prolific ghost writer, penning books under the names of other people, including one for Margaret Truman, daughter of the president.

But her favorite topic was pets. "Dogs don't sue you and cats don't harass you," she liked telling people.

If the books that were published in the wake of L. Ron Hubbard's death struggled to reach an audience because of Scientology's

360

legal tactics, the church was rocked even harder by newspaper and magazine investigations.

A series five years in the making by Joel Sappell and Robert Welkos that appeared over several days in 1990 in the *Los Angeles Times* hit the church right where it was headquartered. It was one of the most thorough newspaper investigations ever done of the church, and introduced many people to the "Xenu" story and other strange Scientology beliefs.

But it was a magazine story the next year that changed everything. Richard Behar's 1991 article on the cover of *TIME* magazine – "The Thriving Cult of Greed and Power" – put Scientology in the national spotlight like nothing since the *60 Minutes* broadcasts years earlier. Behar's story contained a sidebar about his experiences with harassment while he was preparing the story, and it opened with a reference to what Paulette had been through.

Behar's ordeal was just beginning. Scientology chose to draw a line in the sand over the *TIME* story, and filed suit for $416 million, claiming that Behar's story had defamed the church and was a pack of lies. Ultimately, the suit was dismissed, but not before *TIME* spent about $8 million defending itself. Behar suffered some of what Paulette had been through, sitting through 28 days of depositions.

While *TIME* won its legal battle, Scientology's aggressive legal tactics had never been more clearly on display, and the rest of the country's news industry got the message. Some 15 years after the FBI raid and the subsequent publication of documents exposing Scientology's brazen infiltration of government, the country's media greatly reduced its examination of Scientology for fear of a legal catastrophe like *TIME*'s successful defense. Except for a few exceptions – like Richard Leiby at the *Washington Post* – America's mainstream media shied away from Scientology stories for the next fifteen years.

But at the same time, a new outlet for Scientology news was just beginning to grow. The same year Behar's story was published in *TIME*, on an early Internet news service called Usenet, a man name Scott Goering started a newsgroup called "alt.religion.scientology." ARS grew only gradually at first, but within a few years it became the most active place to get information about Hubbard and Scientology.

In December 1994, someone posted information from Scientology's highest-level teachings on ARS, information that the church jealously guarded (so that it could charge high prices for it, critics said). Scientology's lawyers demanded that the material be pulled down, but by then a former church member named Dennis Erlich replied to the original postings, and his replies also contained the material the church claimed was copyrighted. Erlich refused to take down his posts.

In January, Scientology attorney Helena Kobrin tried to have the entire newsgroup taken down by Usenet, but her attempt was met with derision and only made ARS more popular than ever. In February, the church convinced a federal magistrate that its trade secrets were being violated, and Dennis Erlich's home was raided and his computer was hauled away. Other raids occurred, including some in Europe.

Paulette Cooper didn't know that such a major fight with Scientology was going on until a man named Ron Newman, a regular at ARS, called to see if she would object to the entire text of *The Scandal of Scientology* being posted online. She told him that anything that made Scientology unhappy would please her. But she also explained that she no longer owned the copyright to the book and so permission wasn't hers to give—but she also wouldn't object. As far as she was concerned, she said, she'd never spoken to him. She didn't want the harassment starting up again, especially if this time it might be aimed at Paul, who was still doing so well at Lifetime. Newman took the hint and had someone post the book without reference to Paulette's wishes.

For Paulette, it was her first awareness that the battle of critics against Scientology was taking a new form. After talking to Newman, she began lurking at ARS, silently watching the battles taking place there. She couldn't help feeling a thrill when she noticed people talking about her.

"Paulette Cooper was a real hero," one poster said, and Paulette couldn't stay silent any longer. She posted a thanks under her real name, but it wasn't uncommon at ARS for people to assume fake identities to make jokes online. Her post was ignored.

On July 26, 1995 – her 53rd birthday – she finally announced her presence at ARS in a statement that left no doubt that it was really Paulette Cooper. It was her first public utterance about Scientology since her settlement a decade earlier.

She said that she was promoting her newest book (*277 Secrets*

Your Dog Wants You To Know), and that she only spent a few hours online each week through her AOL and Compuserve accounts. She explained that she planned to check in at ARS from time to time, to discuss what was happening with Scientology, "and why I think it's futile to fight them now."

She felt that way because two years earlier, in 1993, Scientology had won its 26-year battle with the IRS to regain its tax-exempt status, sparing the church a billion-dollar tax bill that it had been unable to pay. With its status as a church recognized by the government, and the media chilled by the *TIME* lawsuit, Scientology seemed more invincible than ever, Paulette believed.

In May 1996, she cleared up several ARS misconceptions about *The Scandal of Scientology* and some of the things that had happened to her. She also revealed that she'd been hearing from people who thought she ought to be doing more to publicize Scientology's abuses. "I know some of you have expected me to do more, and some have written asking me to do more. But I feel that I did more than my share, and I want to continue to enjoy my harassment-free life," she wrote.

Reading and occasionally contributing to ARS appealed to Paulette because it seemed only quasi-public. It wasn't the same as talking to the press about Scientology, and the number of people who were even aware of the information published at the newsgroup was relatively small. Paulette wasn't looking for more publicity. What she craved was simply the companionship of other people who understood and wanted to talk about Scientology.

But Paulette got more than she bargained for at ARS. Several of the newsgroup's participants were known for their researching skills. The best way to publicize Scientology's abuses, they believed, was to dig up original documents and cut through the layers of hearsay and gossip about what had really happened in church history.

Two of those researchers, Diane Richardson and Keith Spurgeon, dug into Paulette's story in a way that had never been done before. They soon found some of the discrepancies between the popular understanding of Paulette's story and what records actually showed.

They also dug up the 1976 settlement that Virgil Roberts had worked out for Paulette, went to Boston to pull the Bast tapes out of storage, and also found her 1985 affidavit that accused Michael Flynn of extorting the church.

Placing material from each on ARS, sometimes without any context at all, it appeared to be a drumbeat against Paulette. Other posters seemed bewildered. Why target Paulette now, a decade after she'd stopped fighting Scientology?

The truth was, Paulette Cooper had made some mistakes. She'd walked right into traps set for her multiple times. Long after she had written her book about Scientology as a journalist, she had become an outright foe to the church and talked like one. By the time Richard Bast secretly taped her in 1980, Paulette wasn't even pretending to be an objective journalist anymore. She'd been harmed, and she wanted payback.

By 1984 she also believed that Mike Flynn was no longer

working in her best interest, and she had lost all respect for him when she worked out her own settlement in 1985. Partly, Paulette had a tendency to end up in disputes with the attorneys she hired. (She once totaled it up and she had worked with 40 lawyers on her 19 lawsuits. She remained friends only with Albert Podell and Fred Barnett, and had good things to say about Virgil Roberts and Paul Rheingold. The rest she would rather have forgotten.) But also, she never knew that she'd fallen for another Scientology operation when Marty Rathbun spread information that convinced her that Flynn was going to sabotage her.

Concerned about the way Paulette was being portrayed on ARS, one participant, Shelley Thomson, asked her to go through some of the Bast tape transcripts and explain them for an interview. What did she mean, for example, when she was heard in 1980 talking about "comfortably lying" in depositions?

Paulette explained that it was a reference to preparing in an intelligent way for a deposition – something John Seffern had taught her because he felt she was giving away too much in her previous testimony.

In another line from the 1980 transcript, Paulette was heard describing a plot to have drugs planted in the DC church: "Let me make a few calls back in New York to a couple of my kookiest friends and see if we can't get some LSD tablets also."

How did she account for that? Paulette explained that she was only telling Bast what he wanted to hear – the drug caper was *his* suggestion, she said. And she never really did anything about it.

The Bast tape transcripts were brutal, and at times in her 1996 interview Paulette struggled to explain herself. Still, she stuck around on ARS. On August 1, Paulette announced that Robert Kaufman had died on July 29. He was 63. She had seen him play at a piano recital just the year before, but they had not been close for many years.

In 1997, Paulette began putting accounts of her 1970s harassment online. But over time, she appeared less and less at places like ARS. She had mostly gone quiet again, at least online.

She had found a surprising new avenue for her Scientology stories: She wrote a one-act play about her frame-up. Heavy on one-liners, "The Perils of Paulette" was staged in 1997 as a one-woman performance and won a Chicago Dramatist Award. Then she rewrote it for four players and in 1999 had it read at the New York chapter of the National Academy of Television Arts & Sciences at an HBO screening room. Her script not only presented her story through comedy, but also developed its plot around the notion of a romance with Jerry Levin, the church's spy.

At one point in the play, Paulette has her exasperated, unnamed lawyer say, "Great. A jury's really going to like a kinky 30-year-old woman who puts down a church, isn't married, isn't a virgin, doesn't live at home with her parents, produces books instead of children, smokes pot, and travels all over the world alone."

Over the next several years, Paulette never got entirely away from Scientology. When journalists wrote about the controversies of the church as a new century dawned, they might get an encouraging e-mail from Paulette, urging them on. But she generally kept under the radar.

In 2004, Paul and Paulette moved to Florida. Her parents had been living in Palm Beach for 20 years. She wanted to be close to them as they lived out their last years. Her relationship with her mother, so contentious for so many years, was now as warm as it had been when she was a small child.

Stella admitted, for example, that she'd felt great pride when Paulette, along with *TIME* magazine writer Richard Behar, was given the 'prestigious Conscience in Media' award from the American Society of Journalists & Authors in 1992.

Paulette had always craved the admiration of her parents, even into their old age. But she also had the admiration of many other people. James Randi told Paulette that Martin Gardner had said he applauded her for what she had done. The man who had written the first book she read that exposed L. Ron Hubbard as a charlatan said that? She beamed for days.

Then, she began gradually to speak out again. In 2007, she wrote a lengthy article about her experiences for *Byline* magazine, the publication of the New York Press Club, and it got noticed. By then, media interest in Scientology was growing again, spurred largely by the strange behavior of Tom Cruise, its most famous celebrity member. In 2005, the actor had suddenly become outspoken about the church, and it backfired spectacularly as the press finally began to go after a subject that had been somewhat taboo since the *TIME* lawsuit years before.

In 2006, a lengthy piece by Janet Reitman in *Rolling Stone* got a lot of attention. A BBC documentary in 2007 had also caught fire, in part because its presenter, John Sweeney, lost his cool in a titanic shouting match with Scientology's spokesman, Tommy Davis.

And then, in January 2008, all hell broke loose. A nine-minute interview of Tom Cruise that Scientology had filmed as part of a 2004 celebration of the actor was posted to YouTube by long-time church critic Mark Bunker. Bunker quickly took it down, but the video had already gone viral and spun out to other sites. The interview showed Cruise talking like an enthusiastic Scientologist – which, to outsiders, was incomprehensible and strange.

Scientology knew what a disaster it was, and threw its customary litigation tactics into gear, threatening websites with lawsuits if they didn't immediately remove the video. But that only angered Internet activists, who were very familiar with the church's attempts to curb ARS with the raids on Dennis Erlich, Bob Penny at FACTnet, and others around the world in the 1990s.

After Scientology tried to pull down the Cruise video, the Internet pushed back in the form of Anonymous, a leaderless movement largely made up of web users who channeled their rebellious streaks through posting graphic images and otherwise doing things in the name of hilarity. Now, they had a cause. For many, their first impulse took the form of harassment and vandalism, and Scientology found its websites overwhelmed. The church even received some threats of violence.

Mark Bunker, the old time critic who was the first to put the leaked Tom Cruise video online, then posted a video of himself explaining to Anonymous that the new attention on Scientology was welcome, but that harassment was only making things worse. Nonviolent demonstration was the way to go, Bunker counseled, and he was soon dubbed "Wise Beard Man." The next month, in February 2008, Anonymous began peaceful demonstrations at Scientology facilities around the world.

And Paulette Cooper suddenly started getting a lot more calls.

Her story was still the one writers cited most often when they wanted to refer to Scientology's history of retaliation against journalists and other critics. Paulette was ecstatic about the rise of the anti-Scientology group within the Anonymous movement. She knew that Scientology would be overwhelmed by critics who were so numerous, unidentified, and spread around the world.

In an interview she gave in 2008, she said she was still hopeful that some of the people who had victimized her would someday come forward. "I've always been surprised that the people who did some of the really serious things against me, the ones who really hurt me and my life badly, have never come out and apologized to me. I'm still waiting if you're out there," she said.

In May 2011, Paulette heard that Tom Cruise was going to be given a humanitarian of the year award by the Simon Wiesenthal Center in Los Angeles. It enraged her.

"Who will they award next? Mel Gibson for his anti-Semitic

rants?" she said in a statement that was published by *The Village Voice*.

The *Voice* then followed that up later in the year with a lengthy piece about Paulette's frame-up and harassment. Another story in the *Voice* mentioned that even in 2011, Paulette and her sister Suzy were trying to put together the narrative of their childhood in Belgium. That article was noticed by European newspapers, which did their own stories about Paulette.

After those stories appeared, Paulette received several e-mails from Europe. One of them asked if her father had been a Polish leatherworker.

She dismissed it – she believed that her father had been a music lover and a tailor.

But something about the e-mail stayed with her. She reread it that night. The sender had asked if her mother's last name was originally Minkowski – a fact that very few people knew. She pulled up the news stories, which had been published in Belgium and the Netherlands, but none of them had the name "Minkowski" in them.

She called her sister the next morning. "Wasn't our father a tailor?" she asked.

"He worked in leather," Suzy answered.

A chill ran down her spine. Paulette realized that the e-mail sender knew things about her biological parents that even she didn't know. She answered, and made contact with the family of Sijbren de Hoo. The family still had Sijbren's things, knew his stories, and even had a leather article that Paulette's father had made for him – a bookcover, which they sent to her.

The *Voice* then, with the de Hoo family's help, put together the first full telling of Paulette's actual Holocaust experience. And for the first time, Paulette discovered that her father Chaim Bucholc had been arrested four days *before* she was actually born – he had never set eyes on her. The news devastated her.

And if there were details that crucial to her story that had never before been fully explored, what else in Paulette's story might still need to be set straight?

How, for example, did her fingerprint end up on one of the bomb threat letters? And how were the letters typed on Paulette's typewriter if she didn't do it herself?

Paulette had spent a lot of time wondering how her cousin Joy Heller's stationery might have been stolen from her apartment. Joy kept a pile of it with her other things in Paulette's living room and wrote letters to her mother often. When she wasn't there, Joy would toss her stuff in a corner – and Paulette sometimes did that herself. It was possible that she could have left fingerprints on Joy's stationery as a result.

But the odds of Margie Shepherd or anyone else picking up a piece of Joy's stationery that just happened to have Paulette's fingerprint on it were exceedingly slim.

Besides, trying to source the stationery used for the bomb threats was a red herring. What appeared to tie the second bomb threat letter to Paulette was not the paper it was written on, but the fingerprint that was on that paper. The stationery could have come from anywhere, and not necessarily from Paulette's apartment.

For too long, Paulette wasted time trying to figure out how someone stole her stationery *and* put a fingerprint on it. The simple truth was, there was no proof that it was her stationery anyway.

As for how her fingerprint got on the paper that was used, the best theory still appears to come back to Margie Shepherd's odd behavior the day she visited Paulette and Joy on December 6, 1972, two days before the first bomb threat letter showed up at the New York org.

Margie was carrying a clipboard with a petition, and she claimed to be gathering signatures for the UFW. Both women noticed that Shepherd never took her gloves off, even though the temperature in the apartment was very warm.

Paulette took the clipboard from Margie with her left hand in order to sign it with her right hand. If there was a piece of stationery taped to the underside of the clipboard, Paulette could have left the print from her third finger on her left hand on the page without knowing it. (And just a few years later, the "Operation Freakout" documents described doing this very thing to get Paulette's fingerprint for that scheme.)

Before Margie then handed the clipboard to Joy, she could have put another sheet of petitions under it so Joy would not have also left a fingerprint.

If there was a piece of stationery taped to the underside of the petition, did it already have the bomb threat typed on it? The letter could have been typed at any time in the months leading up to Margie's visit. Nibs had access to Paulette's typewriter in the late summer, a couple of months before Margie showed up. Paulette has always believed that the wording and poor grammar of the note reminded her of the way Nibs wrote – and she spent months working with him to craft "An Inside Look at Scientology" that summer and knew his writing quirks quite well.

Over the years, other theories she had considered – that Bernie and Barbara Green had something to do with the threat letters, for example – she had discarded. But she had never been able to eliminate Nibs.

Could there have been more than one attempt to obtain Paulette's fingerprint? A woman named Lori Taverna, who testified at the 1982 Clearwater hearings, says that she was recruited into Scientology in 1965 and was later chosen to spy for the Guardian's Office in New York by Bruce Raymond. But after being sent several military espionage manuals, she had a change of heart and made it clear she would not do any volunteer work for the GO. Then, in 1972, she says her boyfriend was recruited by Raymond for an operation.

After she pushed him for details, her boyfriend told her about his mission. Raymond had said that a woman in town, a writer, was trying to destroy Scientology. The Guardian's Office had to do something about it, and her boyfriend's job was to get the writer's fingerprint on a piece of stationery or an envelope. Her boyfriend worked at a printing shop, so he had a legitimate cover – he would just be trying to sell her stationery. He said he was told to go to the writer's office, and use his natural charm to get her talking and handling the papers.

Years later, after Taverna heard what had happened to Paulette, she assumed it was her boyfriend who had helped frame her. (He died in 1975.) But there are several problems with the story. Paulette didn't go to an office (she worked at home), and she doesn't remember a man of his description trying to sell her stationery in 1972.

Other leads are promising, but have never fully developed. Paulette wrote in 2007 that she had been told by former Scientologist Arnie Lerma that Margie Shepherd was actually a woman named Linda Kramer. But Lerma says he doesn't remember it that way today – it was Paula Tyler he knew, and Paula Tyler was using her actual name. Len Zinberg, however, also remembers hearing that Margie Shepherd was actually a Linda Kramer, but no one else from the orgs contacted for this book knew anything about her.

Another seeming dead end: While it's tempting to credit former church member Margery Wakefield's affidavit that she heard talk in 1978 about a plot to assassinate Paulette, her details are sketchy at best, involve people whose names she can't remember, and can't be corroborated by anyone else. There's no doubt that L. Ron Hubbard wanted Paulette Cooper's life ruined, but Wakefield's account doesn't really lead anywhere. There's no other evidence that what was left of the Guardian's Office in the late 1970s was planning an outright assassination of Scientology's old nemesis.

More than 30 years after the GO was disbanded, many of the

original operatives are still associated with Scientology and still aren't talking about their Snow White days. Others have died. A few, however, agreed to talk about their days as Scientology spies.

Each of them said they're confident that Jerry Levin was actually Don Alverzo. One former operative says he's certain because Alverzo was the guy who got his hands dirty as Scientology's most trusted spy, and the only one with the unflappable quality that would allow him to live with Paulette Cooper for four months in the summer of 1973 without giving a hint of what was actually going on.

In 1982, at the Clearwater Hearings, Paulette said that documents seized in the raid convinced her that Don Alverzo had posed as Levin. (Alverzo was named an unindicted co-conspirator in the Snow White investigation, but was never charged with a crime. Even the FBI and Justice Department didn't seem to know his real name.) One FBI document indicated that when she was interviewed about the frame-up in 1978, Paulette told the agency that Levin had talked about being a combat helicopter pilot (a detail she didn't remember years later). Independently, and unaware of the FBI document, Merrell Vannier wrote that one of the few details he knew about Alverzo's background was that Alverzo said he had been a combat helicopter pilot in Vietnam.

But in more recent years, Paulette began to have her doubts. Descriptions of Alverzo didn't seem to match her memory of Levin. He may have been around the correct height, but Alverzo was said to have olive skin and dark hair. Levin was fair-skinned and had red hair as well as a slightly effeminate manner. Former GO employees, however, say that Alverzo was a chameleon who could pull off amazing changes in appearance and personality.

For several months, Paulette believed that another good candidate for Jerry Levin was a Boston Guardian's Office operative named Jimmy Mulligan.

Mulligan had been a high-level GO official who was named in the Snow White documents and who would have at least overseen some of the operations against Paulette. (He was also the "Reverend" who Paulette's publisher, Harry Shorten, apologized to in order to settle Scientology's lawsuit against his company, Tower Publications, Inc.) Mulligan was slight in stature and had red hair, and he had an effeminate air – which all matched Levin.

Mulligan died in 1997, but photographs of him were obtained from one of his surviving brothers. When Paulette saw the photos, she knew immediately that Jimmy Mulligan was not Jerry Levin. The investigation had come back to Don Alverzo.

And then, a stunning break: Don Alverzo was identified and located.

In 1978, two prominent Scientologists married each other. Heber Jentzsch was a part time actor and singer who, four years later, would be named president of the Church of Scientology (mostly a spokesman position and not one of actual power in the organization). He married Karen de la Carriere, a top auditor who had been trained personally by L. Ron Hubbard. One of Karen's bridesmaids was a young woman named Molly, who was married to Don Alverzo.

Tony Ortega

Although Heber Jentzsch was pressured by the church to divorce Karen in 1989, she still had the photographs of her wedding. She left Scientology in 2010 and quickly became a vocal critic, particularly over the way her ex-husband, Heber, had been treated, with banishment to Scientology's bizarre internal prison for executives, which had become known as "The Hole."

In 2014, knowing that Paulette Cooper was trying to find what had become of Don Alverzo, Karen pulled out her photographs of herself in her wedding gown with her bridesmaid, Molly Alverzo, and asked a friend who is a private investigator to see if he could track her down.

Through marriage and other records, the private eye found Molly and her husband, and learned his real name, and where he lived and worked. He also tracked down a 2002 photograph of Alverzo, under his real name which was on the Internet.

That photograph was positively ID'd as Alverzo by Merrell Vannier, the former GO operative who, with Alverzo, had broken into the law firm that was representing the *St. Louis Post-Dispatch* in 1974, and by Len Zinberg, the GO volunteer in New York. Other former Scientologists who had been involved in the New York org in the early 1970s remembered him under his real name, and not his GO identity.

Don Alverzo had been found.

Or had he? Another former GO operative who had worked with Alverzo, Mike McClaughry, disagreed, telling us that the man in the 2002 photo was not Alverzo. And Paulette was skeptical that the man in the photo had been Jerry Levin. She remembered Levin as a slightly stocky young man, but the photograph showed a fat, aging older man. When she focused on his face and blocked out his figure, she thought it could be Levin, but she wasn't sure.

But then, McClaughry's wife, Virginia, a skilled researcher, tracked down a 1967 photograph of the man in a newspaper clipping announcing his graduation from Army Aviation School. Mike McClaughry looked at the photo and agreed: There was no longer any question that he was Don Alverzo.

Paulette looked at the same photo and also was convinced: She was "99 percent" sure that the man in the photo was the person who called himself Jerry Levin and lived with her for four months in 1973. This man was Don Alverzo, and Don Alverzo was Jerry Levin.

After a few unsuccessful attempts to catch him at his business office, I finally reached him on the phone, and he pleasantly asked what he could do for me. He was told that a book was being written about Paulette Cooper, and that it was hoped he might be persuaded to talk about his involvement with the New York org in the 1970s.

He said he didn't understand the question. I repeated myself. Paulette Cooper? The Guardian's Office? B-I? That you were known as Don Alverzo?

"I'm sorry, I don't even understand what language you're talking. I guess you have the wrong person."

Like Merrell Vannier had described him, the man was unflappable.

While I was on the hunt for Alverzo, talking with about a dozen former GO agents, it became obvious to me that even after 40 years, some of them had changed little in their attitudes about Paulette Cooper. Although some of them were entirely out of Scientology and had gained some perspective on their previous activities, repeatedly they said that Cooper was still someone they reviled.

"She didn't deserve to be treated the way she was, but she's a bad person," one former GO operative said.

Another person, who had been the "Cooper I/C" – the person "in charge" of Scientology's litigation with Paulette – said he couldn't understand why a book would be written about her. "She's not important," he said, before asking never to be called again and hanging up the telephone.

The other person who infiltrated Paulette's life, Paula Tyler, is less of a mystery. She's still a church member, and lives in Clearwater, Florida. She didn't respond to questions about her role in the operation against Paulette. Like other former GO operatives, Tyler has remained a church member but hasn't played a visible role in the church's management.

Her daughter is a different story. Erin Banks rose through Scientology's public relations ranks, and by 2013 had made it to the national media office. Her comments to newspapers show up when a new building opens in the Midwest, for example. On Scientology's web page describing its PR team, she's listed on the second rank along with her husband, Nick Banks.

When Paulette found that Paula Tyler had a page on Facebook (under a married name), she sent her a message through the social media platform.

"How does it feel to ruin a life?" she said. She didn't get a reply. She sent the same message to Charles Batdorf, the GO operative who had been part of Operation Freakout, and also didn't get a reply – but then Batdorf took down his Facebook page.

The Guardian herself, Mary Sue Hubbard, died of breast cancer in 2002. The GO's ringleader, Jane Kember, is today still involved in Scientology, reportedly taking courses at Saint Hill Manor, Scientology's United Kingdom headquarters in East Grinstead, England. Like other living Snow White veterans, Kember maintains ties to Scientology without holding any official position.

Kember had twin sons, one of whom is in the Sea Organization in Los Angeles. The other one was reportedly never in Scientology.

The Guardian's Office was dismantled after Mary Sue Hubbard and Jane Kember and the other nine defendants in the Snow White Program were sentenced to prison. In 1981, it was time for a new group of loyal Scientologists to take over while L. Ron Hubbard was in hiding.

Bill Franks, now in his late 60s, was made Scientology's executive director international in April 1981 and it became his job later that year to dissolve what was left of the GO. On Hubbard's orders (relayed through David Miscavige), Franks took over the Guardian's Office just long enough to take it apart.

It was Franks who, with Miscavige, met with Mary Sue Hubbard in a Los Angeles hotel to give her the news that she was being sacrificed for the good of her husband and for Scientology. She would step down from her role as Guardian, she would go to prison (for only a year, it turned out), and she would no longer have a position of power in the organization. (Franks' story is confirmed by John Brousseau, who had wired up the two men before they met with Mary Sue, and he listened in from a van about a block away.)

Franks says that in order to dismantle the GO, he first had to understand what it had been doing. So he spent hours going through the spy unit's files, and says it became obvious to him that Hubbard was obsessed with Paulette Cooper.

"A lot of the stuff I read was from Hubbard. He thought Paulette Cooper was working for every group he could imagine that was against Scientology. It was striking," he says. "It was striking that this woman, who I never met – she had just written a book and was a journalist – that there was so much anger. And it was clear, Hubbard said to do anything including getting rid of her, in one memo I read."

Franks claims that Hubbard, in handwritten notes that were later destroyed, ordered assassinations of Scientology critics, including David Mayo, who had once been Hubbard's own Scientology counselor before he was driven out of the church. Others doubt Franks on this score, but Mayo has reportedly told people that he believes he was on an assassination list and he reportedly continues to live under the assumption that Scientology still wants him dead.

Franks is aware that some doubt his memories. But he says there is no question about what he saw—he still vividly remembers Hubbard's hatred for Paulette. "For some reason he had this thing for Paulette. He just thought she was the antichrist," he says.

Robert Kaufman had told her, years before he died in 1996, "No matter what you do in life and how many years down the road it will be, they will never leave you alone. They will always have a spy on you."

20

A spy comes forward

I n February 2011, Marty Rathbun revealed that a *Vanity Fair* reporter had been working for Scientology for 20 years. Rathbun produced a document dated five years earlier – February 14, 2006 – which he said was written by Linda Hamel, the woman who today runs Scientology's spy operations as the Commanding Officer of the Office of Special Affairs International (CO OSA Int) the unit that replaced the Guardian's Office.

In that memo, Hamel reveals that the *VF* reporter was keeping tabs on British journalist Andrew Morton, who at the time was working on an unauthorized biography of Tom Cruise. According to Hamel, the church spy told Morton he wanted to profile him for *Vanity Fair*. Actually, he was trying to gather information about the Cruise book and what Morton might put in it. He then reported what he learned to Hamel.

Rathbun, in revealing that the reporter was a paid spy for the church, marveled that so many journalists had talked to the man over the years about their Scientology projects, and somehow didn't notice that the spy never actually wrote anything about Scientology himself.

One person the reporter regularly checked in with was Paulette Cooper. He told her he was writing an expose on Tony Pellicano, the detective she had worked with many years earlier. She considered the reporter a friend, and he encouraged her when she came to New York to get together with him to talk about politics and the news.

Inevitably, Scientology would come up. From their very first meeting years earlier, he had always said he would one day write about Scientology, though she wondered why he never did. Paulette now realizes that her *Vanity Fair* reporter friend had been keeping tabs on her for years on behalf of Scientology. Once again, she'd been suckered.

But in recent years, she's become more comfortable than ever as something of a legend among the mix of Anonymous activists, old-time critics, and ex-Scientologists who spend a lot of time writing and talking about Scientology. Particularly now, as the church lurches from one major crisis to another. She jokingly tells Paul that if she dies before him, "sprinkle my ashes over the nearest Scientology org so that I have the last word."

In the summer of 2012, Paulette even accepted an invitation to a backyard barbecue, where many of the most notorious Scientology critics were gathering. She was there, with Paul, to be interviewed by Lawrence Wright, who was collecting video for the web version of his book, *Going Clear*, which was coming out in a few months.

And practically the same week that Wright's book hit book-shelves, Paulette was featured in a television program, on the ID network, which recreated her experience being tailed on her way to F. Lee Bailey's office in Boston by Nancy Many. The recognition was gratifying. But still, Paulette said, what she really craved was to hear from the people who had tried so hard to destroy her life.

Over the years, very few had come forward. In the 1980s, she was heckled during a talk she gave to the Investigative Reporters & Editors convention. It was Robert Vaughn Young, who was then one of Scientology's chief spokesmen. He defected from the church in 1996, and later apologized to her. But that was a rare exception.

Then, in July 2013, she heard from someone she had never known.

Len Zinberg decided he needed to atone for what he had done 40 years earlier. He tracked down an e-mail address for Pau-lette Cooper, and sent her a note, describing what he had been keeping secret for so long.

"My name is Len Zinberg, and though we have never met, I was one of those Scientologists who participated in causing you great pain during the 1970's as a volunteer for the then Guardian's office. I want your forgiveness, and realize that, at this late hour, I am totally undeserving of it. I have spent the better part of the last quarter century disentangling myself from the mindfuck that is Scientology..."

He described breaking into Robert Kaufman's apartment and also delivering pages of Paulette's teenage diary to her father. In a subsequent telephone interview, he talked about first getting into Scientology and then becoming a volunteer for the Guardian's Office. He described his relationship with Sylvia Seplowitz, who was sent on the mission to get Kaufman's attention.

Sylvia also agreed to talk about her days doing work for the GO, and described how her mission at the ballet studio to convince Kaufman to come home with her failed. She now lives in Maine, where she teaches art.

Zinberg sent several more messages and then agreed to the interview. He worried that speaking publicly might engender the wrath of the church, but if that was the case, it was something he had become resigned to enduring.

"I am contacting you now because I am a coward and should have done so much earlier…You have suffered more than any human being should, for the simple 'crime' of writing and speaking the truth. Ms. Cooper, I am 66 years old, married, and the father of 2 children who celebrated their Bar/Bat Mitzvah last year. Before I leave this earth, it is my sincerest hope to be worthy of your forgiveness."

Paulette thanked him for his courage in reaching out to her. "Mazel Tov," she said, regarding his children.

She was surprised that more Scientologists hadn't come forward over the years, hadn't, in the intervening decades, felt compelled to reach out to her and explain what they had done. But she was grateful that Len Zinberg had, at least. It was something she'd been waiting to hear for many years.

"Your children would be proud of your e-mail," she wrote to him.

Like Len Zinberg, other people from Paulette's past have left Scientology. Bill – the man who said he believed he was a reincarnation of Jesus Christ – is today a healthier, happier man who long ago left Scientology behind.

Roger, Bill's friend who first introduced him to Scientology, has a more complex relationship with the organization. After briefly dating Paulette, Roger helped the church retaliate against her once it became known that she was writing a book about Scientology. He continued to do volunteer work for the Guardian's Office and then the Office of Special Affairs for many years. But after decades with the church, Roger, like many others, grew disaffected with church leader David Miscavige at the same time that he still admired L. Ron Hubbard and Scientology's original ideas. He left the official church, becoming an independent Scientologist, and continues to admire many of the things about Scientology that brought him into it at the beginning. But he had separated himself far enough from the church to grant an interview for this book. Both Bill and Roger, however, feared retaliation, and each asked to be given pseudonyms.

L. Ron Hubbard Jr. – Nibs – died in 1991 from complications of diabetes. He once said, "To be perfectly frank, my life's been pretty much of a disaster and a miserable mess because of

Scientology – and you can quote me on that."

John Seffern died in 1999 when he went to the VA for a routine injection that turned disastrous when a needle broke off in his arm, causing lethal bleeding.

Paulette's sister Suzy lives in New York. She has two children—named Rachel and Chaim after her parents—and six grandchildren.

Albert Podell remains good friends with Paulette and Paul. It was Podell who was responsible for both of their introductions, and for helping her settle with Scientology in 1985.

Dr. Stanley Cath, the psychiatrist Paulette saw in college and whose office was broken into to get her files, died in 2011. Dr. David Coddon, who administered Paulette's truth serum test, died in 2002. Roy Wallis, the Belfast professor who wrote *The Road to Total Freedom* and tried to help Paulette after interviewing Nibs in 1973, committed suicide in 1990, shooting himself after the breakup of his marriage. Cyril Vosper, author of *The Mind Benders*, died in 2004.

Nat Lorendi, who had administered the first polygraph exam of Paulette, died in 1999. Paulette's prosecutor, John Gordon III, joined a prestigious law firm, and is now retired. Bob Straus left the district attorney's office and became prominent in the field of judicial review. Charles Stillman, Jay Zelermyer, Virgil Roberts, and Paul Rheingold are all still practicing law.

Tony Pellicano, the private investigator who worked with Paulette briefly in 1973 on a book about surveillance, is serving time in prison for illegal wiretapping.

Bruce Brotman left the FBI and made news at his job as head of security at the Louisville International Airport in 2002 when he was accused of helping a 20-year-old female companion go through security unscanned to catch a flight.

Richard Bast died in 2001.

Ted Cooper lived until just a few months before his 100th birthday in 2010. Five years earlier, his wife Stella had died at 95. They had been married for 68 years.

To the end, Ted kept his sense of humor, even as he began to fade. Paulette had told her father that if he lived to see 100, they would buy him a huge cake and have a woman jump out of it. "What kind of cake?" he quipped. After he was widowed, Ted lived next door to Paul and Paulette, and they had breakfast together every day until the end of his life. He attributed this longevity to them, but even though it was nearly 50 years later, the three of them avoided talking about the events of 1973. The subject was still too painful.

James Meisler, the "reverend" of the New York Scientology church who received the bomb threat letters, now lives in Sacramento and works for a company that helps factories automate. He declined, politely, an invitation to be interviewed.

Michael Meisner, the man who turned witness for the FBI after leading so many of the infiltrations of government offices for the Guardian's Office, now lives in New England after retiring from a job in the energy field. He refused to answer questions for this book.

Michael Flynn no longer handles litigation against the

Church of Scientology. He said he couldn't talk about his former cases. But he offered words of admiration for Paulette Cooper, even after her not so kind words about him were brought up. "I still feel nothing but compassion for her. What Hubbard put her through no one should experience," he said.

David Gaiman, the Scientology UK spokesman who tried to intimidate Paulette at the Edinburgh airport in 1970, who provided responses to her questions that became an appendix in *Scandal*, who was named an unindicted co-conspirator by the Justice Department in the Snow White prosecution, and who showed up in the 1980 episode of *60 Minutes* deflecting questions about Hubbard and Scientology spying, continued to be the face of Scientology in England until his death in 2009. His entire family was deeply involved in the church and remain so today; his widow, Sheila, continues to give large sums for Scientology construction projects, his daughter Claire Edwards is a dedicated Sea Org official in Los Angeles, and his daughter Lizzy Calcioli has appeared on British television defending Scientology practices.

But it was his son, Neil, who became the most famous member of the family. Neil Gaiman left Scientology sometime in the 1980s, and since then he's become one of the most successful fantasy and science fiction writers in the world. In 2013, he published a short book, *The Ocean at the End of the Lane*, which was inspired by an incident at his childhood home, where his father took in Scientology boarders who were taking classes at Saint Hill Manor, L. Ron Hubbard's estate in East Grinstead, England. Doing publicity for the book, Gaiman carefully handled interviewer questions about his relationship to Scientology, and in some ways his situation reflected what many ex-members go through. Most people who leave Scientology never speak publicly about their experiences. There are many examples of Scientology retaliating against people who leave, just as it targeted Paulette Cooper.

And by 2013, Scientology was in deep trouble. Longtime, loyal members had been breaking away for several years in a growing revolt against the leadership of David Miscavige. At the same time, antics by Tom Cruise and other Scientology celebrities erased the media's longtime skittishness about covering the church. And increasingly, state and national governments around the world were beginning to take a harder look at Scientology's practices.

Still, there were infrequent victories for the church; in late 2013, Neil Gaiman's nephew, Alessandro Calcioli, and Calcioli's fiancée, Louisa Hodkin, won the right to a religious wedding in a Scientology church as England's highest court decided that Scientology's orgs did qualify officially as "houses of worship." But the British press judged it a calculated ploy to gain recognition, and said they were on to Scientology and its history of bad behavior. Some of the articles even mentioned the long-ago experiences of a writer named Paulette Cooper.

Marty Rathbun, the Scientology executive who had tried to neutralize Paulette as a legal threat, left the church in 2004 and then disappeared. He resurfaced in 2009 by writing a blog that was harshly critical of Scientology leader David Miscavige, who responded by sending waves of private investigators, attorneys, and other operatives to South Texas to stalk and harass Rathbun and his wife Monique, who had never been a member of the church. In 2013, Monique filed a harassment lawsuit against Miscavige and the church, and her list of grievances sounded very familiar to anyone who knew what Paulette Cooper had gone through 40 years earlier. Scientology, Monique alleged, had tried to smear her husband with the use of private investigators, had followed and photographed the Rathbuns wherever they went, and did what they could to make it almost impossible for them to make a living.

Forty years later, it seems Scientology and its methods of retaliation had hardly changed at all.

Paulette and Paul live in Palm Beach with their two small dogs. They have been married for 26 years. She continues to write books – she's up to 22 now – and she has a column about pets in the *Palm Beach Daily News*. Around town, she's known as Paulette Noble, and few of the people she meets have any idea about her past as Paulette Cooper, the woman who took on the Church of Scientology and became its most famous target for retaliation.

She's still "a finely honed…accumulation of nervous energy," as John Marshall described her in 1980. Even at 72, she gives you the feeling that she's never going to catch up on all of the things she's trying to get accomplished.

She bristles when it's suggested that she's done quite well

despite her years of harassment. "Those fifteen years of my life are still so painful I hate to think about it," she says. "That's almost a quarter of my life that was miserable, and one year – 1973 – that was so horrible it still often haunts me and has become the benchmark for my life – before and after the frame-up."

She has never really recovered from the anxiety of those years, of nineteen lawsuits, invasion of her privacy, of having to come up with the money for legal bills, of worrying that anyone she met might be spying for Scientology. "I chased a lot of people away. They didn't want to be friends with me because I was so obsessed with Scientology and it made them nervous," she says.

Some of it, she admits, was balanced out by the constant inquiries from people, many of which she was able to help. E-mails have come from around the world thanking her for exposing Scientology's abuses. And one story she says affected her the most – a man in his fifties who wrote to tell her that years ago her book had given him the courage to leave Scientology. He then got married, had four children, and runs a company employing about 50 people. He told Paulette that he felt she was responsible for his happiness.

"That reminded me of why I did what I did, and why journalists do what we do. We try to tell the truth so it can help others," she says. "Unfortunately, we sometimes pay a terrible price for it."

ACKNOWLEDGMENTS

Since I began writing about Scientology as a reporter for the *Phoenix New Times* in 1995, I have spoken with hundreds of current and former Scientologists about their experiences, particularly after I started writing daily about the church while I was editor at *The Village Voice* (2007-2012) and then later at my own website, The Underground Bunker. But researching and writing *The Unbreakable Miss Lovely* presented a special challenge—finding people who had witnessed or had even taken part in the ordeal that Paulette Cooper was put through between 1969 and 1985.

Paulette herself was my first resource. She had initially contacted me many years ago, when I was writing in Phoenix and then at *New Times Los Angeles*, sending me encouraging emails when I wrote about Scientology. After she and I discovered the details of her childhood for the first time in a story for the *Voice*, I flew down to Florida to present my ideas for a larger project in the fall of 2012, not sure if she would be interested. Despite the misgivings of her delightful husband Paul, she was ready for a book to be written, and she started me off in numerous directions to track down sources. Almost right away, we began to have great luck as "Roger" and "Bruce" were located and each decided, for the first time in 45 years, to talk about Paulette's introduction to Scientology from a man who thought he was Jesus Christ.

While I pumped my own sources for information about finding former Guardian's Office members, I also received a huge boost from the world's foremost academic who studies Scientology, University of Alberta professor Stephen A. Kent. My great thanks also to his student Robin Willey, who dove into Steve's trove of documents and found some crucial items that became very important to this book – the unpublished 1972 harassment diary that Paulette wrote for her attorney Paul Rheingold, for example, giving me unprecedented clarity about what she was going through in those days. And another previously unseen Guardian's Office document from 1971 which showed its day-by-day surveillance of Paulette, more than a year before she had any idea she was being watched so closely.

Personal interviews of people who appear in the book include Paulette's sister, Suzy Bucholc, her cousin Joy Heller, and Joy's former boyfriend, who asked not to be named. The list also includes former attorneys Charles Stillman, Jay Zelermyer, Virgil Roberts, and Michael Flynn (who was limited in what he could discuss), former FBI special agent Christine Hansen, *St. Louis Post-Dispatch* reporter Elaine Viets, polygraph expert Frederic Joshua Barnett, and *National Enquirer* editor Maury Breecher.

The former members of Scientology who appear in this book have all risked harassment and worse by merely picking up the phone. My gratitude and respect go to Len Zinberg, Jim Dincalci, Nan McLean, Nancy Many, John Brousseau, Gerry Armstrong, Bill Franks, Lori Taverna, Ron Haugen, Simi Valley, and Sylvia Seplowitz, among others I cannot name. Many other former members of the organization, including some of its top former officials, have been extremely patient with me over the years as I've tried to absorb L. Ron Hubbard's arcane ideas. Just to mention a few, I want to thank Mike Rinder, Karen de la Carriere, Jeffrey Augustine, Marty Rathbun, Marc and Claire Headley, Kate Bornstein, Tory Christman, Lawrence Wollersheim, Chuck Beatty, Laura DeCrescenzo, Luis and Rocio Garcia, Spanky Taylor, Tiziano Lugli and Jamie Sorrentini, Jason Beghe, Paul Haggis, Tom DeVocht, Hana Eltringham Whitfield, Sara Goldberg, Michael Fairman, Derek Bloch, and Michael Laws.

Thanks should also go to the Church of Scientology itself, which put together a detailed report on Paulette Cooper in 1974, as well as an entire book about the Snow White FBI investigation and prosecutions. These materials were studied closely, and ensure that the church's views are represented accurately in this book.

Other journalists and researchers have been instrumental in this project, including BBC reporter John Sweeney, *Forbes* reporter and author Richard Behar, former *Los Angeles Times* reporter Joel Sappell, *New Yorker* staffer Lawrence Wright and his research assistant Lauren Wolf, filmmaker Alex Gibney, author Bent Corydon, attorneys Scott Pilutik, Graham Berry, Ken Dandar, and Ray Jeffrey, researchers Roxanne Seibert and

Tony Ortega

Gary Hoffman, and performance artist and L. Ron Hubbard great-grandson Jamie DeWolf.

Special thanks go to Jon Atack, the supreme Scientology historian, who not only deepened my curiosity about Scientology's past, but read an early draft of the book in order to make sure it reflected that history correctly.

And finally, a raucous wave to the commenting crew at The Underground Bunker, which keeps me ever on my toes.

Made in the USA
Lexington, KY
10 May 2015